The Poetic Edda

Edda Sæmundar Hinns Froða
The Edda Of Sæmund The Learned

Translated from the Old Icelandic by Benjamin Thorpe

Printed on acid free ANSI archival quality paper.

ISBN: 978-1-78139-492-2

© 2015 Benediction Classics, Oxford.

Contents

Preface .... *vii*

Part 1: The Mythological Lays

Völuspá: The Vala's Prophecy *1*
Vafþrúðnismál: The lay of Vafthrúdnir *17*
Grímnismál: The Lay of Grimnir *29*
Hrafnagaldr Odins: Odin's Ravens' Song *41*
Vegtamskviþa eða Baldrs Draumar *49*
Hávamál: The High One's Lay *55*
Hymiskviða: The Lay of Hymir *87*
Thrymskviþa eðr Hamarsheimt *97*
Alvíssmál: The Lay of the Dwarf Alvis *105*
Harbarðslióð: The Lay of Harbard *113*
För Skirnis eðr Skirnismál *123*
Rígsmál: The Lay of Rig *133*
Ægisdrekka, eða Lokasenna, eða Lokaglepsa *145*
Fiölsvinnsmál: The Lay of Fiölsvith *159*
Hyndlulioð: The Lay of Hyndla *169*
Gróagaldr: The Incantation of Groa *181*
Solarlióð: The Song of the Sun *185*

Part 2: The Heroic Lays

Preface *201*
Völundarkviða: The Lay of Völund *205*
Helgakviþa Hiörvarðs Sonar *215*
Helgakviða Hundingsbana Fyrri *227*
Helgakviða Hundingsbana Önnur *241*

- Sinfiötlalok: Sinfiötli's End **255**
- SigurÞarkviða Fafnisbana Fyrsta eða Gripisspa **257**
- SigurÞarkviða Fafnisbana Önnur **271**
- Fafnismol **279**
- Sigrdrífumál: The Lay of Sigrdrifa **287**
- Fragments of the Lays of Sigurd and Brynhild **297**
- SigurÞarkviða Fafnisbana Þriðja **303**
- Brot af Brynhildarkviða **319**
- GuÞrúnarkviða Fyrsta: The First Lay of Gudrún **325**
- Helreið Brynhildar: Brynhild's Hel-ride **333**
- Drap Niflunga: The Slaughter of the Niflungs. **337**
- Guðrúnarkviða Önnur: The Second Lay of Gudrún **339**
- Guðrunarkviða Þriðja: The Third Lay of Gudrún **351**
- Oddrúnargrátr: Oddrún's Lament **355**
- Atlakviða: The Lay of Atli **363**
- Atlamál in Groenlenzku **375**
- Gudrúnarhvöt: Gudrún's Incitement **399**
- Hamðismal: The Lay of Hamdir. **405**
- Gunnars Slagr: Gunnar's Melody. **413**
- Gróttasöngr: The Lay of Grótti, or The Mill-Song **419**

Preface

(Chiefly from the Vita Sæamundi Multiseii volgo Froda, Autore Arna Magnæo, prefixed to the Copenhagen edition.)

Sæmund, son of Sigfus, the reputed collector of the poems bearing his name, which is sometimes also called the Elder, and the Poetic, Edda, was of a highly distinguished family, being descended in a direct line from King Harald Hildetönn. He was born at Oddi, his paternal dwelling in the south of Iceland, between the years 1054 and 1057, or about 50 years after the establishment by law of the Christian religion in that island; hence it is easy to imagine that many heathens, or baptized favourers of the old mythic songs of heathenism, may have lived in his days and imparted to him the lays of the times of old, which his unfettered mind induced him to hand down to posterity. The youth of Sæmund was passed in travel and study, in Germany and France, and, according to some accounts, in Italy. His cousin John Ögmundson, who later became first bishop of Holum, and after his death was received among the number of saints, when on his way to Rome, fell in with his youthful kinsman, and took him back with him to Iceland, in the year 1076. Sæmund afterwards became a priest at Oddi, where he instructed many young men in useful learning; but the effects of which were not improbably such as to the common people might appear as witchcraft or magic: and, indeed, Sæmund's predilection for the sagas and songs of the old heathen times (even for the magical ones) was so well known, that among his countrymen there were some who regarded him as a great sorcerer, though chiefly in what is called white or innocuous and defensive sorcery, a repute which still clings to his memory among the common people of Iceland, and will long adhere to it through the numerous and popular stories regarding him (some of them highly entertaining) that are orally transmitted from generation to generation.

The following, the first among many, may serve as a specimen. Sæmund was residing, in the south of Europe, with a famous Master, by whom he was instructed in every kind of lore; while, on the other hand, he forgot (apparently through intense study) all that he had previously learned, even to his own name; so that when the holy man John Ögmundson came to his abode, he told him that his name was Koll; but on John insisting that he was no other than Sæmund Sigfusson, born at Oddi in Iceland, and relating to him many particulars regarding himself, he at length became conscious of his own identity, and resolved to flee from the place with his kinsman. For the purpose of deceiving the Master, John continued some time in the place, and often came to visit him and Sæmund: till at last, on dark night, they betook themselves to flight. No sooner had the Master missed them than he sent in pursuit of them; but in vain, and the heavens were too overcast to admit, according to his custom, of reading their whereabouts in the stars. So they traveled day and night and all the following day. But the next night was clear, and the Master at once read in the stars where they were, and set out after them at full speed. Then Sæmund, casting his eyes up at the heavens, said: 'Now is my Master in chase of us, and sees where we are.' And on John asking what was to be done, he answered: 'Take one of my shoes off; fill it with water, and set it on my head.' John did so, and at the same moment, the Master, looking up at the heavens, says to his companion: 'Bad news: the stranger John has drowned my pupil; there is water about his forehead.'

And thereupon returned home. The pair now again prosecute their journey night and day; but, in the following night, the Master again consults the stars, when, to his great amazement, he sees the star of Sæmund directly above his head, and again sets out after the fugitives. Observing this, Sæmund says: 'The astrologer is again after us, and again we must look to ourselves: take my shoe off again, and with your knife stab me in the thigh: fill the shoe with blood, and place it on the top of my head.' John does as directed, and the Master again gazing at the stars, says: 'There is blood now about the star of Master Koll, and the stranger has for certain murdered him': and so returns home. The old man now has once more recourse to his art; but on seeing Sæmund's star shining brightly above him, he exclaimed: 'My pupil is still living: so much the better. I have taught him more than enough; for he outdoes me both in astrology and magic. Let them now proceed in safety; I am unable to hinder their departure.'

Sæmund died at the age of 77, leaving behind him a work on the history of Norway and Iceland, which is now entirely lost. The first who ascribed to Sæmund the collection of poems known as the *Poetic Edda*,[1] was Brynjolf Sveinsson, bishop of Skalholt. This prelate, who was a zealous collector of ancient manuscripts, found in the year 1643, the old vellum codex, which is the most complete of all the known manuscripts of the Edda; of this he caused a transcript to be made, which he entitled *Edda Sæmundi Multiseii*. The transcript came into the possession of the royal historiographer Torfæus; the original, together with other MSS., was presented to the King of Denmark, Frederick III., and placed in the royal library at Copenhagen, where it now is.[2] As many of the Eddaic poems appear to have been orally transmitted in an imperfect state, the collector has supplied the deficiencies by prose insertions, whereby the integrity of the subject is to a certain degree restored.

The collection called *Sæmund's Edda* consists of two parts, viz., the Mythological and the Heroic. It is the former of these which is now offered to the public in an English version. In the year 1797, a translation of this first part, by A.S. Cottle, was published at Bristol. This work I have never met with; nor have I seen any English version of any part of the Edda, which the exception of Gray's spirited but free translation of the *Vegtamskvida*. The present volume closes with a translation of the *Solarlioð*, a poem in which the religion of the country appears in a transition state from Heathenism to Christianity.[3] Some readers will, I doubt not, be desirous of ampler illustration of the mythological poems of the *Edda* than that which is afforded by the Index to this volume; to such I would recommend the translation of the *Prose Edda*, in Mallet's *Northern Antiquities*, published by Bohn, and Thorpe's *Northern Mythology and Popular Traditions*, in 3 vols. Small 8, the 1st vol. Of which contains a good and satisfactory compendium of the Odinic religion. The German scholar will find ample and valuable information on the same subject in the "Altnordische Mythologie" prefixed to Professor Lünings editions of the *Edda*, a work which I have principally used while revising the present translation, and which I regard as unquestionably the best existing.

From a memorandum made at the time, I find that this volume was ready for press in the year 1856, though the idea of offering it to the public was not entertained until about two years ago.

---

1. Bishop P.E. Müller supposes the greater number of the Eddaic poems to be of the 8th century. Sagabibliothek II, p.131.
2. Codex Regius, No. 2365, 4to. The handwriting of this MS. is supposed to be of the beginning of the 14th. century.
3. The Solarlioð is by some supposed to be the composition of Sæmund himself.

On intimating my intention to one or two persons, I was informed that an edition was already in the press, and, consequently, I withdrew from the field. But as that edition seems to be postponed *sine die,* or I had been misinformed regarding it, I have resolved on sending forth my humble production. It is needless to inform my readers that it has no pretension to elegance; but I believe it to be a faithful though homely representation of the original, and may, at all events serve as a stop-gap until made to give place to a worthier work; for that the lack of an edition of the *Edda* seems a chasm in our literature cannot be denied.

If a not unfavourable reception is given it by the British public, the Second, or Heroic part shall be immediately sent to press.

The Editor

Part 1: The Mythological Lays

Völuspá: The Vala's Prophecy

Introduction to the Völuspá

As introductory to the *Völuspá*, the following description of a wandering *Vala* or prophetess may be thought both desirable and interesting: "We find them present at the birth of children, when they seem to represent the Norns. They acquired their knowledge either by means of *seid*, during the night, which all others in the house were sleeping, and uttered their oracles in the morning; or they received sudden inspirations during the signing of certain songs appropriated to the purpose, without which the sorcery could not perfectly succeed. These seid-women were common over all of the North. When invited by the master of a family, they appeared in a peculiar costume, sometimes with a considerable number of followers, e.g., with fifteen young men and fifteen girls. For their soothsaying they received money, gold rings, and other precious things. Sometimes it was necessary to compel them to prophesy. An old description of such a Vala, who went from guild to guild telling fortunes, will give the best idea of these women and their proceedings: -

Thorbiörg, nicknamed the little Vala, during the winter attended the guilds, at the invitation of those who desired to know their fate, or the quality of the coming year. Everything was prepared in the most sumptuous manner for her reception. There was an elevated seat, on which lay a cushion stuffed with feathers. A man was sent to meet her. She came in the evening dressed in a blue mantle fastened with thongs and set with stones down to the lap; round her neck she had a necklace of glass beads, on her head a hood of black lambskin lined with white catskin; in her hand a staff, the head of which was mounted with brass and ornamented with stones; round her body she wore a girdle of agaric *(knöske)*, from which hung a bag containing her conjuring apparatus; on her feet were rough calfskin shoes with long ties and tin buttons, on her hands catskin gloves, white and hairy within. All bade her welcome with a reverent salutation; the master himself conducted her by the hand to her seat. She undertook no prophecy on the first day, but would first pass a night there. In the evening of the following day she ascended her elevated seat, caused the women to place themselves round her, and desired them to sing certain songs, which they did in a strong, clear voice. She then prophesied of the coming year, and afterwards, all that would advanced and asked her such questions as they thought proper, to which they received plain answers." *Northern Mythology I. p.214, Den Ældre Edda I. p. 6.*

In the following grand and ancient lay, dating most probably from the time of heathenism, are set forth, as the utterances of a Vala, or wandering prophetess, as above described, the story of the creation of the world from chaos, of the origin of the giants, the gods, the dwarfs, and the human race, together with other events relating to the mythology of the North, and ending with the destruction of the gods and the world, and their renewal.

Völuspá
The Vala's Prophecy

1. For silence I pray all
sacred children,
great and small,
sons of Heimdall[1]
they will that I Valfather's
deeds recount,
men's ancient saws,
those that I best remember.

2. The Jötuns I remember
early born,
those who me of old
have reared.
I nine worlds remember,
nine trees,
the great central tree,
beneath the earth.

3. There was in times of old,
where Ymir dwelt,
nor sand nor sea,
nor gelid waves;
earth existed not,
nor heaven above,
'twas a chaotic chasm,
and grass nowhere.

4. Before Bur's sons
raised up heaven's vault,
they who the noble
mid-earth shaped.
The sun shone from the south
over the structure's rocks:
then was the earth begrown
with herbage green.

---

1. In the *Rigsmal* we are informed how Heimdall, under the name of Rig, became the progenitor of the three orders of mankind.

5. The sun from the south,
the moon's companion,
her right hand cast
about the heavenly horses.
The sun knew not
where she[2] a dwelling had,
the moon knew not
what power he possessed,
the stars knew not
where they had a station.

6. Then went the powers all
to their judgement-seats,
the all-holy gods,
and thereon held council:
to night and to the waning moon
gave names;
morn they named,
and mid-day,
afternoon and eve,
whereby to reckon years.

7. The Æsir met
on Ida's plain;
they altar-steads and temples
high constructed;
their strength they proved,
all things tried,
furnaces established,
precious things forged,
formed tongs,
and fabricated tools;

8. At tables played at home;
joyous they were;
to them was naught
the want of gold,
until there came
Thurs-maidens three,
all powerful,
from Jötunheim.

---

2. In the Germanic tongues, as in the Semitic, the sun is fem., the moon masc.

9. Then went all the powers
to their judgement-seats,
the all-holy gods,
and thereon held council,
who should of the dwarfs
the race create,
from the sea-giant's blood
and livid bones.

10. Then was Mötsognir
created greatest
of all the dwarfs,
and Durin second;
there in man's likeness
they created many
dwarfs from the earth,
as Durin said.

11. Nýi and Nidi,
Nordri and Sudri,
Austri and Vestri,
Althiöf, Dvalin
Nár and Náin,
Niping, Dáin,
Bivör, Bavör,
Bömbur, Nori,
An and Anar,
Ai, Miödvitnir,

12. Veig and Gandálf,
Vindálf, Thráin,
Thekk and Thorin,
Thror, Vitr, and Litr,
Núr and Nýrád,
Regin and Rádsvid.
Now of the dwarfs I have
rightly told.

13. Fili, Kili,
Fundin, Nali,
Hepti, Vili,
Hanar, Svior,
Billing, Bruni,
Bild, Búri,
Frár, Hornbori,
Fræg and Lóni,
Aurvang, Iari,
Eikinskialdi.

14. Time 'tis of the dwarfs
in Dvalin's band,
to the sons of men,
to Lofar up to reckon,
those who came forth
from the world's rock,
earth's foundation,
to Iora's plains.

15. There were Draupnir,
and Dólgthrasir,
Hár, Haugspori,
Hlævang, Glói,
Skirvir, Virvir,
Skafid, Ai,
Alf and Yngvi,
Eikinskialdi,

16. Fjalar and Frosti,
Finn and Ginnar,
Heri, Höggstari,
Hliódolf, Móin:
that above shall,
while mortals live,
the progeny of Lofar,
accounted be.
******************[3]

---

[3]. Indicates a line that has been lost.

17. Until there came three
mighty and benevolent
Æsir to the world
from their assembly.
They found on earth,
nearly powerless,
Ask and Embla,
void of destiny.

18. Spirit they possessed not,
sense they had not,
blood nor motive powers,
nor goodly colour.
Spirit gave Odin,
sense gave Hoenir,
blood gave Lodur,
and goodly colour.
****

19. I know an ash standing
Yggdrasil hight,
a lofty tree, laved
with limpid water:
thence come the dews
into the dales that fall
ever stands it green
over Urd's fountain.

20. Thence come maidens,
much knowing,
three from the hall,
which under that tree stands;
Urd hight the one,
the second Verdandi,
on a tablet they graved
Skuld the third.
Laws they established,
life allotted
to the sons of men;
destinies pronounced.

21. Alone she[3] sat without,
when came that ancient
dread Æsir's prince;
and in his eyes she gazed.

22. "Of what wouldst thou ask me?
Odin! I know all,
where thou thine eye didst sink
in the pure well of Mim."
Mim drinks mead each morn
from Valfather's pledge.[5]
Understand ye yet, or what?

23. The chief of hosts gave her
rings and necklace,
useful discourse,
and a divining spirit:
wide and far she saw
o'er every world.

24. She the Valkyriur saw
from afar coming,
ready to ride
to the gods' people:
Skuld held a shield,
Skögul was second,
then Gunn, Hild, Göndul,
and Geirskögul.
Now are enumerated
Herian's maidens,
the Valkyriur, ready
over the earth to ride.

25. She that war remembers,
the first on earth,
when Gullveig[6] they
with lances pierced,
and in the high one's[7] hall

---

4. The Vala here speaks of herself in the third person.
5. His eye, here understood to signify the sun.
6. A personification of gold. With the introduction of gold was the end of the golden age.
7. *i.e.*, Odin's: his hall is the world.

her burnt,
thrice burnt,
thrice brought her forth,
oft not seldom;
yet she still lives.

26. Heidi they called her,
whithersoe'r she came,
the well-foreseeing Vala:
wolves she tamed,
magic arts she knew,
magic arts practised;
ever was she the joy
of evil people.

27. Then went the powers all
to their judgement-seats,
the all-holy gods,
and thereon held council,
whether the Æsir should
avenge the crime,
or all the gods
receive atonement.

28. Broken was the outer wall
of the Æsir's burgh.
The Vanir, foreseeing conflict
tramp oér the plains.
Odin cast (his spear),
and mid the people hurled it:
that was the first
warfare in the world.
****

29. Then went the powers all
to their judgement-seats,
the all-holy gods,
and thereon held council:
who had all the air
with evil mingled?
or to the Jötun race
Od's maid had given?

30. There alone was Thor
with anger swollen.
He seldom sits,
when of the like he hears.
Oaths are not held sacred;
nor words, nor swearing,
nor binding compacts
reciprocally made.

31. She knows that Heimdall's
horn is hidden
under the heaven-bright
holy tree.
A river she sees flow,
with foamy fall,
from Valfather's pledge.
Understand ye yet, or what?

32. East sat the crone,
in Iárnvidir,
Fenrir's progeny:
of all shall be
one especially
the moon's devourer,
in a troll's semblance.

33. He is sated with the last breath
of dying men;
the gods' seat he
with red gore defiles:
swart is the sunshine then
for summers after;
all weather turns to storm.
Understand ye yet, or what?

34. There on a height sat,
striking a harp,
the giantess's watch,
the joyous Egdir;
by him crowed,
in the bird-wood,
the bright red cock,
which Fialar hight.

35. Crowed o'er the Æsir
Gullinkambi,
which wakens heroes
with the sire of hosts;
but another crows
beneath the earth,
a soot-red cock,
in the halls of Hel.

36. I saw of Baldr,
the blood-stained god,
Odin's son,
the hidden fate.
There stood grown up,
high on the plain,
slender and passing fair,
the mistletoe.

37. From that shrub was made,
as to me it seemed,
a deadly, noxious dart.
Hödr shot it forth;
But Frigg bewailed,
in Fensalir,
Valhall's calamity.
Understand ye yet, or what?

38. Bound she saw lying,
under Hveralund,
a monstrous form,
to Loki like.
There sits Sigyn,
for her consort's sake,
not right glad.
Understand ye yet, or what?

39. Then the Vala knew
the fatal bonds were twisting,
most rigid,
bonds from entrails made.

40. From the east a river falls,
through venom dales,
with mire and clods,
Slid is its name.

41. On the north there stood,
on Nida-fells,
a hall of gold,
for Sindri's race;
and another stood
in Okolnir,
the Jötuns beer-hall
which Brimir hight.

42. She saw a hall standing,
far from the sun,
in Náströnd;
its doors are northward turned,
venom-drops fall
in through its apertures:
entwined is that hall
with serpent's backs.

43. She there saw wading
the sluggish streams
bloodthirsty men
and perjurers,
and him who the ear beguiles
of another's wife.
There Nidhögg sucks
the corpses of the dead;
the wolf tears men.
Understand ye yet, or what?

44. Further forward I see,
much can I say
of Ragnarök
and the gods' conflict.

45. Brothers shall fight,
and slay each other;
cousins shall
kinship violate.
The earth resounds,
the giantesses flee;
no man will
another spare.

46. Hard is it in the world,
great whoredom,
an axe age, a sword age,
shields will be cloven,
a wind age, a wolf age,
ere the world sinks.

47. Mim's sons dance,
but the central tree takes fire,
at the resounding
Gjallar-horn.
Loud blows Heimdall,
his horn is raised;
Odin speaks
with Mim's head.

48. Trembles Yggdrasil's
ash yet standing;
groans that aged tree,
and the jötun is loosed.
Loud bays Garm
before the Gnupa-cave,
his bonds he rends asunder;
and the wolf runs.

49. Hrym steers from the east,
the waters rise,
the mundane snake is coiled
in jötun-rage.
The worm beats the water,
and the eagle screams:
the pale of beak tears carcases;
Naglfar is loosed.

50. That ship fares from the east:
come will Muspell's
people o'er the sea,
and Loki steers.
The monster's kin goes
all with the wolf;
with them the brother is
of Byleist on their course.

51. Surt from the south comes
with flickering flame;
shines from his sword
the Val-god's sun.
The stony hills are dashed together,
the giantesses totter;
men tread the path of Hel,
and heaven is cloven.

52. How is it with the Æsir?
How with the Alfar?
All Jötunheim resounds;
the Æsir are in council.
The dwarfs groan
before their stony doors,
the sages of the rocky walls.
Understand ye yet, or what?

53. Then arises
Hlin's second grief,
when Odin goes
with the wolf to fight,
and the bright slayer
of Beli with Surt.
Then will Frigg's
beloved fall.

54. Then comes the great
victor-sire's son,
Vidar, to fight
with the deadly beast.
He with his hands will
make his sword pierce
to the heart of the giant's son:
then avenges he his father.

55. Then comes the mighty
son of Hlódyn:
(Odin's son goes
with the monster to fight);
Midgárd's Veor in his rage
will slay the worm.
Nine feet will go
Fiörgyn's son,
bowed by the serpent,
who feared no foe.
All men will
their homes forsake.

56. The sun darkens,
earth in ocean sinks,
fall from heaven
the bright stars,
fire's breath assails
the all-nourishing tree,
towering fire plays
against heaven itself.

57. She sees arise,
a second time,
earth from ocean,
beauteously green,
waterfalls descending;
the eagle flying over,
which in the fell
captures fish.

58. The Æsir meet
on Ida's plain,
and of the mighty
earth-encircler speak,
and there to memory call
their mighty deeds,
and the supreme god's
ancient lore.

59. There shall again
the wondrous
golden tables
in the grass be found,
which in days of old
had possessed
the ruler of the gods,
and Fjölnir's race.

60. Unsown shall
the fields bring forth,
all evil be amended;
Baldr shall come;
Hödr and Baldr,
the heavenly gods,
Hropt's glorious dwellings shall inhabit.
Understand ye yet, or what?

61. Then can Hoenir
choose his lot,
and the two brother's
sons inhabit
the spacious Vindheim.
Understand ye yet, or what?

62. She a hall sees standing
than the sun brighter,
with gold bedecked,
in Gimill:
there shall the righteous
people dwell,
and for evermore
happiness enjoy.

64. Then comes the mighty one
to the great judgement,
the powerful from above,
who rules o'er all.
He shall dooms pronounce,
and strifes allay,
holy peace establish,
which shall ever be.
****

65. There comes the dark
dragon flying from beneath,
the glistening serpent,
from Nida-fells.
On his wings bears Nidhögg,
flying o'er the plain,
a corpse.
Now she will descend.

VafÞrúðnismál: The lay of Vafthrúdnir

Odin visits the Giant *(Jötun)* Vafthrudnir, for the purpose of proving his knowledge. They propose questions relative to the Cosmogony of the Northern creed, on the condition that the baffled party forfeit his head. The Jötun incurs the penalty.

Odin
1. Counsel thou me now, Frigg!
as I long to go
Vafthrudnir to visit;
great desire, I say,
I have, in ancient lore
with that all-wise Jötun to contend.

Frigg
2. At home to bide
Hærfather I would counsel,
in the gods' dwellings;
because no Jötun
is, I believe, so mighty
as is Vafthrudnir.

Odin
3. Much have I journeyed,
much experienced,
mighty ones many proved;
but this I fain would know,
how in Vafthrudnir's
halls it is.

Frigg
4. In safety mayest thou go,
in safety return,
in safety on thy journeyings be;
may thy wit avail thee,
when thou, father of men! shalt
hold converse with the Jötun.

5. Then went Odin
the lore to prove
of that all-wise Jötun.
To the hall he came
which Im's father owned.
Ygg went forthwith in.

Odin
6. Hail to thee, Vafthrudnir!
to thy hall I am now come,
thyself to see;
for I fain would know,
whether thou art a cunning
and all-wise Jötun.

Vafthrudnir
7. What man is this,
that in my habitation
by word addresses me?
Out thou goest not
from our halls,
if thou art not the wiser.

Odin
8. Gagnrad is my name,
from my journey I am come
thirsty to thy halls,
needing hospitality,
for I long have journeyed
and kind reception from thee, Jötun!

Vafthrudnir
9. Why then, Gagnrad!
speakest thou from the floor?
Take in the hall a seat;
then shall be proved
which knows most,
the guest or the ancient talker.

Gagnrad
10. A poor man should,
who to a rich man comes,
speak usefully or hold his tongue:
over-much talk
brings him, I ween, no good,
who visits an austere man.

Vafthrudnir
11. Tell me, Gagnrad!
since on the floor thou wilt
prove thy proficiency,
how the horse is called
that draws each day
forth over human kind?

Gagnrad
12. Skinfaxi he is named,
that the bright day draws
forth over human kind.
Of coursers he is best accounted
among the Reid-goths.
Ever sheds light that horse's mane.

Vafthrudnir
13. Tell me now, Gagnrad!
since on the floor thou wilt
prove thy proficiency,
how that steed is called,
which from the east draws night
o'er the beneficent powers?

Gagnrad
14. Hrimfaxi he is called,
that each night draws forth
over the beneficent powers.
He from his bit lets fall
drops every morn,
whence in the dales comes dew.

Vafthrudnir
15. Tell me, Gagnrad!
since on the floor thou wilt
prove thy proficiency,
how the stream is called,
which earth divides between
the Jötuns and the Gods?

Gagnrad
16. Ifing the stream is called
which earth divides between
the Jötuns and the Gods:
open shall it run
throughout all time.
On that stream no ice shall be.

Vafthrudnir
17. Tell me, Gagnrad!
since on the floor thou wilt
prove thy proficiency,
how that plain is called,
where in fight shall meet
Surt and the gentle Gods?

Gagnrad
18. Vigrid the plain is called,
where in fight shall meet
Surt and the gentle Gods;
a hundred rasts it is
on every side.
That plain is to them decreed.

Vafthrudnir
19. Wise art thou, o guest!
Approach the Jötuns bench,
and sitting let us together talk:
we will our heads
in the hall pledge,
guest! for wise utterance.
****

Gagnrad
20. Tell me first,
if thy wit suffices,
and thou, Vafthrudnir! knowest,
whence first came the earth,
and the high heaven,
thou, sagacious Jötun?

Vafthrudnir
21. From Ymir's flesh
the earth was formed,
and from his bones the hills,
the heaven from the skull
of that ice-cold giant,
and from his blood the sea.

Gagnrad
22. Tell me secondly,
if thy wit suffices,
and thou, Vafthrudnir! knowest,
whence came the moon,
which over mankind passes,
and the sun likewise?

Vafthrudnir
23. Mundilfoeri hight he,
who the moon's father is,
and eke the sun's:
round heaven journey
each day they must,
to count years for men.

Gagnrad
24. Tell me thirdly,
since thou art called wise,
and if thou, Vafthrudnir! knowest,
whence came the day,
which over people passes,
and night with waning moons?

Vafthrudnir
25. Delling hight he
who the day's father is,
but night was of Nörvi born;
the new and waning moons
the beneficent powers created,
to count years for men.

Gagnrad
26. Tell me fourthly,
since they pronounce thee sage,
and if thou, Vafthrudnir! knowest,
whence winter came,
and warm summer
first among the wise gods?

Vafthrudnir
27. Vindsval hight he,
who winter's father is,
and Svasud summer's;
yearly they both
shall ever journey,
until the powers perish.

Gagnrad
28. Tell me fifthly,
since they pronounce thee sage,
and if thou, Vafthrudnir! knowest,
which of the Æsir earliest,
or of Ymir's sons
in days of old existed?

Vafthrudnir
29. Countless winters,
ere earth was formed,
was Bergelmir born;
Thrudgelmir
was his sire,
his grandsire Aurgelmir.

Gagnrad
30. Tell me sixthly,
since thou art called wise,
and if thou, Vafthrudnir! knowest,
whence first came Aurgelmir,
among the Jötun's sons,
thou sagacious Jötun?

Vafthrudnir
31. From Elivagar
sprang venom drops,
which grew till they became a Jötun;
but sparks flew
from the south-world:
to the ice the fire gave life.

Gagnrad
32. Tell me seventhly,
since thou art called wise,
and if thou knowest, Vafthrudnir!
how he children begat,
the bold Jötun,
as he had no giantess's company?

Vafthrudnir
33. Under the armpit grew,
'tis said, of the Hrimthurs,
a girl and boy together;
foot with foot begat,
of that wise Jötun,
a six-headed son.

Gagnrad
34. Tell me eighthly,
since thou art called wise,
and if thou knowest, Vafthrudnir!
what thou doest first remember,
or earliest knowest?
Thou art an all-wise Jötun.

Vafthrudnir
35. Countless winters,
ere earth was formed,
Bergelmir was born.
That I first remember,
when that wise Jötun
in an ark was laid.

Gagnrad
36. Tell me ninthly,
since thou art called wise,
and if thou knowest, Vafthrudnir!
whence the wind comes,
that over ocean passes,
itself invisible to man?

Vafthrudnir
37. Hræsvelg he is called,
who at the end of heaven sits,
a Jötun in an eagle's plumage:
from his wings comes,
it is said, the wind,
that over all men passes.

Gagnrad
38. Tell me tenthly,
since thou all the origin
of the gods knowest, Vafthrudnir!
whence Niörd came
among the Æsir's sons?
O'er fanes and offer-steads
he rules by hundreds,
yet was not among the Æsir born.

Vafthrudnir
39. In Vanaheim
wise powers him created,
and to the gods a hostage gave.
At the world's dissolution
he will return
to the wise Vanir.

Gagnrad
40. Tell me eleventhly,
since all the condition
of the gods thou knowest, Vafthrudnir!
what the Einherjar do
in Hærfather's halls,
until the powers perish?

Vafthrudnir
41. All the Einherjar
in Odin's halls
each day together fight;
the fallen they choose,
and from the conflict ride;
beer with the Æsir drink,
of Sæhrimnir eat their fill,
then sit in harmony together.

Gagnrad
42. Tell me twelfthly,
as thou all the condition
of the gods knowest, Vafthrudnir!
of the Jötuns' secrets,
and of all the gods',
say what truest is,
thou all-knowing Jötun!

Vafthrudnir
43. Of the secrets of the Jötuns
and of all the gods,
I can truly tell;
for I have over
each world travelled;
to nine worlds I came,
to Niflhel beneath:
here die men from Hel.

Gagnrad
44. Much have I journeyed,
much experienced,
mighty ones many proved.
What mortals will live,
when the great "Fimbulwinter"
shall from men have passed?

Vafthrudnir
45. Lif and Lifthrasir;
but they will be concealed
in Hoddmimir's holt.
The morning dews
they will have for food.
From them shall men be born.

Gagnrad
46. Much have I journeyed,
much experienced,
mighty ones many proved.
Whence will come the sun
in that fair heaven,
when Fenrir has this devoured?

Vafthrudnir
47. A daughter shall
Alfrödull bear,
ere Fenrir shall have swallowed her.
The maid shall ride,
when the powers die,
on her mother's course.

Gagnrad
48. Much have I journeyed, (etc.)
who are the maidens
that o'er the ocean travel,
wise of spirit, journey?

Vafthrudnir
49. O'er people's dwellings three descend
of Mögthrasir's maidens,
the sole Hamingiur
who are in the world,
although with Jötuns nurtured.

Gagnrad
50. Much have I journeyed, (etc.)
Which of the Æsir will rule o'er the gods' possession,
when Surt's fire shall be quenched?

Vafthrudnir
51. Vidar and Vali
will the gods' holy fanes inhabit,
when Surt's fire shall be quenched.
Modi and Magni will
Mjöllnir possess,
and warfare strive to end.

Gagnrad
52. Much have I journeyed, (etc.)
What of Odin will
the life's end be,
when the powers perish?

Vafthrudnir
53. The wolf will
the father of men devour;
him Vidar will avenge:
he his cold jaws will cleave,
in conflict with the wolf.

Gagnrad
54. Much have I journeyed, (etc.)
What said Odin
in his son's ear,
ere he on the pile was laid?

Vafthrudnir
55. That no one knoweth,
what thou in days of old
saidst in thy son's ear.
With dying mouth
my ancient saws I have said,
and the gods' destruction.
With Odin I have contended
in wise utterances:
of men thou ever art the wisest!

Grímnismál: The Lay of Grimnir
The subject is wholly mythological

King Hraudung had two sons, one named Agnar, the other Geirröd. Agnar was ten, and Geirröd eight winters old. They both rowed out in a boat, with their hooks and lines, to catch small fish; but the wind drove them out to sea. In the darkness of the night they were wrecked on the shore, and went up into the country, where they found a cottager, with whom they stayed through the winter. The cottager's wife brought up Agnar, and the cottager, Geirröd, and gave him good advice. In the spring the man got them a ship; but when he and his wife accompanied them to the strand, the man talked apart with Geirröd. They had a fair wind, and reached their father's place. Geirröd was at the ship's prow: he sprang on shore, but pushed the ship out, saying, "Go where an evil spirit may get thee." The vessel was driven out to sea, but Geirröd went up to the town, where he was well received; but his father was dead. Geirröd was then taken for king, and became a famous man.

Odin and Frigg were sitting in Hlidskialf, looking over all the world. Odin said, "Seest thou Agnar, thy foster-son, where he is getting children with a giantess in a cave? while Geirröd, my foster-son, is a king residing in his country." Frigg answered, "He is so inhospitable that he tortures his guests, if he thinks too many come." Odin replied that that was the greatest falsehood; and they wagered thereupon. Frigg sent her waiting-maid Fulla to bid Geirröd be on his guard, lest the trollmann who was coming should do him harm, and also say that a token whereby he might be known was, that no dog, however fierce, would attack him. But that King Geirröd was not hospitable was mere idle talk. He, nevertheless, caused the man to be secured whom no dog would assail. He was clad in a blue cloak, and was named Grimnir, and would say no more concerning himself, although he was questioned. The king ordered him to be tortured to make him confess, and to be set between two fires; and there he sat for eight nights. King Geirröd had a son ten years old, whom he named Agnar, after his brother. Agnar went to Grimnir and gave him a full horn to drink from, saying that the king did wrong in causing him to be tortured, though innocent. Grimnir drank from it. The fire had then so approached him that his cloak was burnt; whereupon he said: -

    1. Fire! thou art hot,
    and much too great;
    flame! let us separate.
    My garment is singed,
    although I lift it up,
    my cloak is scorched before it.

2. Eight nights have I sat
between fires here,
and to me no one
food has offered,
save only Agnar,
the son of Geirröd,
who alone shall rule
over the land of the Goths.

3. Be thou blessed, Agnar!
as blessed as the god of men
bids thee to be.
For one draught
thou never shalt
get better recompense.

4. Holy is the land,
which I see lying
to Æsir and Alfar near;
but in Thrundheim
Thor shall dwell
until the powers perish.

5. Ydalir it is called,
where Ullr has
himself a dwelling made.
Alfheim the gods to Frey
gave in days of yore
for a tooth-gift.

6. The third dwelling is,
where the kind powers have
with silver decked the hall;
Valaskjalf 'tis called,
which for himself acquired
the Ás in days of old.

7. Sökkvabekk the fourth is named
oe'r which
the gelid waves resound;
Odin and Saga there,
joyful each day,
from golden beakers quaff.

8. Gladsheim the fifth is named,
there the golden-bright
Valhall stands spacious,
there Hropt selects
each day those men
who die by weapons.

9. Easily to be known is,
by those who to Odin come,
the mansion by its aspect.
Its roof with spears is laid,
its hall with shields is decked,
with corslets are its benches strewed.

10. Easily to be known is,
by those who to Odin come,
the mansion by its aspect.
A wolf hangs
before the western door,
over it an eagle hovers.

11. Thrymheim the sixth is named,
where Thiassi dwelt,
that all-powerful Jotun;
but Skadi now inhabits,
the bright bride of the gods,
her father's ancient home.

12. Breidablik is the seventh,
where Baldr has
built for himself a hall,
in that land,
in which I know exists
the fewest crimes.

13. Himinbjörg is the eighth,
where Heimdall, it is said,
rules o'er the holy fanes:
there the gods' watchman,-
in his tranquil home,
drinks joyful the good mead.

14. Folkvang is the ninth,
there Freyja directs
the sittings in the hall.
She half the fallen chooses each day,
but Odin th' other half.

15. Glitnir is the tenth;
it is on gold sustained,
and eke with silver decked.
There Forseti dwells
throughout all time,
and every strife allays.

16. Noatun is the eleventh,
there Niörd has
himself a dwelling made,
prince of men;
guiltless of sin,
he rules o'er the high-built fane.

17. O'ergrown with branches
and high grass
is Vidar's spacious Landvidi:
There will the son descend,
from the steed's back,
bold to avenge his father.

18. Andhrimnir makes,
in Eldhrimnir,
Sæhrimnir to boil,
of meats the best;
but few know how many
Einherjar it feeds.

19. Geri and Freki
the war-wont sates,
the triumphant sire of hosts;
but on wine only
the famed in arms,
Odin, ever lives.

20. Hugin and Munin
fly each day
over the spacious earth.
I fear for Hugin,
that he come not back,
yet more anxious am I for Munin.

21. Thund roars;
joyful in Thiodvitnir's
water lives the fish;
the rapid river
seems too great
for the battle-steed to ford.

22. Valgrind is the lattice called,
in the plain that stands,
holy before the holy gates:
ancient is that lattice,
but few only know
how it is closed with lock.

23. Five hundred doors,
and forty eke, I think,
are in Valhall.
Eight hundred Einherjar
will at once from each door go
when they issue with the wolf to fight.

34. Five hundred floors,
and forty eke, I think,
has Bilskirnir with its windings.
Of all the roofed
houses that I know,
is my son's the greatest.

25. Heidrun the goat is called,
that stands o'er Odin's hall,
and bites from Lærad's branches.
He a bowl shall fill
with the bright mead;
that drink shall never fail.

26. Eikthyrnir the hart is called,
that stands o'er Odin's hall,
and bites from Lærad's branches;
from his horns fall
drops into Hvergelmir,
whence all waters rise:-

27. Sid and Vid,
Soekin and Eikin,
Svöl and Gunntro,
Fiörm and Fimbulthul,
Rin and Rennandi,
Gipul and Göpul,
Gömul and Geirvimul:
they round the gods' dwellings wind.
Thyn and Vin,
Thöll and Höll,
Grad and Gunnthorin.

28. Vina one is called,
a second Vegsvin,
a third Thiodnuma;
Nyt and Nöt,
Nön and Hrön,
Slid and Hrid,
Sylg and Ylg,
Vid and Van,
Vönd and Strönd,
Giöll and Leipt;
these (two) fall near to men,
but fall hence to Hel,

29. Körmt and Örmt,
and the Kerlaugs twain:
these Thor must wade each day,
when he to council goes
at Yggdrasil's ash;
for the As-bridge
is all on fire,
the holy waters boil.

30. Glad and Gyllir,
Gler and Skeidbrimir,
Sillfrintopp and Sinir,
Gisl and Falhofnir,
Gulltopp and Lettfeti;
on these steeds the Æsir
each day ride,
when they to council go,
at Yggdrasil's ash.

31. Three roots stand
on three ways
under Yggdrasil's ash:
Hel under one abides,
under the second the Hrimthursar,
under the third mankind.

32. Ratatösk is the squirrel named,
which has to run
in Yggdrasil's ash;
he from above
the eagle's words must carry,
and beneath to Nidhögg repeat.

33. Harts there are also four,
which from its summits,
arch-necked, gnaw.
Dain and Dvalin,
Duneyr and Durathror.

34. More serpents lie
under Yggdrasil's ash,
than any one would think
of witless mortals:
Goin and Moin
they are Grafvitnir's sons
Grabak and Grafvöllud,
Ofnir and Svafnir,
will, I ween,
the branches of that tree
ever lacerate.

35. Yggdrasil's ash
hardship suffers
greater than men know of;
a hart bites it above,
and in its side it rots,
Nidhögg beneath tears it.

36. Hrist and Mist
the horn shall bear me
Skeggöld and Skögul,
Hlökk and Herfjötur,
Hildi and Thrudi,
Göll and Geirölul,
Randgrid and Radgrid,
and Reginleif,
these bear beer to the Einherjar.

37. Arvakr and Alsvid,
theirs 'tis up hence
fasting the sun to draw:
under their shoulder
the gentle powers, the Æsir,
have concealed an iron-coolness.

38. Svalin the shield is called,
which stands before the sun,
the refulgent deity:
rocks and ocean must, I ween,
be burnt,
fell it from its place.

39. Sköll the wolf is named,
that the fair-faced goddess
to the ocean chases;
another Hati hight,
he is Hrodvitnir's son;
he the bright maid of heaven shall precede.

40. Of Ymir's flesh
was earth created,
of his blood the sea,
of his bones the hills,
of his hair trees and plants,
of his skull the heaven;

41. And of his brows
the gentle powers
formed Midgard for the sons of men;
but of his brain
the heavy clouds are
all created.

42. Ullr's and all the gods'
favour shall have,
whoever first shall look to the fire;
for open will the dwelling be,
to the Æsir's sons,
when the kettles are lifted off.[1]

43. Ivald's sons
went in days of old
Skidbladnir to form,
of ships the best,
for the bright Frey,
Njörd's benign son.

44. Yggdrasil's ash is
of all trees most excellent,
and of all ships, Skidbladnir,
of the Æsir, Odin,
and of horses, Sleipnir,
Bifröst of bridges,
and of skalds, Bragi,
Habrok of hawks,
and of dogs, Garm, (Brimir of swords.)

---

1. What in this strophe is said of Ullr has apparently reference to a lost myth. It would seem that, through the intervention of the kettles, the Æsir were unable to see Odin's unpleasant position between the two fires.

45. Now I my face have raised
to the gods' triumphant sons,
at that will welcome help awake;
from all the Æsir,
that shall penetrate, to Aegir's bench,
to Aegir's compotation.[2]

46. I am called Grim,
I am called Gangleri,
Herian and Hjalmberi,
Thekk and Thridi,
Thund and Ud,
Helblindi and Har,

47. Sad and Svipall,
and Sanngetall,
Herteit and Hnikar
Bileyg, Baleyg,
Bölverk, Fjölnir,
Grim and Grimnir,
Glapsvid and Fjölsvid,

48. Sidhött, Sidskegg
Sigfödr, Hnikud,
Alfödr, Valfödr,
Atrid and Farmatýr;
by one name
I never have been called,
since among men I have gone.

49. Grimnir I am called
at Geirröd's,
and at Asmund's Jalk
and Kialar, when a sledge I drew;
Thror at the public meetings,
Vidur in battles,
Oski and Omi,
Jafnhar and Biflindi,
Göndlir and Harbard with the gods.

---

[2]. My version of this strophe is not in accordance with those of other interpreters. Odin raises his countenance to heaven, in full confidence that when seen help will forthwith be afforded him. Under the name of Ægir, Gierrod is generally understood: I rather think the meaning to be, that all the Æsir who [sit at] Ægir's compotation will forthwith come to his aid.

50. Svidur and Svidrir
I was at Sökkmimir's called,
and beguiled that ancient Jötun,
when of Midvitnir's
renowned son
I was the sole destroyer.

51. Drunken art thou, Geirröd,
thou hast drunk too much,
thou art greatly by mead beguiled.
Much didst thou lose,
when thou wast
of my help bereft,
of all the Einherjar's
and Odin's favour.

52. Many things I told thee,
but thou hast few remembered:
thy friends mislead thee.
My friend's sword
lying I see,
with blood all dripping.

53. The fallen by the sword
Ygg shall now have;
thy life is now run out:
Wroth with thee are the Disir:
Odin thou now shalt see:
draw near to me if thou canst.

54. Odin I now am named,
Ygg I was called before,
before that, Thund,
Vakr and Skilfing,
Vafudr and Hroptatýr,
with the gods, Gaut and Jalk,
Ofnir and Svafnir,
all which I believe to be names of me alone.

King Geirröd was sitting with his sword lying across his knees, half drawn from the scabbard, but on finding that it was Odin, he rose for the purpose of removing him from the fires, when the sword slipt from his hand with the hilt downwards; and the king having stumbled, the sword pierced him through and killed him. Odin then vanished, and Agnar was king for a long time after.

Hrafnagaldr Odins: Odin's Ravens' Song

This very obscure poem has been regarded as a fragment only of a poem, of which the beginning and end are wanting. With regard to the beginning, the want may possibly be more apparent than real; the strophes 2-5 being in fact a sort of introduction, although they do not at first strike us as such, in consequence of the obscurity of the 1st strophe, which seems very slightly connected with the following ones, in which the gods and dwarfs are described as in council, on account of certain warnings and forebodings of their approaching downfall, or Ragnarök. Another point of difficulty is its title, there being nothing in the whole poem to connect it with Odin's ravens, except the mention of Hugr (Hugin) in the 3rd strophe. Erik Halson, a learned Icelander, after having spent or wasted ten years in an attempt to explain this poem, confessed that he understood little or nothing of it. In its mythology, too, we find parts assigned to some of the personages, of which no traces occur in either Sæmunds' or Snorri's Edda; though we are hardly justified in pronouncing it, with more than one scholar of eminence, a fabrication of later times.

1. Alfather works,
the Alfar discern,
the Vanir know,
the Nornir indicate,
the Ividia brings forth,
men endure,
the Thursar await,
the Valkyriur long.

2. The forebodings the Æsir
suspected to be evil;
treacherous Vættar had
the runes confounded.
Urd was enjoined
to guard Odhroerir,
powerfully to protect it
against the increasing multitude.

3. Hug then goes forth,
explores the heavens,
the powers fear
disaster from delay.
'Twas Thrain's belief
that the dream was ominous;
Dain's thought that
the dream was dark.

4. Among the dwarfs
virtue decays;
worlds sink down
to Ginnung's abyss.
Oft will Asvid
strike them down,
oft the fallen
again collect.

5. Stand no longer shall
earth or sun.
The stream of air
with corruption laden
shall not cease.
Hidden is in Mim's
limpid well
men's certain knowledge.
Understand ye yet, or what?
****

6. In the dales dwells
the prescient Dis,
from Yggdrasil's
ash sunk down,
of alfen race,
Idun by name,
the youngest of Ivaldi's
elder children.

7. She ill brooked
her descent,
under the hoar tree's
trunk confined.
She would not happy be
with Nörvi's daughter,
accustomed to a pleasanter
abode at home.

8. The triumphant gods saw
Nanna sorrowing
in earth's deep sanctuaries;
a wolf's skin they gave her,
in which herself she clad,
changed her feelings,
practised guile,
alter'd her aspect.

9. Vidrir selected
Bifröst's guardian,
of the Giöll-sun's
keeper to inquire
all that she knew
of every world;
Bragi and Lopt
should witness bear.

10. Magic songs they sung,
rode on wolves
the god and gods.
At the heavenly house,
Odin listened,
in Hlidskjalf;
let them go forth
on their long way.

11. The wise god asked
the cupbearer
of the gods' progeny
and their associates,
whether of heaven, or Hel,
or earth, she knew
the origin, duration,
or dissolution?

12. She spoke not,
she could no words
to the anxious gods
bring forth,
nor a sound uttered;
tears flowed from the head's orbs;
with pain repressed
they flow anew.

13. As from the east,
from Elivagar,
the thorn is impelled by
the ice-cold Thurs,
wherewith Dain
all people strikes
over the fair mid-earth;

14. When every faculty is lulled,
the hands sink,
totters with drowsiness
the bright, sword-girt Ás;
drives away the current
the giantess's blandishment
of the mind's agitations
of all people,

15. So to the gods appeared
Jorun to be affected,
with sorrows swollen,
when they no answer got;
they strove the more
the greater the repulse;
still less than they had hoped
did their words prevail.

16. When the leader
of the inquiring travellers,
the guardian of Herian's
loud-sounding horn
took the son of Nal
for his companion,
Grimnir's skald
at the place kept watch.

17. Vingolf reached
Vidur's ministers,
both borne
by Forniots kin.
They entered,
and the Æsir
forthwith saluted,
at Ygg's convivial meeting.

18. Hangatyr they hailed,
of Æsir the most blissful;
potent drink in the high seat
they wished him to enjoy,
and the gods to sit
happy at the feast,
ever with Yggiung
pleasure to share.

19. On benches seated,
at Bölverk's bidding,
the company of gods
were with Sæhrimnir sated.
Skögul at the tables,
from Hnikar's vessel,
measured out mead,
in Mimir's horns.

20. Of many thing inquired,
when the meal was over,
the high gods of Heimdall,
the goddesses of Loki,
whether the maid had uttered
divinations or wise words?
From noon
until twilight's advent.

21. Ill they showed
it had fallen out,
their errand bootless,
little to glory in.
A lack of counsel
seemed likely,
how from the maiden they
might an answer get.

22. Omi answered;
"Night is the time
for new counsels;
till the morrow let reflect
each one competent
to give advice
helpful to the Æsir."

23. Ran along the ways
of mother Rind,
the desired repast
of Fenrisulf.
Went from the guild,
bade the gods farewell
Hropt and Frigg,
as, before Hrimfaxi,

24. The son of Delling
urged on his horse
adorned with
precious jewels.
Over Mannheim shines
the horse's mane,
the steed Dvalin's deluder
drew in his chariot.

25. In the north boundary
of the spacious earth,
under the outmost root
of the noble tree,
went to their couches
Gygiar and Thursar,
spectres, dwarfs,
and Murk Alfs.

26. The powers rose,
the Alfs' illuminator
northwards towards Niflheim
chased the night.
Up Argjöll ran
Ulfrun's son,
the mighty hornblower,
of heaven's heights.

Vegtamskviþa eða Baldrs Draumar

The Lay of Vegtam, or Baldr's Dreams

1. Together were the Æsir
all in council,
and the Asyniur
all in conference,
and they consulted,
the mighty gods,
why Baldr had
oppressive dreams.

2. To that god his slumber
was most afflicting;
his auspicious dreams
seemed departed.
They the Jötuns questioned,
wise seers of the future,
whether this might not
forebode calamity?

3. The responses said
that to death destined was
Ullr's kinsman,
of all the dearest:
that caused grief
to Frigg and Svafnir,
and to the other powers
On a course they resolved:

4. That they would send
to every being,
assurance to solicit,
Baldr not to harm.
All species swore
oaths to spare him;
Frigg received all
their vows and compacts.

5. Valfather fears
something defective;
he thinks the Hamingiur
may have departed;
the Æsir he convenes,
their counsel craves;
at the deliberation
much is devised.

6. Uprose Odin
lord of men,
and on Sleipnir he
the saddle laid;
rode thence down
to Niflhel.
A dog he met,
from Hel coming.

7. It was blood-stained
on its breast,
on its slaughter-craving throat,
and nether jaw.
It bayed
and widely gaped
at the sire of magic song:
long it howled.

8. Forth rode Odin
the ground rattled
till to Hel's lofty
house he came.
Then rode Ygg
to the eastern gate,
where he knew there was
a Vala's grave.

9. To the prophetess he began
a magic song to chant,
towards the north looked,
potent runes applied,
a spell pronounced,
an answer demanded,
until compelled she rose,
and with deathlike voice she said:

Vala
10. "What man is this,
to me unknown
who has for me increased
an irksome course?
I have with snow been decked
by rain beaten,
and with dew moistened:
long have I been dead."

Vegtam
11. "Vegtam is my name,
I am Valtam's son.
Tell thou me of Hel:
from earth I call on thee.
For whom are those benches
strewed o'er with rings,
those costly couches
o'erlaid with gold?"

Vala
12. "Here stands mead,
for Baldr brewed,
over the bright potion
a shield is laid;
but the Æsir race
are in despair.
By compulsion I have spoken
I will now be silent."

Vegtam
13. "Be thou not silent, Vala!
I will question thee,
until I know all.
I will yet know
who will Baldr's
slayer be,
and Odin's son
of life bereave."

Vala
14. "Hödr will hither
his glorious brother send,
he of Baldr will
the slayer be,
and Odin's son
of life bereave.
By compulsion I have spoken;
I will now be silent."

Vegtam
15. "Be not silent, Vala!
I will question thee,
until I know all.
I will yet know
who on Hödr vengeance
will inflict
or Baldr's slayer
raise on the pile."

Vala
16. "Rind a son shall bear,
in the western halls:
he shall slay Odin's son,
when one night old.
He a hand will not wash,
nor his head comb,
ere he to the pile has borne
Baldr's adversary.
By compulsion I have spoken;
I will now be silent."

Vegtam
17. "Be not silent, Vala!
I will question thee,
until I know all.
I will yet know
who the maidens are,
that weep at will,
and heavenward cast
their neck-veils?
Tell me but that:
till then thou sleepest not."

Vala
18. "Not Vegtam art thou,
as I before believed;
rather art thou Odin,
lord of men!"

Odin
19. "Thou art no Vala,
nor wise woman,
rather art thou the mother
of three Thursar."

Vala
20. "Home ride thou, Odin!
and exult.
Thus shall never more
man again visit me,
until Loki free
from his bonds escapes,
and Ragnarök
all-destroying comes."

Hávamál: The High One's Lay

1. All door-ways,
before going forward,
should be looked to;
for difficult it is to know
where foes may sit
within a dwelling.

2. Givers, hail!
A guest is come in:
where shall he sit?
In much haste is he,
who on the ways has
to try his luck.

3. Fire is needful
to him who is come in,
and whose knees are frozen;
food and raiment
a man requires,
who o'er the fell has travelled.

4. Water to him is needful
who for refection comes,
a towel and hospitable invitation,
a good reception;
if he can get it,
discourse and answer.

5. Wit is needful
to him who travels far:
at home all is easy.
A laughing-stock is he
who nothing knows,
and with the instructed sits.

Odin is the *"High One."* The poem is a collection of rules and maxims, and stories of himself, some of them not very consistent with our ideas of a supreme deity.

6. Of his understanding
no one should be proud,
but rather in conduct cautious.
When the prudent and taciturn
come to a dwelling,
harm seldom befalls the cautious;
for a firmer friend
no man ever gets
than great sagacity.

7. A way guest[1]
who to refection comes,
keeps a cautious silence,
(Or/Wit is needful
to him who travels far:
harm seldom befalls the wary;)
with his ears listens,
and with his eyes observes:
so explores every prudent man.

8. He is happy,
who for himself obtains
fame and kind words:
less sure is that
which a man must have
in another's breast.

9. He is happy,
who in himself possesses
fame and wit while living;
for bad counsels
have oft been received
from another's breast.

---

1. In the Copenhagen paper Ms. F. this strophe begins with the following three lines: —
    Wit is needful
    to him who travels far:
    harm seldom befalls the wary:
They are printed in the Stockholm edition of the original Afzelius and Rask, and in the Swedish translations by Afzelius.

10. A better burthen
no man bears on the way
than much good sense;
that is thought better than riches
in a strange place;
such is the recourse of the indigent.

11. A worse provision
on the way he cannot carry
than too much beer-bibbing;
so good is not,
as it is said,
beer for the sons of men.

12. A worse provision
no man can take from table
than too much beer-bibbing:
for the more he drinks
the less control he has
of his own mind.

13. Oblivion's heron 'tis called
that over potations hovers,
he steals the minds of men.
With this bird's pinions
I was fettered
in Gunnlöd's dwelling.

14. Drunk I was,
I was over-drunk,
at that cunning Fjalar's.
It's the best drunkenness,
when every one after it
regains his reason.

15. Taciturn and prudent,
and in war daring
should a king's children be;
joyous and liberal
every one should be
until the hour of his death.

16. A cowardly man
thinks he will ever live,
if warfare he avoids;
but old age will
give him no peace,
though spears may spare him.

17. A fool gapes
when to a house he comes,
to himself mutters or is silent;
but all at once,
if he gets drink,
then is the man's mind displayed.

18. He alone knows
who wanders wide,
and has much experienced,
by what disposition
each man is ruled,
who common sense possesses.

19. Let a man hold the cup,
yet of the mead drink moderately,
speak sensibly or be silent.
As of a fault
no man will admonish thee,
if thou goest betimes to sleep.

20. A greedy man,
if he be not moderate,
eats to his mortal sorrow.
Oftentimes his belly
draws laughter on a silly man,
who among the prudent comes.

21. Cattle know
when to go home,
and then from grazing cease;
but a foolish man
never knows
his stomach's measure.

22. A miserable man,
and ill-conditioned,
sneers at every thing;
one thing he knows not,
which he ought to know,
that he is not free from faults.

23. A foolish man
is all night awake,
pondering over everything;
he then grows tired;
and when morning comes,
all is lament as before.

24. A foolish man
thinks all who on him smile
to be his friends;
he feels it not,
although they speak ill of him,
when he sits among the clever.

25. A foolish man
thinks all who speak him fair
to be his friends;
but he will find,
if into court he comes,
that he has few advocates.

26. A foolish man
thinks he know everything
if placed in unexpected difficulty;
but he knows not
what to answer,
if to the test he is put.

27. A foolish man,
who among people comes,
had best be silent;
for no one knows
that he knows nothing,
unless he talks to much.
He who previously knew nothing

will still know nothing
talk he ever so much.

28. He thinks himself wise,
who can ask questions
and converse also;
conceal his ignorance
no one can,
because it circulates among men.

29. He utters too many
futile words
who is never silent;
a garrulous tongue,
if it be not checked,
sings often to its own harm.

30. For a gazing-stock
no man shall have another,
although he come a stranger to his house.
Many a one thinks himself wise,
if he is not questioned,
and can sit in a dry habit.

31. Clever thinks himself
the guest who jeers a guest,
if he takes to flight.
Knows it not certainly
he who prates at meat,
whether he babbles among foes.

32. Many men
are mutually well-disposed,
yet at table will torment each other.
That strife will ever be;
guest will guest irritate.

33. Early meals
a man should often take,
unless to a friend's house he goes;
else he will sit and mope,
will seem half-famished,
and can of few things inquire.

34. Long is and indirect the way
to a bad friend's,
though by the road he dwell;
but to a good friend's
the paths lie direct,
though he be far away.

35. A guest should depart,
not always stay
in one place.
The welcome becomes unwelcome,
if he too long continues
in another's house.

36. One's own house is best,
small though it be;
at home is every one his own master.
Though he but two goats possess,
and a straw-thatched cot,
even that is better than begging.

37. One's own house is best,
small though it be,
at home is every one his own master.
Bleeding at heart is he,
who has to ask
for food at every meal-tide.

38. Leaving in the field his arms,
let no man go
a foot's length forward;
for it is hard to know
when on the way
a man may need his weapon.

39. I have never found a
man so bountiful,
or so hospitable
that he refused a present;
of his property
so liberal
that he scorned a recompense.

40. Of the property
which he has gained
no man should suffer need;
for the hated oft is spared
what for the dear was destined.
Much goes worse than is expected.

41. With arms and vestments
friends should each other gladden,
those which are in themselves most sightly.
Givers and requiters
are longest friends,
if all (else) goes well.[2]

42. To his friend
a man should be a friend,
and gifts with gifts requite.
Laughter with laughter
men should receive,
but leasing with lying.

43. To his friend
a man should be a friend,
to him and to his friend;
but of his foe
no man shall
the friend's friend be.

44. Know, if thou has a friend
whom thou fully trustest,
and from whom thou woulds't good derive,
thou shouldst blend thy mind with his,
and gifts exchange,
and often go to see him.

45. If thou hast another,
whom thou little trustest,
yet wouldst good from him derive,
thou shouldst speak him fair,
but think craftily,
and leasing pay with lying.

---

2. The sense of this line seems doubtful; I have adopted the version of Finn Magnusen.

46. But of him yet further,
whom thou little trustest,
and thou suspectest his affection;
before him thou shouldst laugh,
and contrary to thy thoughts speak:
requital should the gift resemble.

47. I was once young,
I was journeying alone,
and lost my way;
rich I thought myself,
when I met another.
Man is the joy of man.

48. Liberal and brave men live best,
they seldom cherish sorrow;
but a base-minded man
dreads everything;
the niggardly is uneasy even at gifts.

49. My garments in a field
I gave away
to two wooden men:
heroes they seemed to be,
when they got cloaks:
exposed to insult is a naked man.

50. A tree withers
that on a hill-top stands;
protects it neither bark nor leaves:
such is the man
whom no one favours:
why should he live long?

51. Hotter than fire
love for five days burns
between false friends;
but is quenched
when the sixth day comes,
and friendship is all impaired.

52. Something great
is not (always) to be given,
praise is often for a trifle bought.
With half a loaf
and a tilted vessel
I got myself a comrade.

53. Little are the sand grains,
little the wits,
little the minds of (some) men;
for all men
are not wise alike:
men are everywhere by halves.

54. Moderately wise
should each one be,
but never over-wise:
of those men
the lives are fairest,
who know much well.

55. Moderately wise
should each one be,
but never over-wise;
for a wise man's heart
is seldom glad,
if he is all-wise who owns it.

56. Moderately wise
should each one be,
but never over-wise.
His destiny let know
no man beforehand;
his mind will be freest from care.

57. Brand burns from brand
until it is burnt out;
fire is from fire quickened.
Man to man
becomes known by speech,
but a fool by his bashful silence.

58. He should early rise,
who another's property or life
desires to have.
Seldom a sluggish wolf
gets prey,
or a sleeping man victory.

59. Early should rise
he who has few workers,
and go his work to see to;
greatly is he retarded
who sleeps the morn away.
Wealth half depends on energy.

60. Of dry planks
and roof-shingles
a man knows the measure;
of the fire-wood
that may suffice,
both measure and time.

61. Washed and refected
let a man ride to the Thing,[3]
although his garments be not too good;
of his shoes and breeches
let no one be ashamed,
nor of his horse,
although he have not a good one.

62. Inquire and impart
should every man of sense,
who will be accounted sage.
Let one only know,
a second may not;
if three, all the world knows.

63. Gasps and gapes,
when to the sea he comes,
the eagles over old ocean;
so is a man,

---

3. The public meeting.

who among many comes,
and has few advocates.

64. His power should
every sagacious man
use with discretion;
for he will find,
when among the bold he comes,
that no one alone is the doughtiest.

65. Circumspect and reserved
every man should be,
and wary in trusting friends.
Of the words
that a man says to another
he often pays the penalty.

66. Much too early
I came to many places,
but too late to others;
the beer was drunk,
or not ready:
the disliked seldom hits the moment.

67. Here and there I should
have been invited,
if I a meal had needed;
or two hams had hung,
at that true friend's,
where of one I had eaten.

68. Fire is best
among the sons of men,
and the sight of the sun,
if his health
a man can have,
with a life free from vice.

69. No man lacks everything,
although his health be bad:
one in his sons is happy,
one in abundant wealth,
one in his good works.

70. It is better to live,
even to live miserably;
a living man can always get a cow.
I saw fire consume
the rich man's property,
and death stood without his door.

71. The halt can ride on horseback,
the one-handed drive cattle;
the deaf fight and be useful:
to be blind is better
than to be burnt:[4]
no ones gets good from a corpse.

72. A son is better,
even if born late,
after his father's departure.
Gravestones seldom
stand by the way-side
unless raised by a kinsman to a kinsman.

73. Two are adversaries:
the tongue is the bane of the head:
under every cloak
I expect a hand.
****
****

74. At night is joyful
he who is sure of travelling enjoyment.
(A ship's yards are short.)[5]
Variable is an autumn night.
Many are the weather's changes
in five days,
but more in a month.

---

4. That is dead on the funeral pyre.
5. This line is evidently an interpolation.

75. He (only) knows not
who knows nothing,
that many a one apes another.
One man is rich,
another poor:
let him not be thought blameworthy.

76. Cattle die,
kindred die,
we ourselves also die;
but the fair fame
never dies
of him who has earned it.

77. Cattle die,
kindred die,
we ourselves also die;
but I know one thing
that never dies,
judgement on each one dead.

78. Full storehouses I saw
at Dives' sons':
now bear they the beggar's staff.
Such are riches;
as is the twinkling of an eye:
of friends they are most fickle.

79. A foolish man,
if he acquires
wealth or a woman's love,
pride grows within him,
but wisdom never:
he goes on more and more arrogant.

80. Then 'tis made manifest,
if of runes thou questionest him,
those to the high ones known,
which the great powers invented,
and the great talker[6] painted,
that he had best hold silence.

---

6. Odin.

81. At eve the day is to be praised,
a woman after she is burnt,
a sword after it is proved,
a maid after she is married,
ice after it has passed away,
beer after it is drunk.

82. In the wind one should hew wood,
in a breeze row out to sea,
in the dark talk with a lass:
many are the eyes of day.
In a ship voyages are to be made,
but a shield is for protection,
a sword for striking,
but a damsel for a kiss.

83. By the fire one should drink beer,
on the ice slide;
but a horse that is lean,
a sword that is rusty;
feed a horse at home,
but a dog at the farm.

84. In a maiden's words
no one should place faith,
nor in what a woman says;
for on a turning wheel
have their hearts been formed,
and guile in their breasts been laid;

85. In a creaking bow,
a burning flame,
a yawning wolf,
a chattering crow,
a grunting swine,
a rootless tree,
a waxing wave,
a boiling kettle,

86. A flying dart,
a falling billow,
a one night's ice,
a coiled serpent,
a woman's bed-talk,
or a broken sword,
a bear's play,
or a royal child,

87. A sick calf,
a self-willed thrall,
a flattering prophetess,
a corpse newly slain,
(a serene sky,
a laughing lord,
a barking dog,
and a harlot's grief);

88. An early sown field
let no one trust,
nor prematurely in a son:
weather rules the field,
and wit the son,
each of which is doubtful;

89. A brother's murderer,
though on the high road met,
a half-burnt house,
an over-swift horse,
(a horse is useless,
if a leg be broken),
no man is so confiding
as to trust any of these.

90. Such is the love of women,
who falsehood meditate,
as if one drove not rough-shod,
on slippery ice,
a spirited two-years old
and unbroken horse;
or as in a raging storm
a helmless ship is beaten;

or as if the halt were set to catch
a reindeer in the thawing fell.[7]

91. Openly I now speak,
because I both sexes know:
unstable are men's minds towards women;
'tis then we speak most fair
when we most falsely think:
that deceives even the cautious.

92. Fair shall speak,
and money offer,
who would obtain a woman's love.
Praise the form
of a fair damsel;
he gets who courts her.

93. At love should no one
ever wonder
in another:
a beauteous countenance
oft captivates the wise,
which captivates not the foolish.

94. Let no one wonder at
another's folly,
it is the lot of many.
All-powerful desire
makes of the sons of men
fools even of the wise.

95. The mind only knows
what lies near the heart,
that alone is conscious of our affections.
No disease is worse
to a sensible man
than not to be content with himself.

---

7. From this line it appears that the poem is of Norwegian or Swedish origin, as the reindeer was unknown in Iceland before the middle of the 18th century, when it was introduced by royal command.

96. That I experienced,
when in the reeds I sat,
awaiting my delight.
Body and soul to me
was that discreet maiden:
nevertheless I posses her not.

97. Billing's lass[8]
on her couch I found,
sun-bright, sleeping.
A prince's joy
to me seemed naught,
if not with that form to live.

98. "Yet nearer eve
must thou, Odin, come,
if thou wilt talk the maiden over;
all will be disastrous,
unless we alone
are privy to such misdeed."

99. I returned,
thinking to love,
at her wise desire.
I thought
I should obtain
her whole heart and love.

100. When next I came
the bold warriors were
all awake,
with lights burning,
and bearing torches:
thus was the way to pleasure closed.

---

8. The story of Odin and Billing's daughter is no longer extant; but compare the story of Odin and Rinda in Saxo, p. 126, edit. Muller and Veleschow.

101. But at the approach of morn,
when again I came,
the household all was sleeping;
the good damsel's dog
alone I found
tied to the bed.

102. Many a fair maiden,
when rightly known,
towards men is fickle:
that I experienced,
when that discreet maiden I
strove to seduce:
contumely of every kind
that wily girl
heaped upon me;
nor of that damsel gained I aught.

103. At home let a man be cheerful,
and towards a guest liberal;
of wise conduct he should be,
of good memory and ready speech;
if much knowledge he desires,
he must often talk on good.

104. Fimbulfambi he is called
who little has to say:
such is the nature of the simple.
****

105. The old Jötun I sought;
now I am come back:
little got I there by silence;
in many words
I spoke to my advantage
in Suttung's halls.

106. Gunnlöd gave me,
on her golden seat,
a draught of the precious mead;
a bad recompense
I afterwards made her,
for her whole soul,
her fervent love.

107. Rati's mouth I caused
to make a space,
and to gnaw the rock;
over and under me
were the Jötun's ways:
thus I my head did peril.

108. Of a well-assumed form
I made good use:
few things fail the wise;
for Odhrærir
is now come up
to men's earthly dwellings.

109. 'Tis to me doubtful
that I could have come
from the Jötun's courts,
had not Gunnlöd aided me,
that good damsel,
over whom I laid my arm.

110. On the day following
came the Hrim-thursar,
to learn something of the High One,
in the High One's hall:
after Bölverk they inquired,
whether he with the gods were come,
or Suttung had destroyed him?

111. Odin, I believe,
a ring-oath gave.[9]
Who in his faith will trust?
Suttung defrauded,
of his drink bereft,
and Gunnlöd made to weep!
****

112. Time 'tis to discourse
from the preacher's chair. -
By the well of Urd
I silent sat,
I saw and meditated,
I listened to men's words.

113. Of runes I heard discourse,
and of things divine,
nor of graving them were they silent,
nor of sage counsels,
at the High One's hall.
In the High One's hall.
I thus heard say:

114. I counsel thee, Loddfafnir,
to take advice:
thou wilt profit if thou takest it.
Rise not at night,
unless to explore,
or art compelled to go out.

115. I counsel thee, Loddfafnir,
to take advice,
thou wilt profit if thou takest it.
In an enchantress's embrace
thou mayest not sleep,
so that in her arms she clasp thee.

---

9. In the pagan North oaths were taken on a holy ring or bracelet, as with us on the Gospels, a sacred ring being kept in the temple for the purpose.

116. She will be the cause
that thou carest not
for Thing or prince's words;
food thou wilt shun
and human joys;
sorrowful wilt thou go to sleep.

117. I counsel thee, etc.
Another's wife
entice thou never
to secret converse.

118. I counsel thee, etc.
By fell or firth
if thou have to travel,
provide thee well with food.

119. I counsel thee, etc.
A bad man
let thou never
know thy misfortunes;
for from a bad man
thou never wilt obtain
a return for thy good will.

120. I saw mortally
wound a man
a wicked woman's words;
a false tongue
caused his death,
and most unrighteously.

121. I counsel thee, etc.
If thou knowest thou has a friend,
whom thou well canst trust,
go oft to visit him;
for with brushwood overgrown,
and with high grass,
is the way that no one treads.

122. I counsel thee, etc.
A good man attract to thee
in pleasant converse;
and salutary speech learn while thou livest.

123. I counsel thee, etc.
With thy friend
be thou never
first to quarrel.
Care gnaws the heart,
if thou to no one canst
thy whole mind disclose.

124. I counsel thee, etc.
Words thou never
shouldst exchange
with a witless fool;

125. For from an ill-conditioned man
thou wilt never get
a return for good;
but a good man will
bring thee favour
by his praise.

126. There is a mingling of affection,
where one can tell
another all his mind.
Everything is better
than being with the deceitful.
He is not another's friend
who ever says as he says.

127. I counsel thee, etc.
Even in three words
quarrel not with a worse man:
often the better yields,
when the worse strikes.

128. I counsel thee, etc.
Be not a shoemaker,
nor a shaftmaker,
unless for thyself it be;
for a shoe if ill made,
or a shaft if crooked,
will call down evil on thee.

129. I counsel thee, etc.
Wherever of injury thou knowest,
regard that injury as thy own;
and give to thy foes no peace.

130. I counsel thee, etc.
Rejoiced at evil
be thou never;
but let good give thee pleasure.

131. I counsel thee, etc.
In a battle
look not up,
(like swine
the sons of men become)
that men may not fascinate thee.

132. If thou wilt induce a good woman
to pleasant converse,
thou must promise fair,
and hold to it;
no one turns from good if it can be got.

133. I enjoin thee to be wary,
but not over wary;
at drinking be thou most wary,
and with another's wife;
and thirdly,
that thieves delude thee not.

134. With insult or derision
treat thou never
a guest or wayfarer,
they often little know,
who sit within,
or what race they are who come.

135. Vices and virtues
the sons of mortals bear
in their breasts mingled;
no one is so good
that no failing attends him,
nor so bad as to be good for nothing.

136. At a hoary speaker
laugh thou never;
often is good that which the aged utter,
oft from a shriveled hide
discreet words issue;
from those whose skin is pendent
and decked with scars,
and who go tottering among the vile.

137. I counsel thee, etc.
Rail not at a guest,
nor from thy gate thrust him;
treat well the indigent;
they will speak well of thee.

138. Strong is the bar
that must be raised
to admit all.
Do thou give a penny,
or they will call down on thee
every ill in thy limbs.

139. I counsel thee, etc.
Wherever thou beer drinkest,
invoke to thee the power of earth;
for earth is good against drink,
fire for distempers,
the oak for constipation,
a corn-ear for sorcery
a hall for domestic strife.
In bitter hates invoke the moon;
the biter for bite-injuries is good;
but runes against calamity;
fluid let earth absorb.

RunatalsÞáttr Oðins: Odin's Rune-song.[10]

140. I know that I hung,
on a wind-rocked tree,
nine whole nights,
with a spear wounded,
and to Odin offered,
myself to myself;
on that tree,
of which no one knows
from what root it springs.

141. Bread no one gave me,
nor a horn of drink,
downward I peered,
to runes applied myself,
wailing learnt them,
then fell down thence.

142. Potent songs nine
from the famed son I learned
of Bölthorn, Bestla's sire,
and a draught obtained

---

10. The first eight strophes of this composition require an explanation which I am incompetent to afford. They have had many interpreters and as many interpretations. The idea of Odin hanging on a tree would seem to have been suggested by what we read of the grove at Upsala, or Sigtuna, in which the victims offered to that deity were suspended from the trees. In the guise of an unknown wanderer, Odin may be supposed to have been captured and thus offered to himself. It no doubt refers to some lost legend.

of the precious mead,
drawn from Odhrærir.

143. Then I began to bear fruit,
and to know many things,
to grow and well thrive:
word by word
I sought out words,
fact by fact
I sought out facts.

144. Runes thou wilt find,
and explained characters,
very large characters,
very potent characters,
which the great speaker depicted,
and the high powers formed,
and the powers' prince graved:

145. Odin among the Æsir,
but among the Alfar, Dáin,
and Dvalin for the dwarfs,
Ásvid for the Jötuns:
some I myself graved.

146. Knowest thou how to grave them?
knowest thou how to expound them?
knowest thou how to depict them?
knowest thou how to prove them?
knowest thou how to pray?
knowest thou how to offer?
knowest thou how to send?[11]
knowest thou how to consume?

147. "Tis better not to pray
than too much offer;
a gift ever looks to a return.
'Tis better not to send
than too much consume.
So Thund graved

---

11. Probably, send them (the runes) forth on their several missions.

before the origin of men,
where he ascended,
to whence he afterwards came.

148. Those songs I know
which the king's wife knows not
nor son of man.
Help the first is called,
for that will help thee
against strifes and cares.

149. For the second I know,
what the sons of men require,
who will as leeches live.
****
****
****

150. For the third I know,[12]
if I have great need
to restrain my foes,
the weapons' edge I deaden:
of my adversaries
nor arms nor wiles harm aught.

151. For the forth I know,
if men place
bonds on my limbs,
I so sing
that I can walk;
the fetter starts from my feet,
and the manacle from my hands.

152. For the fifth I know,
I see a shot from a hostile hand,
a shaft flying amid the host,
so swift it cannot fly
that I cannot arrest it,
if only I get sight of it.

---

12. The miraculous powers here ascribed to Odin to himself bear, in many instances, a remarkable similarity to those attributed to him by Snorri.

153. For the sixth I know,
if one wounds me
with a green tree's roots;[13]
also if a man
declares hatred to me,
harm shall consume them sooner than me.

154. For the seventh I know,
if a lofty house I see
blaze o'er its inmates,
so furiously it shall not burn
that I cannot save it.
That song I can sing.

155. For the eighth I know,
what to all is
useful to learn:
where hatred grows
among the sons of men
that I can quickly assuage.

156. For the ninth I know,
if I stand in need
my bark on the water to save,
I can the wind
on the waves allay,
and the sea lull.

157. For the tenth I know,
if I see troll-wives
sporting in air,
I can so operate
that they will forsake
their own forms,
and their own minds.

158. For the eleventh I know,
if I have to lead
my ancient friends to battle,

---

13. The ancient inhabitants of the North believed that the roots of trees were particularly fitted for hurtful *trolldom*, or witchcraft, and that wounds caused thereby were mortal. In India a similar superstition prevails of the hurtfulness of the roots of trees.

under their shields I sing,
and with power they go
safe to the fight,
safe from the fight;
safe on every side they go.

159. For the twelfth I know,
if on a tree I see
a corpse swinging from a halter,
I can so grave
and in runes depict,
that the man shall walk,
and with me converse.

160. For the thirteenth I know,
if on a young man
I sprinkle water,
he shall not fall,
though he into battle come:
that man shall not sink before swords.

161. For the fourteenth I know,
if in the society of men
I have to enumerate the gods,
Æsir and Alfar,
I know the distinctions of all.
This few unskilled can do.

162. For the fifteenth I know
what the dwarf Thiodreyrir sang
before Delling's doors.
Strength he sang to the Æsir,
and to the Alfar prosperity,
wisdom to Hroptatýr.

163. For the sixteenth I know,
if a modest maiden's favour and affection
I desire to possess,
the soul I change
of the white-armed damsel,
and wholly turn her mind.

164. For the seventeenth I know,
that that young maiden will
reluctantly avoid me.
These songs, Loddfafnir!
thou wilt long have lacked;
yet it may be good if thou understandest them,
profitable if thou learnest them.

165. For the eighteenth I know
that which I never teach
to maid or wife of man,
(all is better
what one only knows.
This is the closing of the songs)
save her alone
who clasps me in her arms,
or is my sister.

166. Now are sung the
High-one's songs,
in the High-one's hall,
to the sons of men all-useful,
but useless to the Jötun's sons.
Hail to him who has sung them!

Hail to him who knows them!
May he profit who has learnt them!
Hail to hose who have listened to them!

Hymiskviða: The Lay of Hymir

1. Once the celestial gods
had been taking fish,
and were in compotation,
ere they the truth discovered.[1]
Rods[2] they shook,
and blood inspected,
when they found at Ægir's
a lack of kettles.

2. Sat the rock-dweller
glad as a child,
much like the son
of Miskorblindi.
In his eyes looked
Ygg's son steadfastly.
"Thou to the Æsir shalt
oft a compotation give."

3. Caused trouble to the Jötun
th' unwelcome-worded Ás:
he forthwith meditated
vengeance on the gods.
Sif's husband he besought
a kettle him to bring.
"in which I beer
for all of you may brew."

4. The illustrious gods
found that impossible,
nor could the exalted powers
it accomplish,
till from true-heartedness,
Týr to Hlorridi
much friendly counsel gave.

---

1. To wit, that they were short of kettles for brewing.
2. That is divining rods.

5. "There dwell eastward
of Elivagar
the all-wise Hýmir,
at heaven's end.
My sire, fierce of mood,
a kettle owns,
a capacious caldron,
a rast in depth."

Thor
6. "Knowest thou whether we
can get the liquor-boiler?"

Tý
"Yes, friend! if we
stratagem employ."
Rapidly they drove
forward that day
from Asgard,
till to the giant's home they came.

7. Thor stalled his goats,
splendid of horn,
then turned him to the hall
that Hýmir owned.
The son his granddam found
to him most loathful;
heads she had
nine hundred.

8. But another came
all-golden forth,
fair-browed, bearing
the beer-cup to her son:

9. "Ye Jötuns' kindred!
I will you both,
ye daring pair,
under the kettles place.
My husband is
oftentimes
niggard toward guests,
to ill-humour prone."

10. But the monster,
the fierce-souled Hýmir,
late returned
home from the chase.
He the hall entered,
the icebergs resounded,
as the churl approached;
the thicket on his cheeks was frozen.

11. "Hail to thee, Hýmir!
be of good cheer:
now thy son is come
to thy hall,
whom we expected
from his long journey;
him accompanies
our famed adversary,
the friend of man,
who Veor hight.

12. "See where they sit
under the hall's gable,
as if to shun thee:
the pillar stands before them."
In shivers flew the pillar
at the Jötun's glance;
the beam was first
broken in two.

13. Eight kettles fell,
but only one of them,
a hard-hammered cauldron,
whole from the column.
The two came forth,
but the old Jötun
with eyes surveyed
his adversary.

14. Augured to him
his mind no good,
when he saw
the giantess's sorrow
on the floor coming.
Then were three
oxen taken,
and the Jötun bade
them forthwith be boiled.

15. Each one they made
by the head shorter,
and to the fire
afterwards bore them.
Sif's consort ate,
ere to sleep he went,
completely, he alone,
two of Hýmir's beeves.

16. Seemed to the hoary
friend of Hrúngnir
Hlorridi's refection
full well large:
"We three to-morrow night
shall be compelled
on what we catch
to live."

17. Veor said he would
on the sea row,
if the bold Jötun him
would with baits supply:
"To the herd betake thee,
(if thou in thy courage trustest,
crusher of the rock-dwellers!)
for baits to seek.

18. I expect
that thou wilt
bait from an ox
easily obtain."
The guest in haste
to the forest went,
where stood an all-black
ox before him.

19. The Thursar's bane
wrung from an ox
the high fastness
of his two horns.
"To me thy work seems
worse by far,
ruler of keels!
than if thou hadst sat quiet."

20. The lord of goats
the apes' kinsman besought
the horse of plank
farther out to move;
but the Jötun
declared his slight desire
farther to row.

21. The mighty Hýmir drew,
he alone,
two whales up
with his hook;
but at the stern abaft
Veor cunningly
made him a line.

22. Fixed on the hook
the shield of men,
the serpent's slayer,
the ox's head.

Gaped at the bait
the foe of gods,
the encircler beneath
of every land.[3]

23. Drew up boldly
the mighty Thor
the worm with venom glistening,
up to the side;
with his hammer struck,
on his foul head's summit,
like a rock towering,
the wolf's own brother.

24. The icebergs resounded,
the caverns howled,
the old earth
shrank together:
at length the fish
back into the ocean sank.[4]

25. The Jötun was little glad,
as they rowed back,
so that the powerful Hýmir
nothing spake,
but the oar moved
in another course.

26. "Wilt thou do
half the work with me,
either the whales
home to the dwelling bear,
or the boat
fast bind?"

---

[3]. The great serpent that encircles the earth.
[4]. According to the *Prose Edda*, the giant, overcome with fright, took out his knife and severed Thor's line.

27. Hlorridi went,
grasped the prow,
quickly, with its hold-water, lifted
the water-steed,
together with its oars
and scoop;
bore to the dwelling
the Jötun's ocean-swine,
the curved vessel,
through the wooded hills.

28. But the Jötun
yet ever frowned,
to strife accustomed,
with Thor disputed,
said that no one was strong,
however vigorously
he might row,
unless he his cup could break.

29. But Hlorridi,
when to his hands it came,
forthwith brake
an upright stone in twain;
sitting dashed the cup
through the pillars:
yet they brought it whole
to Hýmir back.

30. Until the beauteous
woman gave
important, friendly counsel,
which she only knew:
"Strike at the head of Hýmir,
the Jötun with food oppressed,
that is harder
than any cup."

31. Rose then on his knee
the stern lord of goats,
clad in all
his godlike power.
Unhurt remained
the old man's helm-block,
but the round wine-bearer
was in shivers broken.

32. "Much good, I know,
has departed from me,
now that my cup I see
hurled from my knees."
Thus the old man spake:
I can never
say again,
beer thou art too hot.

33. Now 'tis to be tried
if ye can carry
the beer-vessel
out of our dwelling."
Tý twice assayed
to move the vessel,
yet at each time
stood the kettle fast.

34. Then Modi's father
by the brim grasped it,
and trod through
the dwelling's floor.
Sif's consort lifted
the kettle on his head,
while about his heels
its rings jingled.

35. They had far journeyed
before Odin's son
cast one look backward:
he from the caverns saw,
with Hýmir from the east,
a troop of many-headed
monsters coming.

36. From his shoulders he
lifted the kettle down;
Mjöllnir hurled forth
towards the savage crew,
and slew
all the mountain-giants,
who with Hýmir
had him pursued.

37. Long they had not journeyed
when of Hlorridi's goats
one lay down
half-dead before the car.
It from the pole had sprung
across the trace;
but the false Loki
was of this the cause.

38. Now ye have heard,
for what fabulist can
more fully tell
what indemnity
he from the giant got:
he paid for it
with his children both.[5]

39. In his strength exulting
he to the gods' counsel came,
and had the kettle,
which Hýmir had possessed,
out of which every god
shall beer with Ægir drink
at every harvest-tide.

---

5. This strophe belongs apparently to another poem.

Thrymskviþa eðr Hamarsheimt

The Lay of Thrym, or the Hammer recovered

1. Wroth was Vingthor,
when he awoke,
and his hammer
missed;
his beard he shook,
his forehead struck,
the son of earth
felt all around him;

2. and first of all
these words he uttered:
"Hear now, Loki!
what I now say,
which no ones knows
anywhere on earth,
nor in heaven above;
the Ás's hammer is stolen!"

3. They went to the fair
Freyja's dwelling,
and he these words
first of all said:
"Wilt thou me, Freyja,
thy feather-garment lend,
that perchance my hammer
I may find?"

Freyja
4. "That I would give thee,
although of gold it were,
and trust it to thee,
though it were of silver."

5. Flew then Loki
the plumage rattled
until he came beyond
the Æsir's dwellings,
and came within
the Jötun's land.

6. On a mound sat Thrym,
the Thursar's lord,
for his greyhounds
plaiting gold bands
and his horses'
manes smoothing.

7. "How goes it with the Æsir
How goes it with the Alfar,
Why art thou come alone
to Jötunheim?"

Loki
8. "Ill it goes with the Æsir,
Ill it goes with the Alfar.
Hast thou Hlorridi's
hammer hidden?"

Thrym
9. "I have Hlorridi's
hammer hidden
eight rasts
beneath the earth;
it shall no man
get again,
unless he bring me
Freyja to wife."

10. Flew then Loki
the plumage rattled
until he came beyond
the Jötun's dwellings,
and came within
the Æsir's courts;
there he met Thor,
in the middle court,
who these words
first of all uttered.

11. "Hast thou had success
as well as labour?
Tell me from the air
the long tidings.
Oft of him who sits
are the tales defective,
and he who lied down
utters falsehood."

Loki
12. "I have had labour
and success:
Thrym has thy hammer,
the Thursar's lord.
It shall no man
get again,
unless he bring him
Freyja to wife."

13. They went the fair
Freyja to find;
and he those words
first of all said:
"Bind thee, Freyja,
in bridal raiment,
we two must drive
to Jötunheim."

13. Wroth then was Freyja,
and with anger chafed,
all the Æsir's hall
beneath her trembled:
in shivers flew the famed
Brisinga necklace.
"Know me to be
of women lewdest,
if with thee I drive
to Jötunheim."

15. Straightway went the Æsir
all to counsel,
and the Asyniur
all to hold converse;
and deliberated
the mighty gods,
how they Hlorridi's
hammer might get back.

16. Then said Heimdall,
of Æsir brightest
he well foresaw,
like other Vanir
"Let us clothe Thor
with bridal raiment,
let him have the famed
Brisinga necklace.

17. "Let by his side
keys jingle,
and woman's weeds
fall round his knees,
but on his breast
place precious stones,
and a neat coif
set on his head."

18. Then said Thor,
the mighty Ás:
"Me the Æsir will
call womanish,
if I let myself be clad
in bridal raiment."

19. Then spake Loki,
Laufey's son:
"Do thou, Thor! refrain
from suchlike words:
forthwith the Jötuns will
Asgard inhabit,
unless thy hammer thou
gettest back."

20. Then they clad Thor
in bridal raiment,
and with the noble
Brisinga necklace,
let by his side
keys jingle,
and woman's weeds
fall round his knees:
and on his breast
places precious stones,
and a neat coif
sat on his head.

21. Then said Loki,
Laufey's son:
"I will with thee
as a servant go:
we two will drive
to Jötunheim."

22. Straightway were the goats
homeward driven,
hurried to the traces;
they had fast to run.
The rocks were shivered,
the earth was in a blaze;
Odin's son drove
to Jötunheim.

23. Then said Thrym,
the Thursar's lord:
"Rise up, Jötuns!
and the benches deck,
now they bring me
Freyja to wife,
Niörd's daughter,
from Noatún.

24. "Hither to our court let bring
gold-horned cows,
all-black oxen,
for the Jötuns' joy.
Treasures I have many,
necklaces many,
Freyja alone
seemed to me wanting."

25. In the evening
they early came,
and for the Jötuns
beer was brought forth.
Thor alone an ox devoured,
salmons eight,
and all the sweetmeats
women should have.
Sif's consort drank
three salds of mead.

26. Then said Thrym,
the Thursar's prince:
"Where hast thou seen brides
eat more voraciously?
I never saw brides
feed more amply,
nor a maiden
drink more mead."

27. Sat the all-crafty
serving-maid close by,
who words fitting found
against the Jötun's speech:
"Freyja has nothing eaten
for eight nights,
so eager was she
for Jötunheim."

28. Under her veil he stooped
desirous to salute her,
but sprang back
along the hall.
"Why are so piercing
Freyja's looks?
Methinks that fire
burns from her eyes."

29. Sat the all-crafty
serving-maid close by,
who words fitting found
against the Jötun's speech:
"Freyja for eight nights
has not slept,
so eager was she
for Jötunheim."

30. In came the Jötun's
luckless sister,
for a bride-gift
she dared to ask:
"Give me from thy hands
the ruddy rings,
if thou wouldst gain
my love,
my love
and favour all."

31. Then said Thrym,
the Thursar's lord:
"Bring the hammer in,
the bride to consecrate;
lay Mjöllnir
on the maiden's knee;
unite us each with other
by the hand of Vör.

32. Laughed Hlorridi's
soul in his breast,
when the fierce-hearted
his hammer recognized.
He first slew Thrym,
the Thursar's lord,
and the Jötun's race
all crushed;

33. He slew the Jötun's
aged sister,
her who a bride-gift
had demanded;
she a blow got
instead of skillings,
a hammer's stroke
for many rings.
So got Odin's son
his hammer back.

Alvíssmál: The Lay of the Dwarf Alvis

Alvis
1. The benches they are decking,
now shall the bride[1] with me
bend her way home.
That beyond my strength I have hurried
will to every one appear:
at home naught shall disturb my quiet.

Vingthor
2. What man is this?
Why about the nose art thou so pale?
Hast thou last night with corpses lain?
To me thou seemst to bear
resemblances to the Thursar.
Thou art not born to carry off a bride.

Alvis
3. Alvis I am named,
beneath the earth I dwell,
under the rock I own a place.
The lord of chariots
I am come to visit.
A promise once confirmed let no one break.[2]

Vingthor
4. I will break it;
for o'er the maid I have,
as father, greatest power.
I was from home
when the promise was given thee.
Among the gods I the sole giver am.

Alvis
5. What man is this,
lays claim to power
over that fair, bright maiden?
For far-reaching shafts

---

1. Thrud, Thor's daughter by his wife Sif. *Skaldskap*.
2. This appears to allude to a promise made to the dwarf; but of which the story is lost.

few will know thee.
Who has decked thee with bracelets?

Vingthor
6. Vingthor I am named,
wide I have wandered;
I am Sidgrani's son:
with my dissent thou shalt not
that young maiden have,
nor that union obtain.

Alvis
7. Thy consent
I fain would obtain.
Rather would I possess
than be without
that snow-white maiden.

Vingthor
8. The maiden's love
shall not, wise guest!
be unto thee denied,
if thou of every world
canst tell
all I desire to know.

Alvis
9. Vingthor! thou canst try,
as thou art desirous
the knowledge of the dwarf to prove.
All the nine worlds
I have travelled over,
and every being known.

Vingthor
10. Tell me, Alvis!
for all men's concerns
I presume thee, dwarf, to know
how the earth is called,
which lies before the sons of men,
in every world.

Alvis
11. Jörd among men "tis called,
but with the Æsir fold;
the Vanir call it vega,
the Jötuns igroen,
the Alfar groandi,
the powers supreme aur.

Vingthor
12. Tell me Alvis! etc.
how the heaven is called,
which is perceptible,
in every world.

Alvis
13. Himinn tis called by men;
but hlýrnir with the gods;
vindofni the Vanir call it,
uppheimr the Jötuns,
the Alfar fagraræfr,
the dwarfs driupansal.

Vingthor
14. Tell me Alvis! etc.
how the moon is called,
which men see
in every world.

Alvis
15. Mani 'tis called by men,
but mylinn with the gods,
hverfanda hvel in Hel they call it,
skyndi the Jötuns,
but the dwarfs skin;
the Alfar name it artali.

Vingthor
16. Tell me, Alvis! etc.
how the sun is called,
which men's sons see
in every world.

Alvis
17. Sol among men 'tis called,
but with the gods sunna,
the dwarfs call it Dvalinn's leika,
the Jötuns eyglo,
the Alfar fagrahvel,
the Æsir's sons alskir.

Vingthor
18. Tell me, Alvis! etc.
how the clouds are called,
which with showers are mingled
in every world.

Alvis
19. Sky they are called by men,
but skurvan by the gods;
the Vanir call them vindflot,
the Jötuns urvan,
the Alfar veðrmegin;
in Hel they are called hialm huliðs.

Vingthor
20. Tell me, Alvis! etc.
how the wind is called,
which widely passes
over every world.

Alvis
21. Windr 'tis called by men,
but vavuðr by the gods,
the wide-ruling powers call it gneggiuð,
the Jötuns æpir
the Alfar dynfari,
in Hel they call it hviðuðr.

Vingthor
22. Tell me Alvis! etc.
how the calm is called,
which has to rest
in every world.

Alvis
23. Logn 'tis called by men,
but lægi by the gods,
the Vanir call it vindslot,
the Jötuns ofhlý,
the Alfar dagsevi,
the Dwarfs call it dags vera.

Vingthor
24. Tell me, Alvis! etc.
what the sea is called,
which men row over
in every world.

Alvis
25. Sær 'tis called by men,
but silægia with the gods;
the Vanir call it vagr,
the Jötuns alheimr,
the Alfar lagastafr,
the Dwarfs call it diupan mar.

Vingthor
26. Tell me, Alvis! etc.
how the fire is called,
which burns before men's sons
in every world.

Alvis
27. Eldr 'tis called by men,
but by the Æsir funi;
the Vanir call it vagr,
the Jötuns frekr,
but the Dwarfs forbrennir;
in Hel they call it hröðuðr.

Vingthor
28. Tell me, Alvis! etc.
how the forest it called,
which grows for the sons of men
in every world.

Alvis
29. Viðr 'tis called by men,
but vallarfax by gods,
Hel's inmates call it hliðÞangr,
the Jötuns eldi,
the Alfar fagrlimi;
the Vanir call it vöndr.

Vingthor
30. Tell me, Alvis! etc.
how the night is called,
that Nörvi's daughter hight,
in every world.

Alvis
31. Nott it is called by men,
but by the gods niol;
the wide-ruling powers call it grima,
the Jötuns olios,
the Alfar svefngaman;
the Dwarfs call it draumniörunn.

Vingthor
32. Tell me, Alvis! etc.
how the seed is called,
which the sons of men sow
in every world.

Alvis
33. Bygg it is called by men,
but by the gods barr,
the Vanir call it vaxtr,
the Jötuns æti,
the Alfar lagastafr;
in Hel 'tis hnipinn called.

Vingthor
34. Tell me, Alvis! etc.
how the beer is called,
which the sons of men drink
in every world.

Alvis
35. Öl it is called by men,
but by the Æsir biorr,
the Vanir call it veig,
hreinna lögr the Jötuns,
but in Hel 'tis called miöðr:
Suttung's sons call it sumbl.

Vingthor
36. In one breast
I have never found
more ancient lore. -
By great wiles thou hast, I tell thee,
been deluded.
Thou art above ground, dwarf! at dawn;
already in the hall the sun is shining!

Harbarðslióð: The Lay of Harbard

Thor journeying from the eastern parts came to a strait or sound, on the other side of which was a ferryman with his boat. Thor cried out: -

1. Who is the knave of knaves,
that by the sound stands yonder?

Harbard
2. Who is the churl of churls,
that cries across the water?

Thor
3. Ferry me across the sound,
to-morrow I'll regale thee.
I have a basket on my back:
there is no better food:
at my ease I ate,
before I quitted home,
herrings and oats,
with which I yet feel sated.

Harbard
4. Thou art in haste
to praise thy meal:
thou surely hast no foreknowledge;
for sad will be thy home:
thy mother, I believe, is dead.

Thor
5. Thou sayest now
what seems to every one
most unwelcome to know
that my mother is dead.

Harbard
6. Thou dost not look like one
who owns three country dwellings,
bare-legged thou standest,
and like a beggar clothed;
thou hast not even breeches.

Thor
7. Steer hitherward thy boat;
I will direct thee where to land.
But who owns this skiff,
which by the strand thou holdest?

Harbard
8. Hildolf he is named
who bade me hold it,
a man in council wise,
who dwells in Radsö sound.
Robbers he bade me not to ferry,
or horse-stealers,
but good men only,
and those whom I well knew.
Tell me then they name,
if thou wilt cross the sound.

Thor
9. I my name will tell,
(although I am an outlaw)
and all my kin:
I am Odin's son,
Meili's brother,
and Magni's sire,
the gods' mighty leader:
With Thor thou here mayst speak.
I will now ask
how thou art called.

10. I am Harbard called;
seldom I my name conceal.

Thor
11. Why shouldst thou thy name conceal,
unless thou crime has perpetrated?

Harbard
12. Yet, thou I may crime have perpetrated,
I will nathless guard my life
against such as thou art;
unless I death-doomed am.

Thor
13. It seems to me a foul annoyance
to wade across the strait to thee,
and wet my garments:
but I will pay thee, mannikin!
for thy sharp speeches,
if o'er the sound I come.

Harbard
14. Here will I stand,
and here await thee.
Thou wilt have found no stouter one
since Hrugnir's death.

Thor
15. Thou now remindest me
how I with Hrugnir fought,
that stout-hearted Jötun,
whose head was all of stone;
yet I made him fall,
and sink before me.
What meanwhile didst thou, Harbard?

Harbard
16. I was with Fjölvari
five winters through,
in the isle
which Algrön hight.
There we could fight,
and slaughter make,
many perils prove,
indulge in love.

Thor
17. How did your women
prove towards you?

Harbard
18. Sprightly women we had,
had they but been meek;
shrewd ones we had,
had they but been kind.
Of sand a rope
they twisted,
and from the deep valley
dug the earth:
to them all I alone was
superior in cunning.
I rested with the sisters seven,
and their love and pleasures shared.
What meanwhile didst thou, Thor?

Thor
19. I slew Thiassi,
that stout-hearted Jötun:
up I cast the eyes
of Allvaldi's son
into the heaven serene:
they are signs the greatest
of my deeds.
What meanwhile didst thou, Harbard?

Harbard
20. Great seductive arts I used
against the riders of the night,[1]
when from their husbands I enticed them.
A mighty Jötun I believed
Hlebard to be:
a magic wand he gave me,
but from his wits I charmed him.

Thor
21. With evil mind then
thou didst good gifts requite.

---

1. Giantesses, witches, etc.

Harbard
22. One tree gets that
which is from another scraped:
each one in such case is for self.
What meanwhile didst thou, Thor?

Thor
23. In the east I was,
and slew the Jötun brides,
crafty in evil,
as they to the mountain went.
Great would have been the Jötun race,
had they all lived;
and not a man
left in Midgard.
What meanwhile didst thou, Harbard?

Harbard
24. I was in Valland,
and followed warfare;
princes I excited,
but never reconciled.
Odin has all the jarls
that in conflict fall;
but Thor the race of thralls.

Thor
25. Unequally thou wouldst divide
the folk among the Æsir,
if thou but hadst the power.

Harbard
26. Thor has strength overmuch,
but courage none;
from cowardice and fear,
thou wast crammed into a glove,
and hardly thoughtest thou was Thor.
Thou durst not then,
through thy terror,
either sneeze or cough,
lest Fjalar it might hear.

Thor
27. Harbard, thou wretch!
I would strike thee dead,
could I but stretch my arm across the sound.

Harbard
28. Why wouldst thou
stretch they arm across the sound,
when there is altogether no offence?
But what didst thou, Thor?

Thor
29. In the east I was,
and a river I defended,
when the sons of Svarang
me assailed,
and with stones pelted me,
though in their success they little joyed:
they were the first
to sue for peace.
What meanwhile didst thou, Harbard?

Harbard
30. I was in the east,
and with a certain lass held converse;
with that fair I dallied,
and long meetings had.
I that gold-bright one delighted;
the game amused her.

Thor
31. Then you had kind damsels there?

Harbard
32. Of thy aid I had need, Thor!
in retaining
that maiden lily-fair.

Thor
33. I would have given it thee,
if I had had the opportunity.

Harbard
34. I would have trusted thee,
my confidence
if thou hadst not betrayed it.

Thor
35. I am not such a heel-chafer
as an old leather shoe in spring.

Harbard
36. What meanwhile didst thou, Thor?

Thor
37. The Berserkers' brides
I on Læssö cudgeled;
they the worst had perpetrated,
the whole people had seduced.

Harbard
38. Dastardly didst thou act, Thor!
when thou didst cudgel women.

Thor
39. She-wolves they were,
and scarcely women.
They crushed my ship,
which with props I had secured,
with iron clubs threatened me,
and drove away Thialfi.
What meanwhile didst thou, Harbard?

Harbard
40. I in the army was,
which was hither sent,
war-banners to raise,
lances to redden.

Thor
41. Of that thou now wilt speak,
as thou wentest forth
us hard terms to offer.

Harbard
42. That shall be indemnified
by a hand-ring,
such as arbitrators give,
who wish to reconcile us.

Thor
43. Where didst thou learn words
than which I never heard
more irritating?

Harbard
44. From men I learned them,
from ancient men,
whose home is in the woods.

Thor
45. Thou givest certainly
a good name to grave-mounds,
when thou callest them
homes in the woods.

Harbard
46. So speak I
of such a subject.

Thor
47. Thy shrewd words
will bring thee evil,
if I resolve the sound to ford.
Louder than a wolf
thou wilt howl, I trow,
if of my hammer thou gettest a touch.

Harbard
48. Sif has a gallant at home;
thou wilt anxious be to find him:
thou shalt that arduous work perform;
it will beseem thee better.

Thor
49. Thou utterest what comes upmost,
so that to me it be most annoying,
thou dastardly varlet!
I believe thou art lying.

Harbard
50. I believe I am telling truth.
Thou art travelling slowly;
thou wouldst have long since arrived,
hadst thou assumed another form.

Thor
51. Harbard! thou wretch!
rather is it thou who has detained me.

Harbard
52. I never thought
that a ferryman could
the course of Asa-Thor retard.

Thor
53. One advice I now will give thee:
row hither with thy boat;
let us cease from threats;
approach the sire of Magni.

Harbard
54. Go farther from the sound,
the passage is refused thee.

Thor
55. Show me then the way,
if thou wilt not ferry me
across the water.

Harbard
56. That's too little to refuse.
"Tis far to go;
"tis to the stock an hour,
and to the stone another;
then keep the left hand way,
until thou reachest Verland;
there will Fjörgyn
find her son Thor,
and point out to him
his kinsmen's ways
to Odin's land.

Thor
57. Can I get there to-day?

Harbard
58. With pain and toil
thou mayest get there,
while the sun is up,
which, I believe, is now nigh.

Thor
59. Our talk shall now be short,
as thou answerest with scoffing only.
For refusing to ferry me I will reward thee,
if another time we meet.

Harbard
60. Just go to where
all the powers of evil may have thee.

För Skirnis eðr Skirnismál

The Journey or Lay of Skirnir

Frey, son of Niörd, had one day seated himself in Hlidskjalf, and was looking over all regions, when turning his eyes to Jötunheim, he there saw a beautiful girl, as she was passing from her father's dwelling to her bower. Thereupon he became greatly troubled in mind. Frey's attendant was named Skirnir; him Niörd desired to speak with Frey; when Skadi said: -

1. Rise up now, Skirnir!
go and request
our son to speak;
and inquire
with whom he so sage
may be offended.

Skirnir
2. Harsh words I have
from your son to fear,
if I go and speak with him,
and to inquire
with whom he so sage
may be offended.

Skirnir
3. Tell me now, Frey,
prince of gods!
for I desire to know,
why alone thou sittest
in the spacious hall
the livelong day?

Frey
4. Why shall I tell thee,
thou young man,
my mind's great trouble?
for the Alfs' illuminator
shines every day,
yet not for my pleasure.

Skirnir
5. Thy care cannot, I think,
be so great,
that to me thou canst not tell it;
for in early days
we were young together:
well might we trust each other.

Frey
6. In Gýmir's courts
I saw walking
a maid for whom I long.
Her arms gave forth light
wherewith shone
all air and water.

7. Is more desirable
to me that maid
than to any youth
in early days;
yet will no one,
Æsir or Alfar,
that we together live.

Skirnir
8. Give me but thy steed,
which can bear me through
the dusk, flickering flame,
and that sword,
which brandishes itself
against the Jötuns' race.

Frey
9. I will give thee my steed,
which can bear thee through
the dusk, flickering flame,
and that sword,
which will itself brandish,
if he is bold who raises it.

Skirnir speaks to the horse....

>10. Dark it is without,
>'tis time, I say, for us to go
>across the misty fells,
>over the Thursar's land:
>we shall both return,
>or the all-potent Jötun
>will seize us both.

Skirnir rides to Jötunheim, to Gýmir's mansion, where fierce dogs were chained at the gate of the enclosure that was round Gýmir's hall. He rides on to where a cowherd was sitting on a mound, and says to him:

>11. Tell me, cowherd!
>as on the mound thou sittest,
>and watchest all the ways,
>how I to the speech may come,
>of the young maiden,
>for Gýmir's dogs?

>12. Either thou art death-doomed,
>or thou art a departed one.
>Speech wilt thou
>ever lack
>with the good maid of Gýmir.

>Skirnir
>13. Better choices than to whine
>there are for him
>who is prepared to die:
>for one day
>was my age decreed,
>and my whole life determined.

>Gerd
>14. What is that sound of sounds,
>which I now sounding hear
>within our dwelling?
>The earth is shaken,
>and with it all
>the house of Gýmir trembles.

A serving-maid.
15. A man is here without,
dismounted from his horse's back:
he lets his steed browse on the grass.

Gerd
16. Bid him enter
into our hall,
and drink of the bright mead;
although I fear
it is my brother's slayer
who waits without.

17. Who is this of the Alfar's,
or of the Æsir's sons,
or of the wise Vanir's?
Why art thou come alone,
through the hostile fire,
our halls to visit?

Skirnir
18. I am not of the Alfar's,
nor of the Æsir's sons,
nor of the wise Vanir's;
yet I am come alone,
through the hostile fire,
your halls to visit.

19. Apples all-golden
I have here eleven:
these I will give thee, Gerd,
thy love to gain,
that thou mayest say that Frey
to thee lives dearest.

Gerd
20. The apples eleven
I never will accept
for any mortal's pleasure;
nor will I and Frey,
while our lives last,
live both together.

Skirnir
21. The ring too I will give thee,
which was burnt
with the young son of Odin.
Eight of equal weight
will from it drop,
every ninth night.

Gerd
22. The ring I will not accept,
burnt thou it may have been
with the young son of Odin.
I have no lack of gold
in Gýmir's courts;
for my father's wealth I share.

Skirnir
23. Seest thou this sword, young maiden!
thin, glittering-bright,
which I have here in hand?
I thy head will sever
from thy neck,
if thou speakest not favourably to me.

Gerd
24. Suffer compulsion
will I never,
to please any man;
yet this I foresee,
if thou and Gýmir meet,
yet will eagerly engage in fight.

Skirnir
25. Seest thou this sword, young maiden!
thin, glittering-bright,
which I have here in hand?
Beneath its edge
shall the old Jötun fall:
thy sire is death-doomed.

26. With a taming-wand I smite thee,
and I will tame thee,
maiden! to my will.
Thou shalt go thither,
where the sons of men
shall never more behold thee.

27. On an eagle's mount
thou shalt early sit,
looking and turned towards Hel.
Food shall to thee more loathsome be
than is to any one
the glistening serpent among men.

28. As a prodigy thou shalt be,
when thou goest forth;
Hrimnir shall at thee gaze,
all being at thee stare;
more wide-known thou shalt become
than the watch among the gods,[1]
if thou from thy gratings gape.

29. Solitude and disgust,
bonds and impatience,
shall thy tears with grief augment.
Set thee down,
and I will tell thee of
a whelming flood of care,
and a double grief.

30. Terrors shall bow thee down
the livelong day,
in the Jötuns' courts.
To the Hrimthursar's halls,
thou shalt each day
crawl exhausted,
joyless crawl;
wail for pastime
shalt thou have,
and tears and misery.

---

1. Heimdall.

31. With a three-headed Thurs
thou shalt be ever bound,
or be without a mate.
Thy mind shall tear thee
from morn to morn:
as the thistle thou shalt be
which has thrust itself
on the house-top.

32. To the wold I have been,
and to the humid grove,
a magic wand to get.
A magic wand I got.

33. Wroth with thee is Odin,
wroth with thee is the Æsir's prince;
Frey shall loathe thee,
even ere thou, wicked maid!
shalt have felt
the gods' dire vengeance.

34. Hear ye, Jötuns!
hear ye, Hrimthursar!
sons of Suttung!
also ye, Æsir's friends!
how I forbid
how I prohibit
man's joy unto the damsel,
man's converse to the damsel.

35. Hrimgrimnir the Thurs is named,
that shall possess thee,
in the grating of the dead beneath;
there shall wretched thralls,
from the tree's roots,
goats' water give thee.
Other drink shalt thou,
maiden! never get,
either for thy pleasure,
or for my pleasure.

36. Þurs[2] I cut for thee,
and three letters more:
ergi, and oenði,
and oÞola.
So will I cut them out,
as I have cut them in,
if there need shall be.

Gerd
37. Hail rather to thee, youth!
and accept an icy cup,
filled with old mead;
although I thought not
that I ever should
love one of Vanir race.

Skirnir
38. All my errand
will I know,
ere I hence ride home.
When wilt thou converse hold
with the powerful
son of Niörd?

Gerd
39. Barri the grove is named,
which we both know,
the grove of tranquil paths.
Nine nights hence,
there to Niörd's son
Gerd will grant delight.

Skirnir then rode home. Frey was standing without, and spoke to him, asking tidings:

40. Tell me, Skirnir!
ere thou thy steed unsaddlest,
and a foot hence goest,
what thou hast accomplished
in Jötunheim,
for my pleasure or thine?

2. *Thurs*, etc., the names of magical runes.

Skirnir
41. Barri the grove is named,
which we both know,
the grove of tranquil paths.
Nine nights hence,
there to Niörd's son
Gerd will grant delight.

Frey
42. Long is one night,
yet longer two will be;
how shall I three endure.
Often a month to me
less has seemed
than half a night of longing.

Rígsmál: The Lay of Rig

In ancient Sagas it is related that one of the Æsir named Heimdall, being on a journey to a certain sea-shore, came to a village, where he called himself Rig. In accordance with this Saga is the following:

1. In ancient days, they say,
along the green ways went
the powerful and upright
sagacious Ás,
the strong and active Rig,
his onward course pursuing.

2. Forward he went
on the mid-way,
and to a dwelling came.
The door stood ajar,
he went in,
fire was on the floor.
There man and wife sat there,
hoary-haired, by the hearth,
Ai and Edda,
in old guise clad.

3. Rig would counsel
give to them both,
and himself seated
in the middle seat,
having on either side
the domestic pair.

4. Then Edda from the ashes
took a loaf,
heavy and thick,
and with bran mixed;
more besides she laid
on the middle of the board;
there in a bowl was broth
on the table set,
there was a calf boiled,
of cates more excellent.

5. Then rose he up,
prepared to sleep:
Rig would counsel
give to them both;
laid him down
in the middle of the bed;
the domestic pair lay
one on either side.

6. There he continued
three nights together,
then departed
on the mid-way.
Nine months then
passed away.

7. Edda a child brought forth:
they with water sprinkled
its swarthy skin,
and named it Thræl.

8. It grew up,
and well it throve;
of its hands
the skin was shriveled,
the knuckles knotty,
****
and fingers thick;
a hideous countenance it had,
a curved back,
and protruding heels.

9. He then began
his strength to prove,
bast to bind,
make of it loads;
then faggots carried home,
the livelong day.

10. Then to the dwelling came
a woman walking,
scarred were her foot-soles,
her arms sunburnt,
her nose compressed,
her name was Thý.

11. In the middle seat
herself she placed;
by her sat
the house's son.
They spoke and whispered,
prepared a bed,
Thræl and Thý,
and days of care.

12. Children they begat,
and lived content:
Their names, I think, were
Hrimr and Fjósnir,
Klur and Kleggi,
Kefsir, Fulnir,
Drumb, Digraldi,
Drött and Hösvir,
Lút and Leggialdi.
Fences they erected,
fields manured,
tended swine,
kept goats,
dug turf.

13. The daughters were
Drumba and Kumba,
Ökkvinkalfa,
and Arinnefia,
Ysia and Ambatt,
Eikintiasna,
Tötrughypia,
and Trönubeina,
whence are sprung
the race of thralls.
****

14. Rig then went on,
in a direct course,
and came to a house;
the door stood ajar:
he went in;
fire was on the floor,
man and wife sat there
engaged at work.

15. The man was planing
wood for a weaver's beam;
his beard was trimmed,
a lock was on his forehead,
his shirt close;
he chest stood on the floor.

16. His wife sat by,
plied her rock,
with outstretched arms,
prepared for clothing.
A hood was on her head,
a loose sark over her breast,
a kerchief round her neck,
studs on her shoulders.
Afi and Amma
owned the house.

17. Rig would counsel
give to them both;
rose from the table,
prepared to sleep;
laid him down
in the middle of the bed,
the domestic pair lay
one on either side.

18. There he continued
three nights together.
Nine months then
passed away.
Amma a child brought forth,
they with water sprinkled it,
and called it Karl.
The mother in linen swathed
the ruddy redhead:
its eyes twinkled.

19. It grew up,
and well throve;
learned to tame oxen,
make a plough,
houses build,
and barns construct,
make carts,
and the plough drive.

20. Then they home conveyed
a lass with pendant keys,
and goatskin kirtle;
married her to Karl.
Snör was her name,
under a veil she sat.
The couple dwelt together,
rings exchanged,
spread couches,
and a household formed.

21. Children they begat,
and lived content.
Hal and Dreng, these were named,
Held, Thegn, Smith,
Breidrbondi,
Bundinskegg,
Bui and Boddi,
Brattskegg and Segg.

22. But (the daughters) were thus called,
by other names:
Snot, Brud, Svanni,
Svarri, Sprakki,
Fliod, Sprund, and Vif,
Feima, Ristil;
whence are sprung
the races of churls.
****

23. Rig then went thence,
in a direct course,
and came to a hall:
the entrance looked southward,
the door was half closed,
a ring was on the door-post.

24. He went in;
the floor was strewed,
a couple sat
facing each other,
Fadir and Modir,
with fingers playing.

25. The husband sat,
and twisted string,
bent his bow,
and arrow-shafts prepared;
but the housewife
looked on her arms,
smoothed her veil,
and her sleeves fastened;

26. Her head-gear adjusted.
A clasp was on her breast;
ample her robe,
her sark was blue;
brighter was her brow,
her breast fairer,
her neck whiter
than driven snow.

27. Rig would counsel
give to them both,
and himself seated
on the middle seat,
having on either side
the domestic pair.

28. Then took Modir
a figured cloth
of white linen,
and the table decked.
She then took
thin cakes
of snow-white wheat,
and on the table laid.

29. She set forth salvers
full, adorned with silver,
on the table game and pork,
and roasted birds.
In a can was wine;
the cups were ornamented.
They drank and talked;
the day was fast departing,
Rig would counsel
give to them both.

30. Rig then rose,
the bed prepared;
there he then remained
three nights together,
then departed
on the mid-way.
Nine months after that
passed away.

31. Modir then brought forth a boy;
in silk they wrapped him,
with water sprinkled him,
and named him Jarl.
Light was his hair,
bright his cheeks,
his eyes piercing
as a young serpent's.

32. There at home
Jarl grew up,
learned the shield to shake,
to fix the string,
the bow to bend,
arrows to shaft,
javelins to hurl,
spears to brandish,
horses to ride,
dogs to let slip,
swords to draw,
swimming to practice.

33. Thither from the forest came
Rig walking,
Rig walking:
runes he taught him,
and his own son declared him,
whom he bade possess
his alodial fields,
his alodial fields,
his ancient dwellings.

34. Jarl then rode thence,
through a murky way,
over humid fells,
till to a hall he came.
His spear he brandished,
his shield he shook,
made his horse curvet,
and his falchion drew,
strife began to raise,
the field to redden,
carnage to make;
and conquer lands.

35. Then he ruled alone
over eight vills,
riches distributed,
gave to all
treasures and precious things;
lank-sided horses,
rings he dispersed,
and collars cut in pieces.[1]

36. The nobles drove
through humid ways,
came to a hall,
where Hersir dwelt;
there they found
a slender maiden,
fair and elegant,
Erna her name.

37. They demanded her,
and conveyed her home,
to Jarl espoused her;
she under the linen[2] went.
They together lived,
and well throve,
had offspring,
and old age enjoyed.

---

1. A common practice: the pieces served as money.
2. The nuptial veil.

38. Bur was the eldest,
Barn the second,
Jod and Adal,
Arfi, Mög,
Nid and Nidjung.
They learned games;
Son and Svein
swam and at tables played.
One was named Kund,
Kon was the youngest.

39. There grew up
Jarl's progeny;
horses they broke,
curved shields,
cut arrows,
brandished spears.

40. But the young Kon
understood runes,
æfin-runes,
and aldr-runes;
he moreover knew
men to preserve,
edges to deaden,
the sea to calm.

41. He knew the voice of birds,
how fires to mitigate,
assuage and quench;
sorrows to allay.
He of eight men had
the strength and energy.

42. He with Rig Jarl
in runes contended,
artifices practiced,
and superior proved;
then acquired
Rig to be called,
and skilled in runes.

43. The young Kon rode
through swamps and forests,
hurled forth darts,
and tamed birds.

44. Then sang the crow,
sitting lonely on a bough!
"Why wilt thou, young Kon:
tame the birds?
Rather shouldst thou, young Kon!
on horses ride
****
****
and armies overcome.

45. Nor Dan nor Danp
halls more costly had,
nobler paternal seats,
then ye had.
They well knew how
the keel to ride,
the edge to prove,
wounds to inflict.

(The rest is wanting......)

Ægisdrekka, eða Lokasenna, eða Lokaglepsa

Ægir's Compotation or Loki's Altercation

Ægir, who is also name Gýmir, had brewed beer for the Æsir, after he had got the great kettle, as has been already related. To the entertainment came Odin and his wife Frigg. Thor did not come, being in the East, but his wife Sif was there, also Bragi and his wife Idun, and Tý, who was one-handed, Fenrisulf having bitten off his hand while being bound. Besides these were Niörd and his wife Skadi, Frey and Freyja, and Odin's son Vidar. Loki too was there, and Frey's attendants, Byggvir and Beyla. Many other Æsir and Alfar were also present.

Ægir had two servants, Fimafeng and Eldir. Bright gold was there used instead of fire-light. The beer served itself to the guests. The place was a great sanctuary. The guests greatly praised the excellence of Ægir's servants. This Loki could not hear with patience, and so slew Fimafeng; whereupon the Æsir shook their shields, exclaimed against Loki, chased him into the forest, and then returned to drink. Loki came again, and found Eldir standing without, whom he thus addressed:

> 1. Tell me, Eldir!
> ere thou thy foot settest
> one step forward,
> on what converse
> the sons of the triumphant gods
> at their potation?

> Eldir
> 2. Of their arms converse,
> and of their martial fame,
> the sons of the triumphant gods.
> Of the Æsir and the Alfar
> that are here within
> not one has a friendly word for thee.

> Loki
> 3. I will go
> into Ægir's halls,
> to see the compotation.
> Strife and hate
> to the Æsir's sons I bear,
> and will mix their mead with bale.

Eldir
4. Knowest thou not that if thou goest
into Ægir's halls
to see the compotation,
but contumely and clamor
pourest forth on the kindly powers,
they will wipe it all off on thee.

Loki
5. Knowest thou not, Eldir,
that if we two
with bitter words contend,
I shall be rich
in answers,
if thou sayest too much?

Loki then went into the hall, but when those present saw who was come in, they all sat silent.

Loki
6. I Lopt am come thirsty
into this hall,
from a long journey,
to beseech the Æsir
one draught to give me
of the bright mead.

7. Why gods! are ye so silent,
so reserved,
that ye cannot speak?
A seat and place
choose for me at your board,
or bid me hie me hence.

Bragi
8. A seat and place
will the Æsir never
choose for thee at their board;
for well the Æsir know
for whom they ought to hold
a joyous compotation.

Loki
9. Odin! dost thou remember
when we in early days
blended our blood together?
When to taste beer
thou didst constantly refuse,
unless to both 'twas offered?

Odin
10. Rise up, Vidar!
and let the wolf's sire
sit at our compotation;
that Loki may not utter
words of contumely
in Ægir's hall.

Vidar then rising, presented Loki with drink, who before drinking thus addressed.

11. Hail, Æsir!
Hail, Asyniur!
And ye, all-holy gods!
all, save that one As,
who sits within there,
Bragi, on yonder bench.

Bragi
12. A horse and falchion
I from my stores will give thee,
and also with a ring reward thee,
if thou the Æsir wilt not
requite with malice.
Provoke not the gods against thee.

Loki
13. Of horse and rings
wilt thou ever, Bragi!
be in want.
Of the Æsir and the Alfar,
that are here present,
in conflict thou art the most backward,
and in the play of darts most timid.

Bragi
14. I know that were I without,
as I am now within,
the hall of Ægir,
I thy head would
bear in my hand,
and so for lying punish thee.

Loki
15. Valiant on thy seat art thou, Bragi!
but so thou shouldst not be,
Bragi, the bench's pride!
Go and fight,
if thou art angry;
a brave man sits not considering.

Idun
16. I pray thee, Bragi!
let avail the bond of children,
and of all adopted sons,
and to Loki speak not
in reproachful words,
in Ægir's hall.

Loki
17. Be silent, Idun!
of all women I declare thee
most fond of men,
since thou thy arms,
carefully washed, didst twine
round thy brother's murderer.

Idun
18. Loki I address not
with opprobrious words,
in Ægir's hall.
Bragi I soothe,
by beer excited.
I desire not that angry ye fight.

Gefion
19. Why will ye, Æsir twain,
here within,
strive with reproachful words?
Lopt perceives not
that he is deluded,
and is urged on by fate.

Loki
20. Be silent, Gefion!
I will now just mention,
how that fair youth
thy mind corrupted,
who thee a necklace gave,
and around whom thou thy limbs didst twine?

Odin
21. Thou art raving, Loki!
and hast lost thy wits,
in calling Gefion's anger on thee;
for all men's destinies,
I ween, she knows
as thoroughly as I do.

Loki
22. Be silent, Odin!
Thou never couldst allot
conflicts between men:
oft hast thou given to those
to whom thou oughtest not
victory to cowards.

Odin
23. Knowest thou that I gave
to those I ought not
victory to cowards?
Thou was eight winters
on the earth below,
a milch cow and a woman,
and didst there bear children.
Now that, methinks, betokens a base nature.

Loki
24. But, it is said, thou wentest
with tottering steps in Samsö,
and knocked at houses as a Vala.
In likeness of a fortune teller,
thou wentest among people;
Now that, methinks, betokens a base nature.

Frigg
25. Your doings
ye should never
publish among men,
what ye, Æsir twain,
did in days of yore.
Ever forgotten be men's former deeds!

Loki
26. Be thou silent, Frigg!
Thou art Fjörgyn's daughter,
and ever hast been fond of men,
since Ve and Vili, it is said,
thou, Vidrir's wife, didst
both to thy bosom take.

Frigg
27. Know thou that if I had,
in Ægir's halls,
a son like Baldr,
out thou shouldst not go
from the Æsir's sons:
thou should'st have been fiercely assailed.

Loki
28. But wilt thou, Frigg!
that of my wickedness
I more recount?
I am the cause
that thou seest not
Baldr riding to the halls.

Freyja
29. Mad art thou, Loki!
in recounting
thy foul misdeeds.
Frigg, I believe,
knows all that happens,
although she says it not.

Loki
30. Be thou silent, Freyja!
I know thee full well;
thou art not free from vices:
of the Æsir and the Alfar,
that are herein,
each has been thy paramour.

Freyja
31. False is thy tongue.
Henceforth it will, I think,
prate no good to thee.
Wroth with thee are the Æsir,
and the Asyniur.
Sad shalt thou home depart.

Loki
32. Be silent, Freyja!
Thou art a sorceress,
and with much evil blended;
since against thy brother thou
the gentle powers excited.
And then, Freyja! what didst thou do?

Niörd
33. It is no great wonder,
if silk-clad dames
get themselves husbands, lovers;
but 'tis a wonder that a wretched Ás,
that has borne children,
should herein enter.

Loki
34. Be silent, Niörd!
Thou wast sent eastward hence,
a hostage from the gods.
Hýmir's daughter had thee
for a utensil,
and flowed into thy mouth.[1]

Niörd
35. 'Tis to me a solace,
as I a long way hence
was sent, a hostage from the gods,
that I had a son,
whom no one hates,
and accounted is a chief among the Æsir.

Loki
36. Cease now, Niörd!
in bounds contain thyself;
I will no longer keep it secret:
it was with thy sister
thou hadst such a son;
hardly worse than thyself.

Tý
37. Frey is best
of all the exalted gods
in the Æsir's courts:
no maid he makes to weep,
no wife of man,
and from bonds looses all.

Loki
38. Be silent, Tý!
Thou couldst never settle
a strife 'twixt two;
of thy right hand also
I must mention make,
which Fenrir from thee tore.

---

1. The events related in this strophe are probably a mere perversion, by the poet, of what we know of Niord's history.

Tý
39. I of a hand am wanting,
but thou of honest fame;
sad is the lack of either.
Nor is the wolf at ease:
he in bonds must bide,
until the gods' destruction.

Loki
40. Be silent, Tý;
to thy wife it happened
to have a son by me.
Nor rag nor penny ever
hadst thou, poor wretch!
for this injury.

Frey
41. I the wolf see lying
at the river's mouth,
until the powers are swept away.
So shalt thou be bound,
if thou art not silent,
thou framer of evil.

Loki
42. With gold thou boughtest
Gýmir's daughter,
and so gavest away thy sword:
but when Muspell's sons
through the dark forest ride,
thou, unhappy, wilt not
have wherewith to fight.

Byggvir
43. Know that were I of noble race,
like Ingun's Frey,
and had so fair a dwelling,
than marrow softer I would bray
that ill-boding crow,
and crush him limb by limb.

Loki
44. What little thing is that I see
wagging its tail,
and snapping eagerly?
At the ears of Frey
thou shouldst ever be,
and clatter under mills.

Byggvir
45. Byggvir I am named,
and am thought alert,
by all gods and men;
therefore am I joyful here,
that all the sons of Hropt
drink beer together.

Loki
46. Be silent, Byggvir!
Thou couldst never
dole out food to men,
when, lying in thy truckle bed,
thou wast not to be found,
while men were fighting.

Heimdall
47. Loki, thou art drunk,
and hast lost thy wits.
Why dost thou not leave off, Loki?
But drunkenness
so rules every man,
that he knows not of his garrulity.

Loki
48. Be silent, Heimdall!
For thee in early days
was that hateful life decreed:
with a wet back
thou must ever be,
and keep watch as guardian of the gods.

Skadi
49. Thou art merry, Loki!
Not long wilt thou
frisk with an unbound tail;
for thee, on a rock's point,
with the entrails of thy ice-cold son,
the gods will bind.

Loki
50. Know, if on a rock's point,
with the entrails of my ice-cold son,
the gods will bind me,
that first and foremost
I was at the slaying,
when we assailed Thiassi.

Skadi
51. Know, if first and foremost
thou wast at the slaying,
when ye assailed Thiassi,
that from my dwellings
and fields shall to thee
ever cold counsels come.

Loki
52. Milder was thou of speech
to Laufey's son,
when to thy bed thou didst invite me.
Such matters must be mentioned,
if we accurately must
recount our vices.

Then Sif came forth, and poured out mead for Loki in an icy cup, saying:

53. Hail to thee, Loki!
and this cool cup receive,
full of old mead:
at least me alone,
among the blameless Æsir race,
leave stainless.

He took the horn, drank, and said:

> 54. So alone shouldst thou be,
> hadst thou strict and prudent been
> towards thy mate;
> but one I know,
> and, I think, know him well,
> a favoured rival of Hlorridi,
> and that is the wily Loki.

> Beyla
> 55. The fells all tremble:
> I think Hlorridi
> is from journeying home.
> He will bid be quiet
> him who here insults
> all gods and men.

> Loki
> 56. Be silent, Beyla!
> Thou art Byggvir's wife,
> and with much evil mingled:
> never came a greater monster
> among the Æsir's sons.
> Thou art a dirty strumpet.

Thor then came in and said:

> 57. Silence, thou impure being!
> My mighty hammer, Mjöllnir,
> shall stop thy prating.
> I will thy head
> from thy neck strike;
> then will thy life be ended.

> Loki
> 58. Now the son of earth
> is hither come.
> Why dost thou chafe so, Thor?
> Thou wilt not dare do so,
> when with the wolf thou hast to fight,
> and he the all-powerful father swallows whole.

Thor
59. Silence, thou impure being!
My mighty hammer, Mjöllnir,
shall stop thy prating.
Up I will hurl thee
to the east region,
and none shall see thee after.

Loki
60. Of thy eastern travels
thou shouldst never
to people speak,
since in a glove-thumb
thou, Einheri! wast doubled up,
and hardly thoughtest thou was Thor.

Thor
61. Silence, thou impure being!
My mighty hammer, Mjöllnir,
shall stop thy prating;
with this right hand I, Hrugnir's bane,
will smite thee,
so that thy every bone be broken.

Loki
62. 'Tis my intention
a long life to live,
though with thy hammer
thou dost threaten me.
Skrymir's thongs
seemed to thee hard,
when at the food thou couldst not get,
when, in full health, of hunger dying.

Thor
63. Silence, thou impure being!
My mighty hammer, Mjöllnir,
shall stop thy prating.
Hrungnir's bane
shall cast thee down to Hel,
beneath the grating of the dead.

Loki

64. I have said before the Æsir,
I have said before the Æsir's sons,
that which my mind suggested:
but for thee alone
will I go out;
because I know that thou wilt fight.

65. Ægir! thou hast brewed beer;
but thou never shalt henceforth
a compotation hold.
All thy possessions,
which are herein,
flame shall play over,
and on thy back shall burn thee.

After this Loki, in the likeness of a salmon, cast himself into the waterfall of Franangr, where the Æsir caught him, and bound him with the entrails of his son Nari; but his other son, Narfi, was changed into a wolf. Skadi took a venomous serpent, and fastened it up over Loki's face. The venom trickled down from it. Sigyn, Loki's wife, sat by, and held a basin under the venom; and when the basin was full, carried the venom out. Meanwhile the venom dropped on Loki, who shrank from it so violently that the whole earth trembled. This causes what are not called earthquakes.

Fiölsvinnsmál: The Lay of Fiölsvith

1. From the outward wall
he saw one ascending to
the seat of the giant race.

Fiölsvith
Along the humid ways
haste the back hence,
here, wretch! is no place for thee.

2. What monster is it
before the fore-court standing,
and hovering round the perilous flame?
Whom dost thou seek?
Of what art thou in quest?
Or what, friendless being! desirest thou to know?

Wanderer
3. What monster is that,
before the fore-court standing,
who to the wayfarer offers not hospitality?
Void of honest fame,
prattler! hast thou lived:
but hence hie thee home.

Fiölsvith
4. Fiölsvith is my name;
wise I am of mind,
though of food not prodigal.
Within these courts
thou shalt never come:
so now, wretch! take thyself off.

Wanderer
5. From the eye's delight
few are disposed to hurry,
where there is something
pleasant to be seen.
These walls, methinks,
shine around golden halls.
Here I could live contented with my lot.

Fiölsvith
6. Tell me, youth;
of whom thou art born,
or of what race hath sprung.

Wanderer
7. Vindkald I am called,
Varkald was my father named,
his sire was Fiölkald.

8. Tell me, Fiölsvith!
that which I will ask thee,
and I desire to know:
who here holds sway,
and has power over
these lands and costly halls?

Fiölsvith
9. Menglöd is her name,
her mother her begat
with Svaf, Thorin's son.
She here holds sway,
and has power over
these lands and costly halls.

Vindkald
10. Tell me, Fiölsvith! etc.
what the grate is called,
than which among the gods
mortals never saw a greater artifice?

Fiölsvith
11. Thrymgiöll it is called,
and Solblindi's
three sons constructed it:
a fetter fastens
every wayfarer,
who lifts it from its opening.

Vindkald
12. Tell me, Fiölsvith! etc.
what that structure is called,
than which among the gods
mortals never saw a greater artifice?

Fiölsvith
13. Gastropnir it is called,
and I constructed it
of Leirbrimir's limbs.
I have so supported it,
that it will ever stand
while the world lasts.

Vindkald
14. Tell me, Fiölsvith! etc.
what those dogs are called,
that chase away the giantesses,
and safety to the fields restore?

Fiölsvith
15. Gifr the one is called,
the other Geri,
if thou that wouldst know.
Eleven watches
they will keep,
until the powers perish.

Vindkald
16. Tell me, Fiölsvith! etc.
whether any man
can enter
while those fierce assailants sleep?

Fiölsvith
17. Alternate sleep
was strictly to them enjoined,
since to the watch they were appointed.
One sleeps by night,
by day the other,
so that no wight can enter if he comes.

Vindkald
18. Tell me, Fiölsvith! etc.
whether there is any food
that men can get,
such that they can run in while they eat?

Fiölsvith
19. Two repasts
lie in Vidofnir's wings,
if thou that wouldst know:
that is alone such food
as men can give them,
and run in while they eat.

Vindkald
20. Tell me, Fiölsvith! etc.
what that tree is called
that with its branches spreads itself
over every land?

Fiölsvith
21. Mimameidr it is called;
but few men know
from what roots it springs:
it by that will fall
which fewest know.
Nor fire nor iron will harm it.

Vindkald
22. Tell me, Fiölsvith! etc.
to what the virtue is
of that famed tree applied,
which nor fire nor iron will harm?

Fiölsvith
23. Its fruit shall
on the fire be laid,
for labouring women;
out then will pass
what would in remain:
so it is a creator of mankind.

Vindkald
24. Tell me, Fiölsvith! etc.
what the cock is called
that sits in that lofty tree,
and all-glittering is with gold?

Fiölsvith
25. Vidofnir he is called;
in the clear air he stands,
in the boughs of Mima's tree:
afflictions only brings,
together indissoluble,
the swart bird at his lonely meal.

Vindkald
26. Tell me, Fiölsvith! etc.
whether there be any weapon,
before which Vidofnir may
fall to Hel's abode?

27. Hævatein the twig is named,
and Lopt plucked it,
down by the gate of Death.
In an iron chest it lies
with Sinmoera,
and is with nine strong locks secured.

Vindkald
28. Tell me, Fiölsvith! etc.
whether he will alive return,
who seeks after,
and will take, that rod?

Fiölsvith
29. He will return
who seeks after,
and will take, the rod,
if he bears that
which few possess
to the dame of the glassy clay.

Vindkald
30. Tell me, Fiölsvith! etc.
whether there is any treasure,
that mortals can obtain,
at which the pale giantess will rejoice?

Fiölsvith
31. The bright sickle
that lies in Vidofnir's wings,
thou in a bag shalt bear,
and to Sinmoera give,
before she will think fit
to lend an arm for conflict.

Vindkald
32. Tell me, Fiölsvith! etc.
what this hall is called,
which is girt round
with a curious flickering flame?

Fiölsvith
33. Hyr it is called,
and it will long
tremble as on a lance's point.
This sumptuous house
shall, for ages hence,
be but from hearsay known.

Vindkald
34. Tell me, Fiölsvith! etc.
which of the Æsir's sons
has that constructed,
which within the court I saw?

Fiölsvith
35. Uni and Iri,
Bari and Ori,
Var and Vegdrasil,
Dorri and Uri,
Delling and Atvard,
Lidskialf, Loki.

Vindkald
36. Tell me, Fiölsvith! etc.
what that mount is called
on which I see
a splendid maiden stand?

Fiölsvith
37. Hyfiaberg 'tis called,
and long has it a solace been
to the bowed-down and sorrowful:
each woman becomes healthy,
although a year's disease she have,
if she can but ascend it.

Vindkald
38. Tell me, Fiölsvith! etc.
how those maids are called,
who sit at Menglöd's knees
in harmony together?

Fiölsvith
39. Hlif the first is called,
the second is Hlifthursa,
the third Thiodvarta,
Biört and Blid,
Blidr, Frid,
Eir and Örboda.

Vindkald
40. Tell me, Fiölsvith! etc.
whether they protect
those who offer to them,
if it should, be needful?

Fiölsvith
41. Every summer
in which men offer to them,
at the holy place,
no pestilence so great shall come
to the sons of men,
but they will free each from peril.

Vindkald
42. Tell me, Fiölsvith! etc.
whether there is any man
that may in Menglöd's
soft arms sleep?

Fiölsvith
43. There is no man
who may in Menglöd's
soft arms sleep,
save only Svipdag;
to him the sun-bright maid
is for wife betrothed.

Vindkald
44. Set the doors open!
Let the gate stand wide;
here thou mayest Svipdag see;
but yet go learn
if Menglöd will
accept my love.

Fiölsvith
45. Hear, Menglöd!
A man is hither come:
go and behold the stranger;
the dogs rejoice;
the house is opened.
I think it must be Svipdag.

Menglöd
46. Fierce ravens shall,
on the high gallows,
tear out thy eyes,
if thou art lying,
that hither from afar is come
the youth unto my halls.

47. Whence art thou come?
Whence hast thou journeyed?
How do thy kindred call thee?
Of thy race and name
I must have a token,
if I was betrothed to thee.

Svipdag
48. Svipdag I am named,
Solbiart was my father named;
thence the winds on the cold ways drove me.
Urd's decree
may no one gainsay,
however lightly uttered.

Menglöd
49. Welcome thou art:
my will I have obtained;
greeting a kiss shall follow.
A sight unlooked-for
gladdens most persons,
when one the other loves.

50. Long have I sat
on my loved hill,
day and night
expecting thee.
Now that is come to pass
which I have hoped,
that thou, dear youth, again
to my halls art come.

Svipdag
51. Longing I have undergone
for thy love;
and thou, for my affection.
Now it is certain,
that we shall pass
our lives together.

Hyndlulioð: The Lay of Hyndla

Freyja rides with her favourite Ottar to Hyndla, a Vala, for the purpose of obtaining information respecting Ottar's genealogy, such information being required by him in a legal dispute with Angantyr. Having obtained this, Freyja further requests Hyndla to give Ottar a portion *(minnisöl)* that will enable him to remember all that has been told him. This she refuses, but is forced to comply by Freyja having encircled her cave with flames. She gives him the potion, but accompanied by a malediction, which is by Freyja turned to a blessing.

Freyja
1. Wake, maid of maids!
Wake, my friend!
Hyndla! Sister!
who in the cavern dwellest.
Now there is a dark of darks;
we will both
to Valhall ride,
and to the holy fane.

2. Let us Heriafather pray
into our minds to enter,
he gives and grants
gold to the deserving.
He gave to Hermod
a helm and corslet,
and from him Sigmund
a sword received.

3. Victory to his sons he gives,
but to some riches;
eloquence to the great,
and to men, wit;
fair wind he gives to traders,
but poesy to skalds;
valor he gives
to many a warrior.

4. She to Thor will offer,
she to him will pray,
that to thee he may
be well disposed;
although he bears ill will
to Jötun females.

5. Now of thy wolves take one
from out the stall;
let him run
with runic rein.[1]

Hyndla
6. Sluggish is thy hog
the god's way to tread:

Freyja
7. I will my noble
palfrey saddle.

Hyndla
8. False art thou, Freyja!
who tempest me:
by thy eyes thou showest it,
so fixed upon us;
while thou thy man hast
 on the dead-road,[2]
the young Ottar,
Innstein's son.

Freyja
9. Dull art thou, Hyndla!
methinks thou dreamest,
since thou sayest that my man
is on the dead-road with me;
there where my hog sparkles
with its golden bristles,
hight Hildisvini,
which for me made

---

1. That is, with a rein inscribed with runes.
2. The road to Valhall.

the two skilful dwarfs,
Dain and Nabbi.
From the saddle we will talk:
let us sit,
and of princely
families discourse,
of those chieftains
who from the gods descend.
They have contested
for the dead's gold,
Ottar the young
and Angantyr.

10. A duty 'tis to act
so that the young prince
his paternal heritage may have,
after his kindred.

11. An offer-stead to me he raised,
with stones constructed;
now is that stone
as glass become.
With the blood of oxen
he newly sprinkled it.
Ottar ever trusted
in the Asyniur.

12. Now let us reckon up
the ancient families,
and the races of
exalted men.
Who are the Skiöldings?
Who are the Skilfings?
Who the Ödlings?
Who the Ylfings?
Who the höld-born?
Who the hers-born?
The choicest race of men
under heaven?

Hyndla
13. Thou, Ottar! art
of Innstein born,
but Innstein was
from Alf the Old,
Alf was from Ulf.
Ulf from Sæfari,
but Sæfari
from Svan the Red.

14. Thy father had a mother,
for her necklaces famed,
she, I think, was named
Hledis the priestess;
Frodi her father was,
and her mother Friant:
all that stock is reckoned
among chieftains.

15. Ali was of old
of men the strongest,
Halfdan before him,
the highest of the Skiöldungs;
(Famed were the wars
by those chieftains led)
his deeds seemed to soar
to the skirts of heaven.

16. By Eimund aided,
chief of men,
he Sigtrygg slew
with the cold steel.
He Almveig had to wife,
first of women.
They begat and had
eighteen sons.

17. From them the Skiöldungs,
from them the Skilfings,
from them the Ödlings,
from them the Ynglings,
from them the höld-born,
from them the hers-born,
the choicest race of men
under heaven.
All that race is thine,
Ottar Heimski!

18. Hildegun
her mother was,
of Svafa born
and a sea-king.
All that race is thine,
Ottar Heimski!
Carest thou to know?
Wishest thou a longer narrative?

19. Dag wedded Thora,
mother of warriors;
of that race were born
the noble champions,
Fradmar, Gyrd,
and the Frekis both,
Am, Jösur, Mar,
Alf the Old.
Carest thou this to know?
Wishest thou a longer narrative?

20. Ketil their friend was named,
heir of Klyp;
he was maternal grandsire
of thy mother.
Then was Frodi
yet before Kari,
but the eldest born
was Alf.

21. Nanna was next,
Nökkvi's daughter;
her son was
thy father's kinsman,
ancient is that kinship.
I knew both
Brodd and Hörfi.
All that race is thine,
Ottar Heimski!

22. Isolf, Asolf,
Ölmod's sons
and Skurhild's
Skekkil's daughter;
thou shalt yet count
chieftains many.
All that race is thine,
Ottar Heimski!

23. Gunnar, Balk,
Grim, Ardskafi,
Jarnskiöld, Thorir,
Ulf, Ginandi,
Bui and Brami,
Barri and Reifnir,
Tind and Tyrfing,
the two Haddingis.
All that race is thine,
Ottar Heimski!

24. To toil and tumult
were the sons
of Arngrim born,
and of Eyfura:
ferocious berserkir,
calamity of every kind,
by land and sea,
like fire they carried.
All that race is thine,
Ottar Heimski!

25. I knew both
Brodd and Hörfi,
they were in the court
of Hrolf the Old;
all descended
from Jörmunrek,
son-in-law of Sigurd.
(Listen to my story)
the dread of nations,
him who Fafnir slew.

26. He was a king,
from Völsung sprung,
and Hiördis
from Hrödung;
but Eylimi
from the Ödlings.
All that race it thine,
Ottar Heimski!

27. Gunnar and Högni,
sons of Giuki;
and Gudrun likewise,
their sister.
Guttorm was not
of Giuki's race,
although he brother was
of them both.
All that race is thine,
Ottar Heimski!

28. Harald Heildetönn,
born of Hrærekir
Slöngvanbaugi;
he was a son of Aud,
Aud the rich
was Ivar's daughter;
but Radbard was
Randver's father.
They were heroes
to the gods devoted.
All that race is thine,
Ottar Heimski!

29. There were eleven
Æsir reckoned,
when Baldr on
the pile was laid;
him Vali showed himself
worthy to avenge,
his own brother:
he the slayer slew.
All that race is thine,
Ottar Heimski!

30. Baldr's father was
son of Bur:
Frey to wife had Gerd,
she was Gymir's daughter,
from Jötuns sprung
and Aurboda;
Thiassi also
was their relation,
that haughty Jötun;
Skadi was his daughter.

31. We tell thee much,
and remember more:
I admonish thee thus much to know.
Wishest thou yet a longer narrative?

32. Haki was not the worst
of Hvedna's sons,
and Hiövard
was Hvedna's father;
Heid and Hrossthiof were
of Hrimnir's race.

33. All the Valas are
from Vidolf;
all the soothsayers
from Vilmeidr,
all the sorcerers
from Svarthöfdi;
all the Jötuns
come from Ymir.

34. We tell thee much,
and more remember,
I admonish thee thus much to know.
Wishest thou yet a longer narrative?

35. There was one born,
in times of old,
with wondrous might endowed,
of origin divine:
nine Jötun maids
gave birth
to the gracious god,
at the world's margin.

36. Gialp gave him birth,
Greip gave him birth,
Eistla gave him birth,
and Angeia;
Ulfrun gave him birth,
and Eyrgiafa,
Imd and Atla,
and Jarnsaxa.

37. The boy was nourished
with the strength of earth,
with the ice-cold sea,
and with Son's blood.
We tell thee much,
and more remember.
I admonish thee thus much to know.
Wishest thou a yet longer narrative?

38. Loki begat the wolf
with Angrboda,
but Sleipnir he begat
with Svadilfari:
one monster seemed
of all most deadly,
which from Byleist's
brother sprang.

39. Loki, scorched up
in his heart's affections,
had found a half-burnt
woman's heart.
Loki became guileful
from that wicked woman;
thence in the world
are all giantesses come.

40. Ocean towers with storms
to heaven itself,
flows o'er the land;
the air is rent:
thence come snows
and rapid winds;
then it is decreed
that the rain should cease.

41. There was one born
greater than all,
the boy was nourished
with the strength of earth;
he was declared a ruler,
mightiest and richest,
allied by kinship
to all princes.

42. Then shall another come,
yet mightier,
although I dare not
his name declare.
Few may see
further forth
than when Odin
meets the wolf.

Freyja
43. Bear thou the memory-cup
to my guest,
so that he may all
the words repeat
of this discourse,
on the third morn,
when he and Angantyr
reckon up races.

Hyndla
44. Go thou quickly hence,
I long to sleep;
more of my wondrous power
thou gettest not from me.
Thou runnest, my hot friend,
out at nights,
as among he-goats
the she-goat goes.

45. Thou hast run thyself mad,
ever longing;
many a one has stolen
under thy girdle.
Thou runnest, my hot friend,
out at nights,
as among he-goats
the she-goat goes.

Freyja
46. Fire I strike
over thee, dweller of the wood!
so that thou goest not
ever away from hence.

Hyndla
47. Fire I see burning,
and the earth blazing;
many will have
their lives to save.
Bear thou the cup
to Ottar's hand,
the mead with venom mingled,
in an evil hour!

Freyja
48. Thy malediction
shall be powerless;
although thou, Jötun-maid!
dost evil threaten.
He shall drink
delicious draughts.
All the gods I pray
to favour Ottar.

Gróagaldr: The Incantation of Groa

Son
1. Wake up, Groa!
wake up, good woman!
at the gates of death I wake thee!
if thou remembrest,
that thou thy son badest
to thy grave-mound to come.

Mother
2. What now troubles
my only son?
With what affliction art thou burthened,
that thou thy mother callest,
who to dust is come,
and from human homes departed?

Son
3. A hateful game
thou, crafty woman, didst set before me,
whom my father has in his bosom cherished,
when thou bides me go
no one knows whither,
Menglöd to meet.

Mother
4. Long is the journey,
long are the ways,
long are men's desires.
If it so fall out,
that thou thy will obtainest,
the event must then be as it may.

Son
5. Sing to me songs
which are good.
Mother! protect thy son.
Dead on my way
I fear to be.
I seem to young in years.

Mother
6. I will sing to thee first
one that is thought most useful,
which Rind sang to Ran;
that from thy shoulders thou shouldst cast
what to thee seems irksome:
let thyself thyself direct.

7. A second I will sing to thee,
as thou hast to wander
joyless on the ways.
May Urd's protection
hold thee on every side,
where thou seest turpitude.

8. A third I will sing to thee.
If the mighty rivers
to thy life's peril fall,
Horn and Rud,
may they flow down to Hel,
and for thee ever be diminished.

9. A fourth I will sing to thee.
If foes assail thee
ready on the dangerous road,
their hearts shall fail them,
and to thee be power,
and their minds to peace be turned.

10. A fifth I will sing to thee.
If bonds be
cast on thy limbs,
friendly spells I will let
on thy joints be sung,
and the lock from thy arms shall start,
(and from thy feet the fetter.)

11. A sixth I will sing to thee.
If on the sea thou comest,
more stormy than men have known it,
air and water
shall in a bag attend thee,
and a tranquil course afford thee.

12. A seventh I will sing to thee.
If on a mountain high
frost should assail thee,
deadly cold shall not
thy carcase injure,
nor draw thy body to thy limbs.

13. An eighth I will sing to thee.
If night overtake thee,
when out on the misty way,
that the dead Christian woman
no power may have
to do thee harm.

14. A ninth I will sing to thee.
If with a far-famed spear-armed Jötun
thou words exchangest,
of words and wit
to thy mindful heart
abundance shall be given.

15. Go now ever
where calamity may be,
and no harm shall obstruct thy wishes.
On a stone fast in the earth
I have stood within the door,
while songs I sang to thee.

16. My son! bear hence
thy mother's words,
and in thy breast let them dwell;
for happiness abundant
shalt thou have in life,
while of my words thou art mindful.

Solarlióð: The Song of the Sun

This singular poem, the authorship of which is, in some manuscripts, assigned to Sæmund himself, may be termed a Voice from the Dead, given under the form of a dream, in which a deceased father is supposed to address his son from another world. The first 7 strophes seem hardly connected with the following ones, which, as far as the 32nd consist chiefly in aphorisms with examples, some closely resembling those in the *Hávamál*. In the remaining portion is given the recital of the last illness of the supposed speaker, his death, and the scenes his soul passed through on the way to its final home.

The composition exhibits a strange mixture of Christianity and Heathenism, whence it would seem that the poet's own religion was in a transition state. Of the allusions to Heathenism it is, however, to be observed that they are chiefly to persons and actions of which there is no trace in the Odinic mythology, as known to us, and are possibly the fruits of the poet's own imagination. The title of the poem is no doubt derived from the allusion to the Sun at the beginning of the strophes 39-45.

For an elaborate and learned commentary, with an interlinear version of *the Song of the Sun*, the reader may consult *Les Chants de Sol*, by Professor Bergmann, Strassbourg & Paris, 1858.

1. Of life and property
a fierce freebooter
despoiled mankind;
over the ways
beset by him
might no one living pass.

2. Alone he ate
most frequently,
no one invited he to his repast;
until weary,
and with failing strength,
a wandering guest
came from the way.

3. In need of drink
that way-worn man,
and hungry feigned to be:
with trembling heart
he seemed to trust
him who had been so evil-minded.

4. Meat and drink
to the weary one he gave,
all with upright heart;
on God he thought,
the traveller's wants supplied;
for he felt he was an evil-doer.

5. Up stood the guest,
he evil meditated,
he had not been kindly treated;
his sin within him swelled,
he while sleeping murdered
his wary cautious host.

6. The God of heaven
he prayed for help,
when being struck he woke;
but he was doomed the sins of him
on himself to take,
whom sackless he had slain.

7. Holy angels came
from heaven above,
and took to them his soul:
in a life of purity
it shall ever live
with the almighty God.
****

8. Riches and health
no one may command,
though all go smoothly with him.
To many that befalls
which they least expect.
No one may command his tranquility.

9. Unnar and Sævaldi
never imagined
that happiness would fall on them,
yet naked they became,
and of all bereft,
and, like wolves, ran to the forest.
****

10. The force of pleasure
has many a one bewailed.
Cares are often caused by women;
pernicious they become,
although the mighty God
them pure created.

11. United were
Svafud and Skarthedin,
neither might without the other be,
until to frenzy they were driven
for a woman;
she was destined for their perdition.

12. On account of that fair maid,
neither of them cared
for games or joyous days;
no other thing
could they in memory bear
then that bright form.

13. Sad to them were
the gloomy nights,
no sweet sleep might they enjoy:
but from that anguish
rose hate intense
between the faithful friends.

14. Hostile deeds
are in most places
fiercely avenged.
To the holm they went,[1]
for that fair woman,
and each one found his death.
****

15. Arrogance should no one entertain:
I indeed have seen
that those who follow her,

---

1. That is, *they engaged in single combat*; the spot for such encounters being called a *holm*, consisting of a circular space marked out by stones.

for the most part,
turn from God.

16. Rich were both,
Radey and Vebogi,
and thought only of their well-being;
now they sit
and turn their sores
to various hearths.

17. They in themselves confided,
and thought themselves alone to be
above all people;
but their lot
Almighty God was pleased
otherwise to appoint.

18. A life of luxury they led,
in may ways,
and had gold for sport.
Now they are requited,
so that they must walk
between frost and fire.

19. To thy enemies
trust thou never,
although they speak thee fair:
promise them good:
'tis good to have another's injury
as a warning.

20. So it befell
Sörli the upright,
when he placed himself in Vigolf's power;
he confidently trusted him,
his brother's murderer,
but he proved false.

21. Peace to them he granted,
with heart sincere;
they in return promised him gold,
feigned themselves friends.,

while they together drank;
but then came forth their guile.

22. Then afterwards,
on the second day,
when they in Rýgiardal rode,
they with swords wounded him
who sackless was,
and let his life go forth.

23. His corpse they dragged
(on a lonely way,
and cut up piecemeal) into a well,
and would it hide;
but the holy Lord
beheld from heaven.

24. His soul summoned home
the true God
into his joy to come;
but the evil doers
will, I ween, late
be from torments called.
****

25. Do thou pray the Disir
of the Lord's words
to be kind to thee in spirit:
for a week after,
all shall then go happily,
according to thy will.

26. For a deed of ire
that thou has perpetrated,
never atone with evil:
the weeping thou shalt
sooth with benefits:
that is salutary to the soul.

27. On God a man
shall for good things call,
on him who has mankind created.

Greatly sinful is
every man
who late finds the Father.

28. To be solicited, we opine,
is with all earnestness
for that which is lacking:
of all things may be destitute
he who for nothing asks:
few heed the wants of the silent.

29. Late I came,
though called betimes,
to the supreme Judge's door;
thitherward I yearn;
for it was promised me,
he who craves it shall of the feast partake.

30. Sins are the cause
that sorrowing we depart
from this world:
no one stands in dread,
if he does no evil:
good it is to be blameless.

31. Like unto wolves
all those seem
who have a faithless mind:
so he will prove
who has to go
through ways strewed with gleeds.

32. Friendly counsels,
and wisely composed, seven
I have imparted to thee:
consider thou them well,
and forget them never:
they are all useful to learn.
****

33. Of that I will speak,
how happy I was
in the world,
and secondly,
how the sons of men
reluctantly become corpses.

34. Pleasure and pride
deceive the sons of men
who after money crave;
shining riches
at last become a sorrow:
many have riches driven to madness.

35. Steeped in joys
I seemed to men;
for little did I see before me:
our worldly sojourn
has the Lord created
in delights abounding.

36. Bowed down I sat,
long I tottered,
of life was most desirous;
but He prevailed
who was all-powerful:
onward are the ways of the doomed.

37. The cords of Hel
were tightly
bound round my sides;
I would rend them,
but they were strong.
'Tis easy free to go.

38. I alone knew,
how on all sides
my pains increased.
The maids of Hel each eve
with horror bade me
to their home.

39. The sun I saw,
true star of day,
sink in its roaring home;
but Hel's grated doors
on the other side I heard
heavily creaking.

40. The sun I saw
with blood-red beams beset:
(fast was I then from this world declining)
mightier she appeared,
in many ways
than she was before.

41. The sun I saw,
and it seemed to me
as if I saw a glorious god:
I bowed before her,
for the last time,
in the world of men.

42. The sun I saw:
she beamed forth so
that I seemed nothing to know;
but Giöll's streams
roared from the other side
mingled much with blood.

43. The sun I saw,
with quivering eyes,
appalled and shrinking;
for my heart
in great measure was
dissolved in languor.

44. The sun I saw
seldom sadder;
I had then almost from the world declined:
my tongue was
as wood become,
and all was cold without me.

45. The sun I saw
never after,
since that gloomy day;
for the mountain-waters
closed over me,
and I went called from torments.

46. The star of hope,
when I was born,
fled from my breast away;
high it flew,
settled nowhere,
so that it might find rest.

47. Longer than all
was that one night,
when stiff on my straw I lay;
then becomes manifest
the divine word:
"Man is the same as earth."

48. The Creator God can
it estimate and know,
(He who made heaven and earth)
how forsaken
many go hence,
although from kindred parted.

49. Of his works
each has the reward:
happy is he who does good.
Of my wealth bereft,
to me was destined
a bed strewed with sand.

50. Bodily desires
men oftentimes seduce,
of them has many a one too much:
water of baths
was of all things to me
most loathsome.

51. In the Norns' seat
nine days I sat,
thence I was mounted on a horse:
there the giantess's sun
shone grimly
through the dripping clouds of heaven.

52. Without and within,
I seemed to traverse all
the seven nether worlds:
up and down,
I sought an easier way,
where I might have the readiest paths.
****

53. Of that is to be told,
which I first saw,
when I to the worlds of torment came:-
scorched birds,
which were souls,
flew numerous as flies.

54. From the west I saw
Von's dragons fly,
and Glæval's paths obscure:
their wings they shook;
wide around me seemed
the earth and heaven to burst.

55. The sun's hart I saw
from the south coming,
he was by two together led:
his feet stood on the earth,
but his horns
reached up to heaven.

56. From the north riding I saw
the sons of Nidi,
they were seven in all:
from full horns,
the pure mead they drank
from the heaven-god's well.

57. The wind was silent,
the waters stopped their course;
then I heard a doleful sound:
for their husbands
false-faced women
ground earth for food.

58. Gory stones
those dark women
turned sorrowfully;
bleeding hearts hung
out of their breasts,
faint with much affliction.

59. Many a man I saw
wounded go
on those gleed-strewed paths;
their faces seemed
to me all reddened
with reeking blood.

60. Many men I saw
to earth gone down,
who holy service might not have;
heathen stars
stood above their heads,
painted with deadly characters.

61. I saw those men
who much envy harbour
at another's fortune;
bloody runes
were on their breasts
graved painfully.

62. I there saw men
many not joyful;
they were all wandering wild:
this he earns,
who by this world's vices
is infatuated.

63. I saw those men
who had in various ways
acquired other's property:
in shoals they went
to Castle-covetous,
and burthens bore of lead.

64. I saw those men
who many had
of life and property bereft:
through the breasts
of those men passed
strong venomous serpents.

65. I saw those men
who the holy days
would not observe:
their hands were
on hot stones
firmly nailed.

66. I saw those men
who from pride
valued themselves too highly;
their garments
ludicrously were
in fire enveloped.

67. I saw those men
who had many
false words of others uttered:
Hel's ravens
from their heads
their eyes miserably tore.

68. All the horrors
thou wilt not get to know
which Hel's inmates suffer.
Pleasant sins
end in painful penalties:
pains ever follow pleasure.
****

69. I saw those men
who had much given
for God's laws;
pure lights were
above their heads
brightly burning.

70. I saw those men
who from exalted mind
helped the poor to aid:
angels read
holy books
above their heads.

71. I saw those men
who with much fasting had
their bodies wasted:
God's angels
bowed before them:
that is the highest joy.

72. I saw those men
who had put food
into their mothers' mouth:
their couches were
on the rays of heaven
pleasantly placed.

73. Holy virgins
had cleanly washed
the souls from sin
of those men,
who for a long time had
themselves tormented.

74. Lofty cars I saw
towards heaven going;
they were on the way to God:
men guided them
who had been murdered
wholly without crime.

75. Almighty Father!
greatest Son!
holy Spirit of heaven!
Thee I pray,
who hast us all created;
free us all from miseries.
****

76. Biugvör and Listvör
sit at Herðir's doors,
on resounding seat;
iron gore
falls from their nostrils,
which kindles hate among men.

77. Odin's wife
rows in earth's ship,
eager after pleasures;
her sails are
reefed late,
which on the ropes of desire are hung.

78. Son! I thy father
and Solkatla's sons
have alone obtained for thee
that horn of hart,
which from the grave-mound bore
the wise Vigdvalin.

79. Here are runes
which have engraven
Niörd's daughters nine,
Radvör the eldest,
and the youngest Kreppvör,
and their seven sisters.

80. How much violence
have they perpetrated
Svaf and Svaflogi!
bloodshed they have excited,
and wounds have sucked,
after an evil custom.

81. This lay,
which I have taught thee,
thou shalt before the living sing,
the Sun-Song,
which will appear
in many parts no fiction.

82. Here we part,
but again shall meet
on the day of men's rejoicing.
Oh Lord!
unto the dead grant peace,
and to the living comfort.

83. Wondrous lore
has in dream to thee been sung,
but thou hast seen the truth:
no man has been
so wise created
that has before heard the Sun-Song.

Part 2: The Heroic Lays

Preface

In the preface to the first or mythological part of this translation of *Sæmund's Edda*, I announced my intention of publishing the second or heroic portion, should that first part be not unfavourably received. That condition has been fulfilled, for not only has its reception here been favourable, but in the United States of America it has been noticed in terms highly gratifying to the translator. I now therefore do not hesitate to publish the second part.

The limits within which I deem it necessary to confine myself, from my desire to produce a small work at a moderate cost, admit only of a very brief notice of the poems contained in this portion of the Edda: *The Lay of Völund (Völundarkvida)* celebrates the story of Völund's doing and sufferings during his sojourn in the territory of the Swedish king Nidud. (Ger. Wieland, Fr. Veland and Galans) is the Scandinavian and Germanic Vulcan (Hephaistos) and Dædalus. In England his story, as a skillful smith, is traceable to a very early period. In the Anglo-Saxon poem of Beowulf we find that hero desiring, in the event of his falling in conflict with Grendel, that his corslet may be sent to Hygelac, being, as he says, the work of Weland: and king Ælfred, in his translation of *Boethius de Consolatione*, renders the words *fidelis ossa Fabricii*, etc. by Hwæt *(hwær) sint nu Þæs foremæran* and *Þæs wisan goldsmiðes ban Welondes*? (Where are now the bones of the famous and wise goldsmith Weland?), evidently taking the proper name of Fabricius for an appellative equivalent to faber. In the *Exeter Book*, too, there is a poem in substance closely resembling the Eddaic lay. In his novel of *Kenilworth*, Walter Scott has been guilty of a woeful perversion of the old tradition, travestied from the Berkshire legend of Wayland Smith. As a land-boundary we find Weland's smithy in a charter of king Eadred a.d. 955. Ampler details concerning Weland are to be found in Mr. Price's preface to *Warton's History of English Poetry* 8vo., edit.; Müller, Sagabibliothek, II. pp. 157 sqq.; Grimm, *Deutsche Mythologie*, pp. 349 sqq. edit. 1844; Müller, *Aldeutsche Religion*, p. 311. Much interesting matter will also be found in Weber and Jamieson's *Illustrations of Northern Antiquities*. Bishop Müller, derives the name from O. Nor. Vél, thinking that it is only according to the Norse pronunciation that it has a signification, viz. art, wile, guile, and *lundr*, mind, disposition, and is thence inclined to assign a Northern origin to the story. But may not the form Völundr be merely a Northern adaptation of the German Wieland or Anglo-Saxon Weland? On the *Lay of Helgi Hiörvard's Son* there is nothing to remark beyond what appears in the poem itself.

The *Lays of Helgi Hundingcide* form the first of the series of stories relating to the Völsung race, and the Giukungs, or Niflungs.

The connection of the several personages celebrated in these poems will appear plain from the following tables.

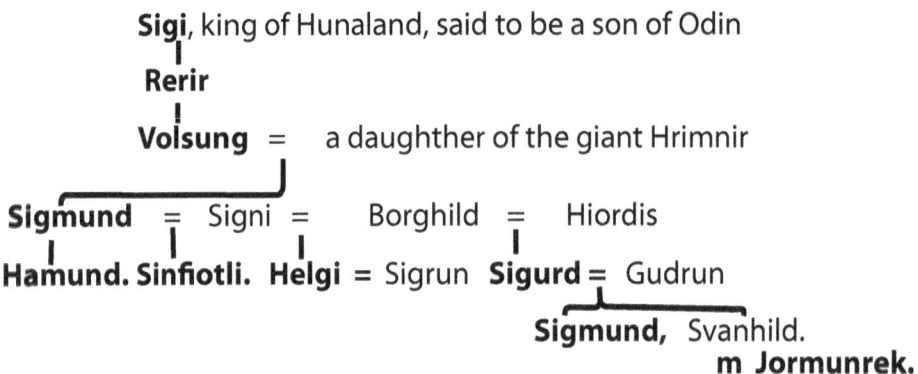

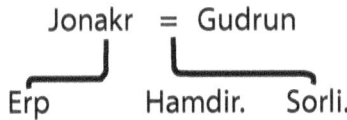

The Eddaic series of the Völsung and Niflung lays terminates with the *Lay of Hamdir*; the one entitled *Gunnar's Melody* is no doubt a comparatively late composition; yet being written in the true ancient spirit of the North is well deserving of a place among the Eddaic poems. Nor, indeed, is the claim of the *Lay of Grotti* to rank among the poems collected by Sæmund, by any means clear, we know it only from its existence in the *Skalda*; yet on account of its antiquity, its intrinsic worth, and its reception in other editions of the Edda, both in original and translation, the present work would seem, and justly so, incomplete without it.

Had the limits, within which I am desirous to confine my humble attempt at a version of the *Poetic Edda*, permitted, I would have assigned a portion of this preface to some notice of the relation between the Northern poems relating to the Völsungs and Giukungs, or Niflungs, and the same subject as it appears in the *Nibelunge Not*; but as the latter is familiar to many readers and accessible to all, in the original old German, in modern German, and in more than one excellent English version, I omit all further mention of the subject.

In compliance with the expressed wish of the Publishers, I subscribe my name as the translator of *Sæmund's Edda*.

Benjamin Thorpe

Völundarkviða: The Lay of Völund

There was a king in Sweden named Nidud: he had two sons and a daughter, whose name was Böd-vild. There were three brothers, sons of a king of the Finns, one was called Slagfid, the second Egil, the third Völund. They went on snow-shoes and hunted wild-beasts. They came to Ulfdal, and there made themselves a house, where there is a water called Ulfsíar. Early one morning they found on the border of the lake three females sitting and spinning flax. Near them lay their swan-plumages: they were Valkyriur. Two of them, Hladgud-Svanhvit and Hervör-Alvit, were daughters of King Hlödver; the third was Ölrún, a daughter of Kiár of Valland. They took them home with them to their dwelling. Egil had Ölrún, Slagfid Svanhvit, and Völund Alvit. They lived there seven years, when they flew away seeking conflicts, and did not return. Egil then went on snow-shoes in search of Ölrún, and Slagfid in search of Svanhvit, but Völund remained in Ulfdal. He was a most skilful man, as we learn from old traditions. King Nidud ordered him to be seized, so as it is here related.

1. Maids flew from the south,
through the murky wood,
Alvit the young,
fate to fulfil.

2. One of them,
of maidens fairest,
to his comely breast
Egil clasped.
Svanhvit was the second,
she a swan's plumage bore;
but the third,
their sister,
the white neck clasped
of Völund.

3. There they stayed
seven winters through;
but all the eighth
were with longing seized;
and in the ninth
fate parted them.
The maidens yearned
for the murky wood,
the young Alvit,
fate to fulfil.

4. From the chase came
the ardent hunters,
Slagfid and Egil,
found their house deserted,
went out and in,
and looked around.
Egil went east
after Ölrún,
and Slagfid west
after Svanhvit;

5. But Völund alone
remained in Ulfdal.
He the red gold set
with the hard gem,
well fastened all the rings
on linden bast,
and so awaited
his bright consort,
if to him
she would return.

6. It was told to Nidud,
the Niarars' lord,
that Völund alone
remained in Ulfdal.
In the night went men,
in studded corslets,
their shields glistened
in the waning moon.

7. From their saddles they alighted
at the house's gable,
thence went in
through the house.
On the bast they saw
the rings all drawn,
seven hundred,
which the warrior owned.

8. And they took them off,
and they put them on,
all save one,
which they bore away.
Came then from the chase
the ardent hunter,
Völund, gliding[1]
on the long way.

9. To the fire he went,
bear's flesh to roast.
Soon blazed the brushwood,
and the arid fir,
the wind-dried wood,
before Völund.

10. On the bearskin sat,
his rings counted,
the Alfar's companion:
one was missing.
He thought that Hlödver´s
daughter had it,
the young Alvit,
and that she was returned.

11. So long he sat
until he slept;
and he awoke
of joy bereft:
on his hands he felt
heavy constraints,
and round his feet
fetters clasped.

12. "Who are the men
that on the rings' possessor
have laid bonds?
and me have bound?"

---

1. On snow-shoes.

13. Then cried Nidud,
the Niarars' lord:
"Whence gottest thou, Völund!
Alfars' chief![2]
our gold,
in Ulfdal?"

14. "No gold was here
in Grani's path,
far I thought our land
from the hills of Rhine.
I mind me that we more
treasures possessed,
when, a whole family,
we were at home.

15. Hladgud and Hervör
were of Hlödver born;
know was Ölrún,
Kiar's daughter,
she entered
into the house,
stood on the floor,
her voice moderated:
"Now is he not mirthful,
who from the forest comes."

King Nidud gave to his daughter Bödvild the ring which had been taken from the bast in Völund's house; but he himself bore the sword that had belonged to Völund. The queen said:

16. His teeth he shows,
when the sword he sees,
and Bödvild's ring
he recognizes:
threatening are his eyes
as a glistening serpent's:
let be severed
his sinews' strength;

---

2. The designation of Alfars' chief, or prince, applied to Volund, who, as we learn from the prose introduction, was a son of a king of the Finns, may perhaps be accounted for by the circumstance that the poem itself hardly belongs to the Odinic Mythology, and was probably composed when that system was in its decline and giving place to the heroic or romantic.

>   and set him then
>   in Sævarstad.

This was done; he was hamstrung and then set on a certain small island near the shore, called Sævarstad. He there forged for the king all kinds of jewelry work. No one was allowed to go to him, except the king. Völund said:

> 17. "The sword shines
>   in Nidud's belt,
>   which I whetted
>   as I could most skillfully,
>   and tempered,
>   as seemed to me most cunningly.
>   That bright blade for ever is
>   taken from me:
>   never shall I see it
>   borne into Völund's smithy.
>
> 18. Now Bödvild wears
>   my consort's
>   red-gold rings:
>   for this I have no indemnity."
>   He sat and never slept,
>   and his hammer plied;
>   but much more speedy vengeance
>   devised on Nidud.
>
> 19. The two young sons
>   of Nidud ran
>   in at the door to look,
>   in Sævarstad.
>   To the chest they came,
>   for the keys asked;
>   manifest was their grudge,
>   when therein they looked.
>
> 20. Many necklaces were there,
>   which to those youths appeared
>   of the red gold to be,
>   and treasures.
>   "Come ye two alone,
>   to-morrow come;

that gold shall
be given to you.

21. Tell it not to the maidens,
nor to the household folk,
nor to any one,
that ye have been with me."
Early called
one the other,
brother, brother:
"Let us go see the rings."

22. To the chest they came,
for the keys asked;
manifest was their grudge,
when therein they looked.
Of those children he
the heads cut off,
and under the prison's mixen
laid their bodies.

23. But their skulls
beneath the hair
he in silver set,
and to Nidud gave;
and of their eyes
precious stones he formed,
which to Nidud's
wily wife he sent.

24. But of the teeth
of the two
breast-ornaments he made,
and to Bödvild sent.
Then did Bödvild
praise the ring:
to Völund brought it,
when she had broken it:
"I dare to no one tell it,
save alone to thee."

Völund
25. "I will so repair
the fractured gold,
that to thy father
it shall fairer seem,
and to thy mother
much more beautiful,
and to thyself,
in the same degree."

26. He then brought her beer,
that he might succeed the better,
as on her seat
she fell asleep.
"Now have I
my wrongs avenged,
all save one
in the wood perpetrated."[3]

27. "I wish," said Völund,
"that on my feet I were,
of the use of which
Nidud's men have deprived me."
Laughing Völund
rose in the air:
Bödvild weeping
from the isle departed.
She mourned her lover's absence,
and for her father's wrath.

28. Stood without
Nidud's wily wife;
then she went in
through the hall;
but he on the enclosure
sat down to rest.
"Art thou awake
Niarars' lord!"

---

3. The translation of this line is founded solely on a conjectural emendation of the text. The wrong alluded to may be the hamstringing.

29. "Ever am I awake,
joyless I lie to rest,
when I call to mind
my children's death:
my head is chilled,
cold are to me thy counsels.
Now with Völund
I desire to speak."

30. "Tell me, Völund,
Alfars' chief!
of my brave boys
what is become?"

31. "Oaths shalt thou
first to me swear,
by board of ship,
by rim of shield,
by shoulder of steed,
by edge of sword,
that thou wilt not slay
the wife of Völund,
nor of my bride
cause the death;
although a wife I have
whom ye know,
or offspring
within thy court.

32. To the smithy go,
which thou has made,
there wilt thou the bellows find
with blood besprinkled.
The heads I severed
of thy boys,
and under the prison's mixen
laid their bodies.

33. But their skulls
beneath the hair
I in silver set,
and to Nidud gave;
and of their eyes
precious stones I formed,
which to Nidud's
wily wife I sent.

34. Of the teeth
of the two,
breast-ornaments I made,
and to Bödvild sent.
Now Bödvild goes
big with child,
the only daughter
of you both."

35. "Word didst thou never speak
that more afflicted me,
or for which I would
more severely punish thee.
There is no man so tall
that he from thy horse can take thee,
or so skilful
that he can shoot thee down,
thence where thou floatest
up in the sky."

36. Laughing Völund
rose in air,
but Nidud sad
remained sitting.

37. "Rise up Thakrád,
my best of thralls!
bid Bödvild,
my fair-browed daughter,
in bright attire come,
with her sire to speak.

38. Is it, Bödvild! true
what has been told to me,
that thou and Völund
in the isle together sat?"

39. "True it is, Nidud!
what has been told to thee,
that Völund and I
in the isle together sat,
in an unlucky hour:
would it had never been!
I could not
against him strive,
I might not
against him prevail."

Helgakviþa Hiörvarðs Sonar

The Lay of Helgi Hiörvard´s son

There was a king named Hiörvard, who had four wives, one of whom was named Alfhild, their son was named Hedin; the second was named Særeid, their son was Humlung; the third was named Sinriód, their son was Hymling. King Hiörvard made a vow that he would have to wife the most beautiful woman he knew of, and was told that King Svafnir had a daughter of incomparable beauty, named Sigrlinn. He had a jarl named Idmund, whose son Atli was sent to demand the hand of Sigrlinn for the king. He stayed throughout the winter with King Svafnir. There was a jarl there named Franmar, who was the foster-father of Sigrlinn, and had a daughter named Alöf. This jarl advised that the maiden should be refused, and Atli returned home. One day when the jarl's son Atli was standing in a grove, there was a bird sitting in the boughs above him, which had heard that his men called the wives which King Hiörvard had the most beautiful. The bird talked, and Atli listened to what it said. The bird said:

> 1. Hast thou seen Sigrlinn,
> Svafnir's daughter,
> of maidens fairest,
> in her pleasant home?
> though fair
> the wives of Hiörvard
> seem to men
> in Glasis-lund.
>
> Atli
> 2. With Atli,
> Idmund's son,
> sagacious bird!
> wilt thou further speak?
>
> Bird
> I will if the prince
> will offer to me,
> and I may choose what I will
> from the king's court.

Atli
3. Choose not Hiörvard
nor his sons,
nor the fair
daughters of that prince,
nor the wives
which the king has.
Let us together bargain;
that is the part of friends.

Bird
4. A fane I will chose,
offer-steads many,
gold-horned cows
from the chief's land,
if Sigrlinn
sleep in his arms,
and unconstrained
with that prince shall live.

This took place before Atli's journey; but after his return, when the king asked his tidings, he said:

5. Labor we have had,
but errand none performed;
our horses failed us
in the vast fell;
we had afterwards
a swampy lake to ford;
then was denied us
Svafnir's daughter
with rings adorned,
whom we would obtain.

The king commanded them to go a second time, and also went himself. But when they had ascended a fell, and saw in Svavaland the country on fire, and a great reek from the horses of cavalry, the king rode down the fell into the country, and took up his night-quarters by a river. Atli kept watch, and crossed the river, and came to a house, on which sat a great bird to guard it, but was asleep. Atli shot the bird dead with an arrow. In the house he found the king's daughter Sigrlinn, and Alöf daughter of Franmar, and brought them both away with him. The jarl Franmar had taken the form of an eagle, and protected them from a hostile army by sorcery. There was a king named Hrodmar, a wooer of Sigrlinn: he had slain the king of Svavaland, and ravaged and burnt the country. Hiörvard obtained Sigrlinn, and Atli Alöf. Hiörvard and Sigrlinn had a son tall and comely: he was taciturn and had no fixed name. As he was sitting on a mound he saw nine Valkyriur, one of whom was of most noble aspect. She said:

> 6. Late wilt thou, Helgi!
> rings possess,
> a potent warrior,
> or Rödulsvellir,
> so at morn the eagle sang
> if thou art ever silent;
> although thou, prince!
> a fierce mood mayest show.
>
> Helgi
> 7. What wilt thou let accompany
> the name of Helgi,
> maid of aspect bright!
> since that thou art please to give me?
> Think well over
> what thou art saying.
> I will not accept it,
> unless I have thee also.
>
> Valkyria
> 8. Swords I know lying
> in Sigarsholm,
> fewer by four
> than five times ten:
> one of them is
> of all the best,
> of shields the bale,
> with gold adorned.
>
> 9. A ring is on the hilt,
> courage in the midst,
> in the point terror
> for his use who owns it:
> along the edge
> a blood-stained serpent lies,
> and on the guard
> the serpent casts its tail.

There was a king named Eylimi; Svava was his daughter; she was a Valkyria and rode through air and water. It was she who gave Helgi that name, and afterwards often protected him in battle. Helgi said:

10. Hiörvard! thou art not
a king of wholesome counsel,
leader of people!
renowned though thou mayest be.
Thou has let fire devour
the homes of princes,
though harm to thee
they none have done.

11. But Hródmar shall
of the rings dispose,
which our relations
have possessed.
That chief recks little
of his life;
he thinks only to obtain
the heritage of the dead.

Hiörvard answers, that he will supply Helgi with an army, if he will avenge his mother's father. Helgi thereupon seeks the sword that Svava had indicated to him. Afterwards he and Atli went and slew Hrodmar, and performed many deeds of valor. He killed the Jötun Hati, as he sat on a crag. Helgi and Atli lay with their ships in Hatafiörd. Atli kept watch in the first part of the night. Hrimgerd, Hati's daughter, said:

12. Who are the chieftains
in Hatafiörd?
With shields are
your ships bedecked;
boldly ye bear yourselves,
few things ye fear, I ween:
tell me how
your king is named.

Atli
13. Helgi is his name;
but thou nowhere canst
to the chief do harm;
iron forts are
around the prince's fleet;
giantesses may not assail us.

Hrímgerd
14. How art thou named?
most powerful champion!
How do men call thee?
Thy king confides in thee,
since in the ship's fair prow
he grants thee place.

Atli
15. Atli I am named,
fierce I shall prove to thee;
towards giantesses I am most hostile.
The humid prow
I have oft occupied,
and the night-riders slain.

16. How art thou called?
corpse-greedy gigantess!
hag! name thy father.
Nine rasts shouldst thou
be underground,
and a forest grow on thy breast.

Hrímgerd
17. Hrímgerd I am called,
Hati was my father called,
whom I knew the mightiest Jötun.
He many women had
from their dwellings taken,
until him Helgi slew.

Atli
18. Thou wast, hag!
before the prince's ships,
and layest before them in the fiörd's mouth.
The chieftain's warriors
thou wouldst to Rán consign,
had a bar not crossed thee.

Hrimgerd
19. Now, Atli! thou art wrong,
methinks thou art dreaming;
thy brows thou lettest over thy eyelids fall.
My mother lay
before the prince's ships;
I Hlödvard's sons drowned in the ocean.

20. Thou wouldst neigh, Atli!
if thou wert not a gelding.
See! Hrímgerd cocks her tail.
Thy heart, methinks, Atli!
is in thy hinder part,
although thy voice is clear.

Atli
21. I think I shall the stronger prove,
if thou desirest to try;
and I can step from the port to land.
Thou shalt be soundly cudgeled,
if I heartily begin,
and let thy tail fall, Hrímgerd!

Hrimgerd
22. Just come on shore, Atli!
if in thy strength thou trustest,
and let us meet in Varinsvik.
A rib-roasting
thou shalt get, brave boy!
if in my claws thou comest.

Atli
23. I will not come
before the men awake,
and o'er the king hold watch.
It would not surprise me,
if from beneath our ship
some hag arose.

Hrimgerd
24. Keep watch, Atli!
and to Hrimgerd pay the blood-fine
for Hati's death.
If one night she may
sleep with the prince,
she for the slain will be indemnified.

Helgi
25. Lodin is named he who shall thee possess,
thou to mankind art loathsome.
In Tholley dwells that Thurs,
that dog-wise Jötun,
of all rock-dwellers the worst:
he is a fitting man for thee.

Hrimgerd
26. Helgi would rather have
her who last night
guarded the port and men,
the gold-bright maiden.
She methought had strength,
she stept from port to land,
and so secured your fleet.
She was alone the cause
that I could not
the king's men slay.

Helgi
27. Hear now, Hrimgerd!
If I may indemnify thee,
say fully to the king:
was it one being only,
that saved the prince's ships,
or went many together?

Hrimgerd
28. Three troops of maidens;
though one maid foremost rode,
bright, with helmed head.
Their horses shook themselves,
and from their manes there sprang

> dew into the deep dales,
> hail on the lofty trees,
> whence comes fruitfulness to man.
> To me all that I saw was hateful.
>
> Atli
> 29. Look eastward now, Hrimgerd!
> whether Helgi has not stricken thee
> with death-bearing words.
> By land and water
> the king's fleet is safe,
> and the chief's men also.
>
> 30. It is now day, Hrimgerd!
> and Atli has the detained
> to thy loss of life.
> A ludicrous haven-mark
> 'twill, indeed, be,
> where thou a stone-image standest.

King Helgi was a renowned warrior. He came to King Eylimi and demanded his daughter Svava. Helgi and Svava were united, and loved each other ardently. Svava remained at home with her father, but Helgi was engaged in warfare. Svava was a Valkyria as before. Hedin was at home with his father, King Hiörvard in Norway. Returning home alone from the forest on a Yule-eve, Hedin met a troll-wife riding on a wolf, with serpents for reins, who offered to attend him, but he declined her offer; whereupon she said: "Thou shalt pay for this at the Bragi-cup."[1] In the evening solemn vows were made, and the són-hog was led forth, on which the guests laid their hands, and then made solemn vows at the Bragi-cup. Hedin bound himself by a vow to possess Svava, the beloved of his brother Helgi; but repented it so bitterly that he left home and wandered through wild paths to the southern lands, and there found his brother Helgi. Helgi said:

> 31. Welcome art thou, Hedin!
> What new tidings
> canst thou give
> from Norway?

---

1. At guilds the Bragi-cup *(Bragafull)* was drunk. It was the custom at the funeral feast of kings and jarls, that the heir should sit on a lower seat, until the Bragafull was brought in, that he should then rise to receive it, make a vow, and drink the contents of the cup *(full)*. He was then led to his father's high seat. At an offering guild, the chief signed with the figure of Thor's hammer both the cup and the meat. First was drunk Odin's cup, for victory and power to the king; then Niord's cup, and Frey's for a good year and peace; after which it was the customer with many to drink a Bragafull. The peculiarity of this cup was, that it was a cup of vows, that on drinking it a vow was made to perform some great and arduous deed, that might be made a subject for the song of the skald.

Why art thou, prince!
from the land driven,
and alone art come
to find us?

Hedin
32. Of a much greater crime
I am guilty.
I have chosen
a royal daughter,
thy bride,
at the Bragi-cup.

Helgi
33. Accuse not thyself;
true will prove
words at drinking uttered
by us both.
Me a chieftain has
to the strand summoned;
within three nights
I must be there.
'Tis to me doubtful
whether I return;
then may well such befall,
is it so must be.

Hedin
34. Thou saidst, Helgi!
that Hedin well
deserved of thee,
and great gifts:
It would beseem thee better
thy sword to redden,
than to grant
peace to thy foes.

Helgi so spoke, for he had a foreboding that his death was at hand, and that his fylgiur (attendant spirit) had accosted Hedin, when he saw the woman riding on a wolf. There was a king named Alf, a son of Hrodmar, who had appointed a place of combat with Helgi in Sigar's plain within three days. Then said Helgi:

35. On a wolf rode,
at evening twilight,
a woman who him
offered to attend.
She well knew,
that the son of Sigrlinn
would be slain,
on Sigar's plain.

There was a great conflict, in which Helgi got his death-wound.

36. Helgi sent
Sigar riding,
after Eylimi's
only daughter:
he bade her quickly
be in readiness,
if she would find
the king alive.

Sigar
37. Helgi has me
hither sent,
with thee, Svava!
thyself to speak.
Thee, said the king,
he fain would see,
ere the noble-born
breathes forth his last.

Svava
38. What has befallen Helgi,
Hiörvard's son?
I am sorely
by afflictions stricken.
Has the sea him deluded,
or the sword wounded?
On that man I will
harm inflict.

Sigar
39. This morning fell,
at Frekastein,
the king who beneath the sun
was of all the best.
Alf has
complete victory,
though this time
it should not have been!

Helgi
40. Hail to thee, Svava!
Thy love thou must divide;
this in this world, methinks,
is our last meeting.
They say the chieftain's
wounds are bleeding.
The sword came
too near my heart.

41. I pray thee, Svava!
weep not, my wife!
if thou wilt
my voice obey
that for Hedin thou
a couch prepare,
and the young prince
in thy arms clasp.

Svava
42. I had said,
in our pleasant home,
when for me Helgi
rings selected,
that I would not gladly,
after my king's departure,
an unknown prince
clasp in my arms.

Hedin
43. Kiss me, Svava!
I will not return,
Rógheim to behold,
nor Rödulsfiöll,
before I have avenged
Hiörvard´s son,
who was of kings
under the sun the best.

Helgi and Svava were, it is said, born again.

Helgakviða Hundingsbana Fyrri

The First Lay of Helgi Hundingcide

1. It was in the times of yore,
when the eagles screamed,
holy waters fell
from the heavenly hills;
then to Helgi,
the great of soul,
Borghild gave birth
in Brálund.

2. In the mansion it was night:
the Norns came,
who should the prince's
life determine.
They him decreed
a prince most famed to be,
and of leaders
accounted best.

3. With all their might they span
the fatal threads,
when that (he) burghs should overthrow[1]
in Brálund.
They stretched out
the golden cord,
and beneath the middle
of the moon's mansion fixed it.

4. East and west
they hid the ends,
where the prince had
lands between;
towards the north
Neri's sister
cast a chain,
which she bade last for ever.

---

1. That is, when they came to spin that period of his destiny.

5. One thing disquieted
the Ylfing's offspring,
and the woman
who had the child brought forth.
Sitting on a lofty tree,
on prey intent,
a raven to a raven said:
"I know something.

6. Stands cased in mail
Sigmund's son,
one day old:
now is our day come.
His eyes are piercing
as a warrior's;
a wolf's friend is he:
we shall rejoice!"

7. He to the folk appeared
a noble chief to be;
among men 'twas said
that happy times were come;
went the king himself
from the din of war,
noble garlic to bring
to the young prince;

8. Gave him the name of Helgi,
and Hringstadir,
Sólfiöll, Snæfiöll,
and Sigarsvellir,
Hringstäd, Hátún,
and Himinvangar,
a sword ornate,
to Sinfiölti´s brother.

9. Then grew up,
in his friends' bosom,
the high-born youth,
in joyous splendor.
He paid and gave
gold for deserts;
nor spared the chief
the blood-stained sword.

10. A short time only the leader let
warfare cease.
When the prince was
fifteen winters old,
he caused the fierce
Hunding to fall,
who long had ruled
over lands and people.

11. The sons of Hunding
afterwards demanded
from Sigmund's son
treasure and rings;
because they had
on the prince to avenge
their great loss of wealth,
and their father's death.

12. The prince would neither
the blood-fine pay,
nor for the slain
indemnity would give.
They might expect, he said,
a terrific storm
of grey arrows,
and Odin's ire.

13. The warriors went
to the trysting place of swords,
which they had appointed
at Logafiöll.
Broken was Frodi's peace
between the foes:
Vidrir's hounds went
about the isle
slaughter-greedy.

14. The leader sat
under the Arastein,
after he had slain
Alf and Eyiólf,
Hiörvard and Hávard,
sons of Hunding:
he had destroyed all
Geirmimir's race.

15. Then gleamed a ray
from Logafiöll,
and from that ray
lightnings issued;
then appeared,
in the field of air,
a helmed band
of Valkyriur:
their corslets were
with blood besprinkled,
and from their spears
shone beams of light.

16. Forthwith inquired
the chieftain bold,
from the wolf-congress
of the southern Dísir,
whether they would,
with the warriors,
that night go home? -
then was a clash of arms!

17. One from her horse,
Högni's daughter,
stilled the crash of shields,
and to the leader said:
"We have, I ween,
other objects
than with princely warriors
to drink beer.

18. My father has
his daughter promised
to the fierce
son of Granmar;
but I have, Helgi!
Declared Hödbrodd,
the proud prince,
like to a cat's son.

19. That chief will come
in a few days,
unless thou him call
to a hostile meeting;
or the maiden take
from the prince."

Helgi
20. Fear thou not
Isung's slayer;
there shall be first a clash of foes,
unless I am dead.

21. Thence sent messengers
the potent prince
through air and over water,
succors to demand,
and abundance
of ocean's gleam
to men to offer,
and to their sons.

22. "Bid them speedily
to the ships to go,
and those from Brandey
to hold them ready."
There the king abode,
until thither came
warriors in hundreds
from Hedinsey.

23. From the strands also,
and from Stafnsnes,
a naval force went out,
with gold adorned.
Helgi then of Hiörleif asked:
"Hast thou mustered
the valiant people?"

24. But the young king
the other answered:
"Slowly" said he "are counted
from Trönuey
the long-beaked ships,
under the seafarers,
which sail without
in Öresund,

25. Twelve hundred
faithful men;
though in Hátún
there is more than half
of the king's host
We are to war inured."

26. Then the steersman threw
the ship's tents aside,
that the princes'
people might awake,
and the noble chiefs
the dawn might see;
and the warriors
hauled the sails
up to the mast
in Varinsfiörd.

27. There was a dash of oars,
and clash of iron,
shield against shield resounded;
the vikings rowed;
roaring went,
under the chieftains
the royal fleet
far from the land.

28. So might be heard,
when together came
the tempest's sister[2]
and the long keels,
as when rock and surge
on each other break.

29. Higher still bade Helgi
the deep sail be hauled.
No port gave shelter
to the crews;
when Ægir's
terrific daughter
the chieftains' vessels
would o'erwhelm.

30. But from above
Sigrún intrepid,
saved them
and their fleet also;
from the hand of Rán
powerfully was wrested
the royal ship
at Gnípalund.

31. At eve they halted
in Unavágar;
the splendid ships
might into port have floated,
but the crews,
from Svarinshaug,

---

2. Kolgu Systir. Kolgat was one of the daugthers of Ægir and Ran; they were the waves.

in hostile mood,
espied the host.

32. Then demanded
the god-born Gudmund:
"Who is the chieftain
that commands the fleet,
and that formidable force
brings to our land?"

33. Sinfiötli said,
slinging up on the yard
a red-hued shield
with golden rim;
He at the strait kept watch,
and able was to answer,
and with nobles
words exchanged

34. "Tell it at eve,
when you feed your pigs,
and your dogs
lead to their food,
that the Ylfings
from the east are come,
ready to fight
at Gnípalund.

35. Hödbrodd will
Helgi find
in the fleet's midst,
a king hard to make flee,
who has oft
the eagles sated,
while thou wast at the mills,
kissing the thrall-wenches.

Gudmund

36. Little dost thou remember
of ancient saws,
when of the noble
thou falsehoods utterest.
Thou hast been eating
wolves' dainties,
and of thy brother
wast the slayer;
wounds hast thou often
sucked with cold mouth;
every where loathed,
thou hast crawled in caverns.

Sinfiötli

37. Thou was a Vala-crone
in Varinsey,
cunning as a fox,
a spreader of lies.
Thou saidst thou no man
wouldst ever marry,
no corsleted warrior,
save Sinfiötli.

38. A mischievous crone was thou,
a giantess, a Valkyria,
insolent, onstrous,
in Alfather's hall.
All the Einheriar
fought with each other,
deceitful woman!
for thy sake.
Nine wolves we begat
in Sagunes;
I alone was
father of them all.

Gudmund
39. Father thou wast not
of Fenriswolves,
older than all,
as far as I remember;
since by Gnípalund,
the Thurs-maidens
thee emasculated
upon Thorsnes.

40. Thou was Siggeir's stepson,
at home under the benches layest,
accustomed to the wolf's howl
out in the forests:
calamity of every kind
came over thee,
when thou didst lacerate
thy brother's breast.
Notorious thou mad'st thyself
by thy atrocious works.

Sinfiötli
41. Thou was Grani's bride
at Brávöllr,
hadst a golden bit,
ready for the course.
Many a time have I
ridden thee tired,
hungry and saddled,
through the fells, thou hag!

Gudmund
42. A graceless lad
thou wast thought to be,
when Gulnir's goats
thou didst milk.
Another time thou wast
a giantess's daughter,
a tattered wretch.
Wilt thou a longer chat?

Sinfiölti
43. I rather would
at Frekastein
the ravens cram
with thy carcase,
than thy dogs
lead to their meat,
or thy hogs feed.
May the fiend deal with thee!

Helgi
44. "Much more seemly, Sinfiölti!
would it be for you both
in battle to engage,
and the eagles gladden,
than with useless
words to contend,
however princes[3]
may foster hate.

45. Not good to me appear
Granmar's sons,
yet 'tis right that princes
should speak the truth:
they have shown,
at Móinsheimar,
that they have courage
to draw the sword."

46. Rapidly they their horses
made to run,
Svipud and Svegiud,
to Sólheimar,
over dewy dales,
dark mountain-sides;
trembled the sea of mist,
where the men went.

---

3. Literally *ring-breakers,* or *–dispensers.*

47. The king they met
at the burgh's gate,
to the prince announced
the hostile advent.
Without stood Hödbrodd
with helmet decked:
he the speed noticed
of his kinsmen.
"Why have ye Hníflúngs
such wrathful countenance?"

48. "Hither to the shore are come
rapid keels,
towering masts,
and long yards,
shields many,
and smooth-shaven oars,
a king's noble host,
joyous Ylfings.

49. Fifteen bands
are come to land;
but there are out at sea,
before Gnípulund,
seven thousand
blue-black ocean-beasts
with gold adorned;
there is by far
their greatest multitude.
Now will Helgi not
delay the conflict."

Hödbrodd
50. "Let a bridled steed
to the chief assembly run,
but Sporvitnir
to Sparinsheid;
Melnir and Mylnir
to Myrkvid;
let no man
stay behind
of those
who swords can brandish.

51. Summon to you Högni,
and the sons of Hring,
Atli and Yngvi,
Alf the old;
they will gladly
engage in conflict.
We will let the Völsungs
find resistance."

52. It was a whirlwind,
when together came
the fallow[4] blades
at Frekastein:
ever was Helgi
Hundingsbani
foremost in the host,
where men together fought:
ardent for battle,
disdaining flight;
the chieftain had
a valiant heart.

53. Then came a maid from heaven,
helmed, from above
the clash of arms increased
for the king's protection.
Then said Sigrún
well skilled to fly
to the host of heroes
from Hugin's grove[5]

54. "Unscathed shalt thou, prince!
possess thy people,
pillar of Yngvi's race!
and life enjoy;
thou hast laid low
the slow of flight,
the chief who caused
the dread warrior's death.

---

4. It would appear that their swords were of bronze.
5. Hugin's grove. The raven's grove, i.e., the battle-field, strewed with corpses, the raven's food.

And thee, o king!
well beseem both
red-gold rings
and a powerful maid:
unscathed shalt thou, prince!
both enjoy,
Högni's daughter,
and Hringstadir,
victory and lands:
then is conflict ended."

Helgakviða Hundingsbana Önnur

The Second Lay of Helgi Hundingcide

King Sigmund, son of Völsung, had to wife Borghild of Brálund. They named their son Helgi, after Helgi Hiörvard's son. Helgi was fostered by Hagal. There was a powerful king named Hunding, after whom the land was called Hundland. He was a great warrior, and had many sons, who were engaged in warfare. There was enmity, both open and concealed, between King Hunding and King Sigmund, and they slew each others kinsmen. King Sigmund and his kindred were called Völsungs, and Ylfings. Helgi went forth and secretly explored the court of King Hunding. Heming, Hunding's son, was at home. On departing Helgi met a herdsman, and said:

> 1. "Say thou to Heming,
> that Helgi bears in mind
> who the mailed warrior was,
> whom the men laid low,
> when the grey wolf
> ye had within,
> and King Hunding
> that it was Hamal."

Hamal was the son of Hagal. King Hunding sent men to Hagal in search of Helgi, and Helgi had no other way to save himself than by taking the clothes of a female slave and going to grind. They sought but did not find him. Then said Blind the Baleful:

> 2. Sharp are the eyes of Hagal's thrall-wench;
> of no churlish race is she
> who at the mill stands.
> The mill-stones are split,
> the receiver flies asunder.
> Now a hard fate has
> befallen the warrior,
> when a prince must
> barley grind:
> much more fitting
> to that hand
> is the falchion's hilt
> than a mill-handle.

Hagal answered and said: -

> 3. No wonder 'tis
> that the receiver rattles,
> when a royal damsel
> the handle turns.
> She hovered
> hither than the clouds,
> and, like the vikings,
> dared to fight,
> until Helgi
> made her captive.
> She is a sister of
> Sigar and Högni;
> therefore has fierce eyes
> the Ylfing maid.
> **********************

Helgi escaped and went on board a ship of war. He slew King Hunding, and was afterwards named Helgi Hundingsbani. He lay with his force in Brunavágar, and carried on 'strand-högg'[1] and ate raw flesh. There was a king named Högni, whose daughter was Sigrún: she was a Valkyria, and rode through air and over the sea. She was Svava regenerated. Sigrún rode to Helgi, and said:

> 4. What men cause a ship
> along the coasts to float?
> where do ye warriors a home possess?
> what await ye
> in Brunavágar?
> whither desire ye
> to explore a way?

> Helgi
> 5. Hamal causes a ship
> along the coasts to float;
> we have home
> in Hlésey;
> a fair wind we await
> in Brunavágar;
> eastward we desire
> to explore a way.

---

1. Slaughtering and carrying off the cattle on the sea-shore.

Sigrún
6. Were, o prince!
hast thou wakened war,
or fed the birds
on conflict's sisters?[2]
Why is thy corslet
sprinkled with blood?
Why beneath the helm
eat ye raw flesh?

Helgi
7. It was the Ylfings' son's
last achievement,
if thou desirest to know
west of the ocean,
that I took bears
in Bragalund,
and the eagles' race
with our weapons sated.
Now, maiden! I have said
what the reasons were,
why at sea
we little cooked meat ate.

Sigrún
8. To a battle thou alludest.
Before Helgi has
King Hunding
been doomed to fall.
In conflict ye have engaged,
when your kindred ye avenged,
and stained with blood
the falchion's edge.

Helgi
9. Why dost thou suppose,
sagacious maiden!
that it was they,
who their kin avenged?
Many a warrior's

---

2. The *Valkyriur*.

bold sons there are,
and hostile
to our kindred.

Sigrún
10. I was not far,
leader of people!
eager, at many
a chieftain's end:
yet crafty I account
Sigmund's son,
when in val-runes[3]
the slaughter he announces.

11. A while ago I saw thee
commanding war-ships,
when thou hadst station
on the bloody prow,
and the cold sea
waves were playing.
Now, prince! thou wilt
from me conceal it,
but Högni's daughter
recognizes thee.
****

Granmar was the name of a powerful prince who dwelt at Svarinshaug. He had many sons: one was called Hödbrodd, the second Gudmund, the third Starkadr. Hödbrodd was at the assembly of kings, and there betrothed himself to Sigrún, the daughter of Högni. But when she was informed of it, she rode with the Valkyriur through the air and over the sea in quest of Helgi. Helgi was at Logafiöll, warring against the sons of Hunding, where he slew Alf and Eyiólf, Hiörvard and Hervard. Being over-fatigued with the conflict, he was sitting under the Arastein, where Sigrún found him, and running to him, threw her arms round his neck, and, kissing him, told him her errand so as it is related in the first *Völsungakviða*.

12. Sigrún sought
the joyous prince,
Helgi's hand
she forthwith grasped,
kissed and addressed
the helm-decked king.

3. Dark words of deadly import.

13. Then was the chieftain's mind
to the lady turned.
She declared that she had loved,
with her whole heart,
Sigmund's son,
before she had seen him.

14. "To Hödbrodd I was
in th' assembly betrothed,
but I another
prince would have:
yet, chieftain! I foresee
my kindred's wrath:
I have my father's
promise broken."

15. Högni's daughter spoke not
at variance with her heart:
she said that Helgi's
affection she must possess.

Helgi
16. Care thou not
for Högni´s wrath,
nor for the evil
mind of thy kin.
Thou shalt, young maiden!
live with me:
of a good race thou art,
as I perceive.

Helgi then collected a large fleet and proceeded to Frekastein, and at sea experienced a perilous storm. Lightnings came over them, and the flashes entered the ships. They saw that nine Valkyriur were riding in the air, and recognized Sigrún among them. The storm then abated and they reached land in safety. The sons of Granmar were sitting on a hill as the sips were sailing towards the land. Gudmund leapt on a horse, and rode to explore on the hill by the haven. The Völsungs then lowered their sails, and Gudmund spoke as it is before written in the *Helgakvida*:

"Who is the leader
that commands the fleet,
and an appalling host
leads to our land?"

This said Gudmund, Granmar's son.

> 17. Who is the warrior
> that commands the ships,
> and lets his golden banner
> wave o'er his prow?
> No peace seems to me
> in that ship's front;
> it casts a warlike glow
> around the vikings.

Sinfiölti, Sigmund's son, answered:

> 18. Here may Hödbrodd
> Helgi learn to know,
> the hard of fight,
> in the fleet's midst:
> he the possession
> hold of thy race;
> he the fishes' heritage
> has to him subjected.
>
> Gudmund
> 19. Therefore ought we first,
> at Frekastein,
> to settle together,
> and decide our quarrels!
> Hödbrod! 'tis time
> vengeance to take,
> if an inferior lot
> we long have borne.
>
> Sinfiötli
> 20. Rather shalt thou, Gudmund!
> tend goats,
> and steep mountain-tops
> shalt climb,
> have in thy hand
> a hazel staff,
> that will better please thee
> than judgments of the sword.

Gudmund rode home with intelligence of the hostile arrangement; whereupon the sons of Granmar collected a host, and many kings came thither. Among them were Högni, the father of Sigrún, with his sons Bragi and Dag. There was a great battle, and all the sons of Högni, and all their chiefs were slain, except Dag, who obtained peace, and swore oaths to the Völsungs. Sigrún, going among the slain, found Hödbrodd at the point of death. She said:

> 23. Not will Sigrún
> of Sefafiöll,
> King Hödbrodd!
> sink in thy arms:
> thy life is departed.
> Oft the axe's blade
> the head approaches
> of Granmar's sons.

She then met Helgi, and was overjoyed. He said:

> 24. Not to thee, all-wise maiden!
> are all things granted,
> though, I say, in somewhat
> are the Norns to blame.
> This morn have fallen
> at Frekastein
> Bragi and Högni:
> I was their slayer.
>
> 25. But at Styrkleifar
> King Starkadr,
> and at Hlebiörg
> the son of Hrollaug.
> That prince I saw
> of all most fierce,
> whose trunk yet fought
> when the head was far.
>
> 26. On the earth lie
> the greater number
> of thy kinsmen,
> to corpses turned.
> Thou hast not fought the battle,
> yet 'twas decreed,
> that thou, potent maiden!
> shouldst cause the strife.

Sigrún then wept. Helgi said:

> 27. Sigrún! console thyself;
> a Hild thou hast been to us.
> Kings cannot conquer fate:
> gladly would I have them living
> who are departed,
> if I might clasp thee to my breast.

Helgi obtained Sigrún, and they had sons. Helgi lived not to be old. Dag, the son of Högni, sacrificed to Odin, for vengeance for his father. Odin lent Dag his spear. Dag met with his relation Helgi in a place called Fiöturlund, and pierced him through with his spear. Helgi fell there, but Dag rode to the mountains and told Sigrún what had taken place.

> 28. Loath am I, sister!
> sad news to tell thee;
> for unwillingly I have
> my sister caused to weep.
> This morning fell,
> in Fiöturlund,
> the prince who was
> on earth the best,
> and on the necks
> of warriors stood.

Sigrún
> 29. Thee shall the oaths
> all gnaw,
> which to Helgi
> thou didst swear,
> the limped
> Leiptr's water,
> and at the cold dank
> wave-washed rock.

> 30. May the ship not move forward,
> which under thee should move,
> although the wished-for wind
> behind thee blow.
> May the horse not run,
> which under thee should run,
> although from enemies
> thou hast to flee!

31. May the sword not bite
which thou drawest,
unless it sing
round thy own head.
Then would Helgi's death
be on thee avenged,
if a wolf thou wert,
out in the woods,
of all good bereft,
and every joy,
have no sustenance,
unless on corpses thou shouldst spring.

Dag
32. Sister! thou ravest,
and hast lost thy wits,
when on thy brother thou
callest down such miseries.
Odin alone is cause
of all the evil;
for between relatives
he brought the runes of strife.

33. Thy brother offers thee
rings of red gold,
all Vadilsvé
and Vigdalir:
have half the land,
thy grief to compensate,
woman ring-adorned!
thou and thy sons.

Sigrún
34. So happy I shall not sit
at Sefafiöll,
neither at morn nor night,
as to feel joy in life,
if o'er the people plays not
the prince's beam of light;
if his war-steed runs not
under the chieftain hither,
to the gold bit accustomed;
if in the king I cannot rejoice.

35. So had Helgi
struck with fear
all his foes
and their kindred,
as before the wolf
the goats run frantic
from the fell,
of terror full.

36. So himself Helgi
among warriors bore,
as the towering ash
is among thorns,
or as the fawn,
moistened with dew,
that more proudly stalks
than all the other beasts,
and its horns glisten
against the sky.

A mound was raised for Helgi; but when he came to Valhall, Odin offered him rule over all jointly with himself. Helgi said:

37. Thou, Hunding! shalt
for every man
a foot-bath get,
and fire kindle;
shalt bind the dogs,
to the horses look,
to the swine give wash,
ere to sleep thou goest.

A female slave passing at evening by Helgi's mound, saw him riding towards it with many men:

38. Is it a delusion
which methinks I see,
or the powers' dissolution,
that ye, dead men, ride,
and your horses
with spurs urge on,
or to warriors is
a home journey granted?

Helgi
39. 'Tis no delusion
which thou thinkst to see,
nor of mankind the end,
although thou seest us,
although our horses we
with spurs urge on,
nor to warriors is
a home-journey granted.

The slave went home and said to Sigrún:

40. Sigrún! go forth
from Sefafiöll,
if the people's chief
thou desirest to meet.
The mound is opened,
Helgi is come,
his wounds still bleed;
the prince prayed thee
that thou wouldst still
the trickling blood.

Sigrún entered the mound to Helgi and said:

41. Now am I as glad,
at our meeting,
as the voracious
hawks of Odin,
when they of slaughter know;
of warm prey,
or, dewy-feathered, see
the peep of day.

42. I will kiss
my lifeless king,
ere thou thy bloody corslet
layest aside.
Thy hair is, Helgi!
tumid with sweat of death;
my prince is all
bathed in slaughter-dew;

cold, clammy are the hands
of Högni's son.
How shall I, prince! for this
make thee amends?

Helgi
43. Thou art alone the cause,[4]
Sigrún of Sefafiöll!
that Helgi is
with sorrow's dew suffused.
Thou weepest, gold-adorned!
cruel tears,
sun-bright daughter of the south!
ere to sleep thou goest;
each one falls bloody
on the prince's breast,
wet, cold, and piercing,
with sorrow big.

44. We shall surely drink
delicious draughts,
though we have lost
life and lands.
No one shall
a song of mourning sing,
though on my breast
he wounds behold.
Now are women
in the mound enclosed,
daughters of kings,
with us the dead.

---

[4]. The superstition commemorated in this strophe is, no doubt, the origin of some very beautiful ballads in the later literature of Scandinavia and Germany referring to this superstition:
"When thou, my dear, art cheerful,
    "And easy in thy mind,
"The coffin where I slumber
    "Is all with roses lined.
"But oft as thou 'rt in sorrow,
    "And bow'd with grief so sore,
"Is all the while my coffin
    "Brim full of blood and gore."

Sigrún prepares a bed in the mound.

> 45. Here, Helgi! have I for thee
> a peaceful
> couch prepared,
> for the Ylfings' son.
> On thy breast I will,
> chieftain! repose,
> as in my hero's lifetime
> I was wont.
>
> Helgi
> 46. Nothing I now declare
> unlooked for,
> at Sefafiöll
> late or early,
> since in a corpse's
> arms thou sleepest,
> Högni's fair daughter!
> in a mound,
> and thou art living,
> daughter of kings!
>
> 47. Time 'tis for me to ride
> on the reddening ways:
> let the pale horse
> tread the aerial path.
> I towards the west must go
> over Vindhiálm's bridge,
> ere Salgofnir
> awakens heroes.

Helgi and his attendants rode their way, but Sigrún and hers proceeded to their habitation. The following evening Sigrún ordered her serving-maid to hold watch at the mound; but at nightfall, when Sigrún came thither, she said:

> 48. Now would be come,
> if he to come intended,
> Sigmund's son,
> from Odin's halls.
> I think the hope lessens
> of the king's coming,

    since on the ash's boughs
    the eagles sit,
    and all the folk
    to the dreams' tryst are hastening.

    Serving-maid
    49. Be not so rash
    alone to go,
    daughter of heroes!
    to the house of draugs:[5]
    more powerful are,
    in the night-season,
    all dead warriors,
    then in the light of day.

Sigrún's life was shortened by grief and mourning. It was a belief in ancient times that men were regenerated, but that is now regarded as an old crone's fancy. Helgi and Sigrún are said to have been regenerated. He was then called Helgi Haddingiaskadi, and she Kara Hálfdan's daughter, as it is said in the *Songs of Kara*; and she also was a Valkyria.

---

5. Probably house of draffs; place of swine, swill, lees.

Sinfiötlalok: Sinfiötli's End

Sigmund Völsung's son was a king in Frankland. Sinfiötli was the eldest of his sons, the second was Helgi, the third Hámund. Borghild, Sigmund's wife, had a brother named Gunnar; but Sinfiötli her step-son and Gunnar both courted one woman, on which account Sinfiötli slew Gunnar. When he came home, Borghild bade him go away, but Sigmund offered the blood-fine, which it was incumbent on her to accept. At the funeral feast Borghild presented the beer: she took a large horn full of poison, and offered it to Sinfiötli; who, when he looked into the horn, and saw that there was poison in it, said to Sigmund: "the drink ferments!" Sigmund took the horn and drank up the contents. It is said that Sigmund was so strong that no poison could hurt him, either outwardly or inwardly; but that all his sons could endure poison outwardly. Borghild bore another horn to Sinfiötli, and prayed him to drink, when all took place as before. Yet a third time she offered him the horn, using reproachful words on his refusing to drink. He said as before to Sigmund, but the latter answered: "Let is pass through thy lips, my son." Sinfiötli drank and instantly died. Sigmund bore him a long way in his arms, and came to a long and narrow firth, where there was a little vessel and one man in it. He offered Sigmund to convey him over the firth; but when Sigmund had borne the corpse to the vessel, the boat was full-laden. The man then said that Sigmund should go before through the firth. He then pushed off his boat and instantly departed.

King Sigmund sojourned long in Denmark, in Borghild's kingdom, after having espoused her. He then went south to Frankland, to the kingdom he there possessed. There he married Hiördís, the daughter of Eylimi. Sigurd was their son. King Sigmund fell in a battle with the sons of Hunding. Hiördís was afterwards married to Alf, son of King Hiálprek, with whom Sigurd grew up in childhood. Sigmund and his sons exceeded all other men in strength, and stature, and courage, and all accomplishments, though Sigurd was foremost of all; and in old traditions he is mentioned as excelling all men, and as the most renowned of warlike kings.

256

SigurÞarkviða Fafnisbana Fyrsta eða Gripisspa

The First Lay of Sigurd Fafnicide
or
Gripir's Prophecy

Gripir was the name of the son of Eylimi, the brother of Hiördis. He ruled over lands, and was of all men wisest and prescient of the future. Sigurd rode alone, and came to Gripir's dwelling. Sigurd was of a distinguished figure. He found a man to address outside the hall, whose name was Geitir. Sigurd applied to him, and asked:

>1. Who here inhabits,
>in these towers?
>what nation's king
>do people name him?

>Geitir
>Gripir is named
>the chief of men,
>he who rules
>a firm realm and people.

>Sigurd
>2. Is the wise king
>of the land at home?
>Will the chief with me
>come and converse?
>With him needs speech
>an unknown man:
>I desire speedily
>Gripir to see.

>Geitir
>3. The glad king will
>of Geitir ask,
>who the man is
>that demands speech of Gripir.

Sigurd
Sigurd I am named,
born of Sigmund,
and Hiördis is
the chieftain's mother.

4. Then went Geitir,
Gripir to inform:
"Here is a man without,
a stranger, come;
of aspect he
is most distinguished.
He desires, king!
with thee to speak."

5. Goes from the hall
the lord of men,
and the stranger prince
kindly greets:
"Welcome, Sigurd!
better had it been earlier;
but do thou, Geitir!
take charge of Grani."

6. They began to talk,
and much to tell,
when the sagacious men
together met.
"Tell me, if thou knowest,
my mother's brother!
how will Sigurd's
life fall out?"

Gripir
7. Thou wilt foremost be
of men beneath the sun,
exalted high above
every king;
liberal of gold,
but of flight sparing,
of aspect comely,
and wise of words.

Sigurd
8. Say thou, sage king!
more than I ask,
thou wise one, to Sigurd,
if thou thinkst to see it:
what will first happen
for my advancement,
when from thy dwelling
I shall have departed?

Gripir
9. First wilt thou, prince!
avenge thy father,
and for the wrongs of Eylimi
wilt retaliate;
thou wilt the cruel
sons of Hunding
boldly lay low;
thou wilt have victory.

Sigurd
10. Say, noble king!
kinsman mine!
with all forethought,
as we hold friendly converse;
seest thou of Sigurd
those bold achievements,
that will highest soar
under heaven's regions?

Gripir
11. Thou alone wilt slay
that glistening serpent,
which greedy lies
on Gnítaheid;
thou shalt of both
the slayer be,
Regin and Fafnir.
Gripir tells truly.

Sigurd
12. Riches will abound,
if I so bring
conflict among men,
as thou for certain sayest.
Apply thy mind,
and at length say
what will yet
my life befall.

Gripir
13. Thou wilt find
Fafnir's lair,
and thence wilt take
splendid riches,
with gold wilt load
Grani's back.
Thou wilt to Giuki ride,
the war-famed prince.

Sigurd
14. Yet must thou, prince!
in friendly speech,
foresighted king!
more relate.
I shall be Giuki's guest,
and I shall thence depart:
what will next
my life befall?

Gripir
15. A king's daughter
will on a mountain sleep,
fair, in corslet cased,
after Helgi's death.
Thou wilt strike
with a keen sword,
wilt the corslet sever
with Fafnir's bane.

Sigurd
16. The corslet is ript open,
the maid begins to speak.
When awakened
from her sleep,
on what will she chiefly
with Sigurd converse hold,
which to the prince's
benefit may tend?

Gripir
17. She to thee, powerful one!
runes will teach,
all those which men
ought to know;
and in every man's
tongue to speak,
and medicines for healing.
May good await thee, king!

Sigurd
18. Now that is past,
the knowledge is acquired,
and I am ready thence
away to ride.
Apply thy mind,
and at length say
what more will
my life befall.

Gripir
19. Thou wilt find
Heimir's dwellings,
and the glad guest wilt be
of that great king.
Vanished is, Sigurd!
that which I foresaw;
no further mayest thou
Gripir question.

Sigurd
20. Now bring me grief
the words thou speakest;
for thou foreseest, king!
much further;
thou knowest of too great
calamity to Sigurd;
therefore thou, Gripir!
wilt not utter it.

Gripir
21. Of thy life
the early portion
lay before me
clearest to contemplate.
I am not truly
accounted sage,
nor of the future prescient:
that which I knew is gone.

Sigurd
22. No man I know
on the earth's surface,
who greater prescience has
than thou, Gripir!
Thou mayest not conceal it,
unhappy though it be,
or if ill betide
my life.

Gripir
23. Not with vices will
thy life be sullied;
let that, noble prince!
in thy mind be borne;
for while mankind exists,
thy name,
director of spear-storm!
will be supreme.

Sigurd
24. The worst seems to me,
that Sigurd is compelled
from the king to part
in such uncertainty.
Show me the way
all is decreed before
great chieftain! if thou wilt,
my mother's brother!

Gripir
25. To Sigurd I will now
openly tell,
since the chieftain me
thereto compels:
thou wilt surely find
that I lie not.
A certain day is
for thy death decreed.

Sigurd
26. I would not importune
the mighty prince,
but rather Gripir's
good counsel have.
Now I fain would know,
though grateful it may not be,
what prospect Sigurd has
lying before him.

Gripir
27. There is with Heimir
a maiden fair of form,
she is by men
Brynhild named,
daughter of Budli;
but the dear king
Heimir nurtures
the hard-souled damsel.

Sigurd
28. What is it to me,
although the maiden be
of aspect fair?
nurtured with Heimir?
That thou, Gripir! must
fully declare;
for thou forseest
my whole destiny.

Gripir
29. She will thee bereave
of almost every joy,
the fair-faced
foster-child of Heimir.
Thou wilt not sleep
nor of affairs discourse,
nor men regard;
only this maiden thou wilt see.

Sigurd
30. What remedy for Sigurd
will be applied;
tell me that, Gripir!
if it seem good to thee.
Shall I obtain the damsel?
with dowry purchase
the lovely
royal daughter?

Gripir
31. Ye will each swear
unnumbered oaths,
solemnly binding,
but few will keep.
Hast thou been Guiki's
guest one night,
thou wilt have forgotten
the fair ward of Heimir.

Sigurd
32. How is that, Gripir!
explain it to me:
seest thou such fickleness
in the king's mind,
that with that maiden I
shall my engagement break,
whom with my whole heart
I thought to love?

Gripir
33. Prince! thou wilt be snared
in another's wiles,
thou wilt pay the penalty
of Grimhild's craft;
the bright-haired maiden,
her daughter,
she to thee will offer.
This snare for the king she lays.

Sigurd
34. Shall I then with Gunnar
form relationship,
and with Gudrun
join in wedlock?
Well wived then
the king would be,
if the pangs of perjury
caused me no pain.

Gripir
35. Thee will Grimhild
wholly beguile;
she will implore thee
Brynhild to demand
for the hand of Gunnar,
king of Goths:
the journey thou wilt forthwith promise
to the king's mother.

Sigurd
36. Evils are at hand,
I can that perceive;
Sigurd's wits
will have wholly perished,
if I shall demand,
for another's hand,
a noble maiden
whom I well love.

Gripir
37. All of you will
swear mutual oaths,
Gunnar, and Högni,
and thou the third;
and ye will forms exchange,
when on the way ye are,
Gunnar and thou:
Gripir lies not.

Sigurd
38. To what end is that?
why shall we exchange
forms and manner,
when on the way we are?
Another fraud
will surely follow this,
altogether horrible.
But say on, Gripir!

Gripir
39. Thou wilt have Gunnar's semblance,
and his manners,
thy own eloquence,
and great sagacity;
there thou wilt betroth
the high-minded
ward of Heimir:
no one can that prevent.

Sigurd
40. To me that seems worse,
that among men I shall
be a false traitor called,
if such take place.
I would not
deception practise
on a royal maid
the most excellent I know.

Gripir
41. Thou wilt repose,
leader of hosts!
pure as the maiden,
as she thy mother were;
therefore exalted,
lord of men!
while the world endures
thy name will be.

42. The nuptials will
of both be solemnized,
of Sigurd and of Gunnar,
in Giuki's halls;
then will ye forms exchange,
when ye home return;
yet to himself will have
each his own senses.

Sigurd
43. Will then Gunnar,
chief among men,
the noble woman wed?
Tell me that, Gripir!
although three nights by me
the chieftain's bride
glad of heart has slept?
The like has no example.

44. How for happiness
shall hereafter be
this affinity?
Tell me that, Gripir!
Will the alliance
for Gunnar's solace
hereforth prove,
or even for mine?

Gripir
45. Thou wilt the oaths remember,
and must silence keep,
and let Gudrun enjoy
a happy union.
Brynhild nathless will herself think
an ill-married woman.
She will wiles devise
to avenge herself.

Sigurd
46. What atonement will
that woman take,
for the frauds we
shall have practised on her?
From me the maiden has
oaths sworn,
but never kept,
and but little joy.

Gripir
47. She to Gunnar will
plainly declare,
that thou didst not well
the oaths observe,
when the noble king,
Guiki's heir,
with his whole soul,
in thee confided.

Sigurd
48. What will then follow?
let me know that.
Will that tale
appear as true,
or that the noble woman
falsely accuses me,
and herself also.
Tell me that, Gripir!

Gripir
49. From spite towards thee,
and from o'erwhelming grief,
the powerful dame
will not most wisely act.
To the noble woman
do thou no further harm,
though thou the royal bride
with guiles has circumvented.

Sigurd
50. Will the prudent Gunnar,
Guthorm, and Högni,
at her instigation,
then proceed?
Will Giuki's sons
on their relative
redden their swords?
Tell me further, Gripir!

Gripir
51. Then will Gudrun be
furious at heart,
when her brothers shall
on thy death resolve.
In nothing then
will that wise woman
take delight.
Such is Grimhild's work.

52. In this thou shalt find comfort,
leader of hosts!
This fortune is allotted
to the hero's life:
a more renowned man
on earth shall never be,
under the sun's abode,
than thou wilt be accounted.

Sigurd
53. Now part we, now farewell!
Fate may not be withstood.
Now hast thou, Gripir!
done as I prayed thee:
thou wouldst have fain
a happier end foretold me
of my life's days,
hadst thou been able.

SigurÞarkviða Fafnisbana Önnur

The Second Lay of Sigurd Fafnicide

Sigurd went to Hiálprek's stud and chose himself a horse, which was afterwards named Grani. Regin, Hreidmar's son, was then come to Hiálprek; he was the most skilful of men, and a dwarf in stature; he was wise, cruel, and versed in magic. Regin undertook the rearing and instruction of Sigurd, and bore him great affection. He informed Sigurd of his parentage, and how it befell that Odin, and Hoenir, and Loki came to Andvarafors (the waterfall of Andvari). In the fall there was an abundance of fish. There was a dwarf named Andvari, who had long lived in the fall in the likeness of a pike, and in which he supplied himself with food. "Our brother", continued Regin, "was named Otr, who often went in to the fall in the likeness of an otter. He had caught a salmon, and was sitting on the bank of the river with his eyes shut eating it, when Loki killed him with a stone. The Æsir thought themselves very lucky, and stripped off the otter's skin. That same evening they sought entertainment with Hreidmar, and showed their prize. Thereupon we laid hands on them, and imposed on them, as the redemption of their lives, that they should fill the otter's skin with gold, and cover it over with red gold. They thereupon sent Loki to procure gold. He went to Ran, and obtained her net, and thence proceeded to Andvarafors, and cast the net before a pike, which leapt into the net. Whereupon Loki said:

1\. What fish is this,
that in the river swims,
and cannot from harm itself protect?
Redeem thy life
from Hel,
and find me the water's flame.[1]

The Pike
2\. Andvari I am named,
Oin was my father named;
many a cataract have I passed.
A luckless Norn
in times of old decreed,
that in the water I should wade.

Loki
3\. Tell me, Andvari!
if thou wilt enjoy

---

1. One of many periphrases for gold.

life in the halls of men,
what retribution get
the sons of mortals,
if with foul words they assail each other.

Andvari
4. Cruel retribution get
the sons of mortals,
who in Vadgelmir wade:
for the false words
they have against other uttered,
the punishments too long endure.

Loki viewed all the gold that Andvari owned; but when he had produced the gold, he retained a single ring, which Loki also took from him. The dwarf went into his stone and said:

5. That gold
which the dwarf possessed,
shall to two brothers
be cause of death,
and to eight princes,
of dissension.
From my wealth no one
shall good derive.

The Æsir produced the gold to Hreidmar, and with it crammed the otter's skin full, and set it up on the feet. They then had to heap up the gold and cover it; but when that was done, Hreidmar, stepping forward, observed a whisker, and required it to be covered; whereupon Odin drew forth the ring *Andvara-naut*, and covered the hair. Loki said:

6. There is gold for thee,
and thou hast a great redemption
for my life.
For thy son
no blessing is decreed;
of both it shall prove the bane.

Hreidmar
7. Gifts thou hast given,
friendly gifts thou hast given not;
with a kind heart thou hast not given.
Of your lives ye should

have been deprived,
had I foreknown that peril.

8. But that is worse,
what I seem to know,
a strife of kinsmen for a woman.
Princes yet unborn
I think them to be,
for whose hate that gold is destined.

9. The red gold, I trust,
I shall possess
while I am living:
of thy threats
I entertain no fear;
so take yourselves hence home.

Fafnir and Regin demanded of Hreidmar their share of the blood-fine for their slain brother Otr, which he refused, and Fafnir stabbed his father with a sword while sleeping. Hreidmar called out to his daughters:

10. Lyngheid and Lofnheid!
Know my life is departing.
To many things need compels.[2]

Lyngheid
Few sisters will,
although they lose a father,
avenge a brother's crime.

11. Then bring forth a daughter,
wolf-hearted fury!
if by a chief
thou have not a son.
Get for the maid a spouse,
in thy great need;
then will her son
thy wrong avenge.

Hreidmar then died, and Fafnir took all the gold. Regin then requested to have his share of the pat-

---

2. To wit, *to avenge my death on your brothers.*

rimony, but met with a refusal from Fafnir. Regin thereupon sought counsel of his sister Lyngheid, how he might obtain the patrimony. She said:

> 12. Thou of thy brother shall
> mildly demand
> thy patrimony and a better spirit.
> It is not seemly,
> that with the sword thou shouldst
> demand thy property of Fafnir.

The foregoing is what Regin related to Sigurd. One day, when he came to Regin's dwelling, he was kindly received, and Regin said:

> 13. Hither is come
> the son of Sigmund
> to our hall,
> that man of energy:
> courage he has greater
> than I aged man:
> now of a conflict have I hope
> from the fierce wolf.[3]

> 14. I will nurture
> the bold-hearted prince:
> now Yngvi's kinsman
> is to us come;
> he will be a king
> under the sun most powerful;
> over all lands
> will his destinies resound.

Sigurd was thence forward constantly with Regin, who related to him how Fafnir lay on Gnítaheid in the likeness of a serpent. He had an "Ægis-helm"[4] at which all living beings were terror-stricken. Regin forged a sword for Sigurd, that was named Gram, and was so sharp that immersing it in the Rhine, he let a piece of wool down the stream, when it clove the fleece asunder as water. With that sword Sigurd clove in two Regin's anvil. After that Regin instigated Sigurd to slay Fafnir. He said:

> 15. Loud will laugh
> Hunding's sons,
> they who Eylimi

---

3. Sigurd.
4. A terrific helm or headpiece.

of life deprived,
if the prince is
more desirous
to seek red rings,
than to avenge his father.

King Hiálprek collected a fleet to enable Sigurd to avenge his father. They encountered a great storm, and were driven past a certain promontory. A man was standing on the cliff who said:

16. Who ride yonder,
on Rævil's horses,
the towering billows,
the roaring main:
the sail-steeds are
with sweat bedewed,
the wave-coursers will not
the wind withstand.

Regin
17. Here am I Sigurd
in sea-trees;
a fair wind is given us
for death itself:
higher than our prows
the steep waves dash,
the rolling horses plunge.
Who is it that inquires?

Hnikar
18. They called me Hnikar,
when I Hugin gladdened,
young Völsung!
and battles fought.
Now thou mayest call me
the ancient of the rock,
Feng, or Fiölnir.
I desire a passage.

They turn to the land, the old man goes on board, and the storm abates. Sigurd said:

19. Tell me, Hnikar!
since thou knowest the omens
both of gods and men,
which omens are best
if to fight 'tis needful
at the swing of glaves?

Hnikar
20. Good omens there are many,
if men but knew them,
at the swing of glaves,
a faithful fellowship, I think,
is the dark raven's,
with the sworded warrior.

21. The second is
if, when thou art gone out,
and about to depart,
thou seest two
renown-seeking men
standing in the fore-court.

22. The third omen is,
if wolves thou hearest
howl under the ash-boughs,
it will victory to the announce
over helmed warriors,
if thou seest them go before thee.

23. No man should
fight against
the moon's
late-shining sister.
They have victory,
who can see keenly
at the play of swords,
or to form the wedge-array.

24. Most perilous it is,
if with thy foot thou strikest,
when thou to battle goest.
Wily Dísir stand
on either side of thee,
and wish to see thee wounded.

25. Combed and washed
let every brave man be,
and at morning fed;
for 'tis uncertain
whither he at eve may come.
'Tis bad to succumb to fate.

Sigurd fought a great battle with Lýngvi, Hunding's son, and his brothers, in which Lýngvi and his three brothers fell. After the battle Regin said:

26. Now is the bloody eagle,
with the trenchant blade,
graven on the back
of Sigmund's slayer.
No son of king,
who the earth reddens,
and the raven gladdens,
is more excellent.

Sigurd returned home to Hiálprek, when Regin instigated him to slay Fafnir.

Fafnismol

Sigurth and Regin went up to the Gnitaheith, and found there the track that Fafnir made when he crawled to water. Then Sigurth made a great trench across the path, and took his place therein. When Fafnir crawled from his gold, he blew out venom, and it ran down from above on Sigurth's head. But when Fafnir crawled over the trench, then Sigurth thrust his sword into his body to the heart. Fafnir writhed and struck out with his head and tail. Sigurth leaped from the trench, and each looked at the other. Fafnir said:

> 1. "Youth, oh, youth! of whom then, youth, art thou born?
> Say whose son thou art,
> Who in Fafnir's blood thy bright blade reddened,
> And struck thy sword to my heart."

Sigurth concealed his name because it was believed in olden times that the word of a dying man might have great power if he cursed his foe by his name. He said:

> 2. "The Noble Hart my name, and I go
> A motherless man abroad;
> Father I had not, as others have,
> And lonely ever I live."

Fafnir spake:
> 3. "If father thou hadst not, as others have,
> By what wonder wast thou born?
> (Though thy name on the day of my death thou hidest,
> Thou knowest now thou dost lie.)"

Sigurth spake:
> 4. "My race, methinks, is unknown to thee,
> And so am I myself;
> Sigurth my name, and Sigmund's son,
> Who smote thee thus with the sword."

Fafnir spake:
> 5. "Who drove thee on? why wert thou driven
> My life to make me lose?
> A father brave had the bright-eyed youth,
> For bold in boyhood thou art."

Sigurth spake:
6. "My heart did drive me, my hand fulfilled,
And my shining sword so sharp;
Few are keen when old age comes,
Who timid in boyhood be."

Fafnir spake:
7. "If thou mightest grow thy friends among,
One might see thee fiercely fight;
But bound thou art, and in battle taken,
And to fear are prisoners prone."

Sigurth spake:
8. "Thou blamest me, Fafnir, that I see from afar
The wealth that my father's was;
Not bound am I, though in battle taken,
Thou has found that free I live."

Fafnir spake:
9. "In all I say dost thou hatred see,
Yet truth alone do I tell;
The sounding gold, the glow-red wealth,
And the rings thy bane shall be."

Sigurth spake:
10. "Some one the hoard shall ever hold,
Till the destined day shall come;
For a time there is when every man
Shall journey hence to Hel."

Fafnir spake:
11. "The fate of the Norns before the headland
Thou findest, and doom of a fool;
In the water shalt drown if thou row 'gainst the wind,
All danger is near to death."

Sigurth spake:
12. "Tell me then, Fafnir, for wise art famed,
And much thou knowest now:
Who are the Norns who are helpful in need,
And the babe from the mother bring?"

Fafnir spake:
13. "Of many births   the Norns must be,
Nor one in race they were
Some to gods, others   to elves are kin,
And Dvalin's daughters some."

Sigurth spake:
14. "Tell me then, Fafnir,   for wise thou art famed,
And much thou knowest now:
How call they the isle   where all the gods
And Surt shall sword-sweat mingle?"

Fafnir spake:
15. "Oskopnir is it,   where all the gods
Shall seek the play of swords;
Bilrost breaks   when they cross the bridge,
And the steeds shall swim the flood.

16. "The fear-helm I wore   to afright mankind,
While guarding my gold I lay;
Mightier seemed I   than any man,
For a fiercer never I found."

Sigurth spake:
17. "The fear-helm surely   no man shields
When he faces a valiant foe;
Oft one finds,   when the foe he meets,
That he is not the bravest of all."

Fafnir spake:
18. "Venom I breathed   when bright I lay
By the hoard my father had;
(There was none so mighty   as dared to meet me,
And weapons nor wiles I feared.)"

Sigurth spake:
19. "Glittering worm,   thy hissing was great,
And hard didst show thy heart;
But hatred more   have the sons of men
For him who owns the helm."

Fafnir spake:
20. "I counsel thee, Sigurth,   heed my speech,
And ride thou homeward hence;
The sounding gold,   the glow-red wealth,
And the rings thy bane shall be."
(V. "For it often happens that he who gets a deathly wound yet avenges himself.")

Sigurth spake:
21. "Thy counsel is given,   but go I shall
To the gold in the heather hidden;
And, Fafnir, thou   with death dost fight,
Lying where Hel shall have thee."

Fafnir spake:
22. "Regin betrayed me,   and thee will betray,
Us both to death will he bring;
His life, methinks,   must Fafnir lose,
For the mightier man wast thou."

Regin had gone to a distance while Sigurth fought Fafnir, and came back while Sigurth was wiping the blood from his sword. Regin said:

23. "Hail to thee, Sigurth!   Thou victory hast,
And Fafnir in fight hast slain;
Of all the men   who tread the earth,
Most fearless art thou, methinks."

Sigurth spake:
24. "Unknown it is,   when all are together,
(The sons of the glorious gods,)
Who bravest born shall seem;
Some are valiant   who redden no sword
In the blood of a foeman's breast."

Regin spake:
25. "Glad art thou, Sigurth,   of battle gained,
As Gram with grass thou cleanest;
My brother fierce   in fight hast slain,
And somewhat I did myself."

Sigurth spake:
26. "Afar didst thou go   while Fafnir reddened
With his blood my blade so keen;
With the might of the dragon   my strength I matched,
While thou in the heather didst hide."

Regin spake:
27. "Longer wouldst thou   in the heather have let
Yon hoary giant hide,
Had the weapon availed not   that once I forged,
The keen-edged blade thou didst bear."

Sigurth spake:
28. "Better is heart   than a mighty blade
For him who shall fiercely fight;
The brave man well   shall fight and win,
Though dull his blade may be.

29. "Brave men better   than cowards be,
When the clash of battle comes;
And better the glad   than the gloomy men
Shall face what before him lies.

30. "Thy rede it was   that I should ride
Hither o'er mountains high;
The glittering worm   would have wealth and life
If thou hadst not mocked at my might."

Then Regin went up to Fafnir and cut out his heart with his sword, that was named Rithil, and then he drank blood from the wounds. Regin said:

31. "Sit now, Sigurth,   for sleep will I,
Hold Fafnir's heart to the fire;
For all his heart   shall eaten be,
Since deep of blood I have drunk."

Sigurth took Fafnir's heart and cooked it on a spit. When he thought that it was fully cooked, and the blood foamed out of the heart, then he tried it with his finger to see whether it was fully cooked. He burned his finger, and put it in his mouth. But when Fafnir's heart's-blood came on his tongue, he understood the speech of birds. He heard nut-hatches chattering in the thickets. A nut-hatch said:

32. "There sits Sigurth,   sprinkled with blood,
And Fafnir's heart   with fire he cooks;
Wise were the breaker   of rings, I ween,
To eat the life-muscles   all so bright."

A second spake:
33. "There Regin lies,   and plans he lays
The youth to betray   who trusts him well;
Lying words   with wiles will he speak,
Till his brother the maker   of mischief avenges."

A third spake:
34. "Less by a head   let the chatterer hoary
Go from here to Hel;
Then all of the wealth   he alone can wield,
The gold that Fafnir guarded."

A forth spake:
35. "Wise would he seem   if so he would heed
The counsel good   we sisters give;
Thought he would give,   and the ravens gladden,
There is ever a wolf   where his ears I spy."

A fifth spake:
36. "Less wise must be   the tree of battle
Than to me would seem   the leader of men,
If forth he lets   one brother fare,
When he of the other   the slayer is."

A sixth spake:
37. "Most foolish he seems   if he shall spare
His foe, the bane of the folk;
There Regin lies,   who hath wronged him so,
Yet falsehood knows he not."

A seventh spake:
38. "Let the head from the frost-cold   giant be hewed,
And let him of rings be robbed;
Then all the wealth   which Fafnir's was
Shall belong to thee alone."

Sigurth spake:
39. "Not so rich a fate   shall Regin have
As the tale of my death to tell;
For soon the brothers   both shall die,
And hence to Hel shall go."

Sigurth hewed off Regin's head, and then he ate Fafnir's heart, and drank the blood of both Regin and Fafnir. Then Sigurth heard what the nut-hatch said:

40. "Bind, Sigurth, the golden   rings together,
Not kingly is it   aught to fear;
I know a maid,   there is none so fair,
Rich in gold,   if thou mightest get her.

41. "Green the paths   that to Gjuki lead,
And his fate the way   to the wanderer shows;
The doughty king   a daughter has,
That thou as a bride   mayst, Sigurth, buy."

42. Another spake:
"A hall stands high   on Hindarfjoll,
All with flame   is it ringed without;
Warriors wise   did make it once
Out of the flaming   light of the flood.[1]

43. "On the mountain sleeps   a battle-maid,
And about her plays   the bane of the wood[2];
Ygg with the thorn   hath smitten her thus,
For she felled the fighter   he fain would save.

44. "There mayst thou behold   the maiden helmed,
Who forth on Vingskornir   rode from the fight;
The victory-bringer   her sleep shall break not,
Thou heroes' son[3],   so the Norns have set."

Sigurth rode along Fafnir's trail to his lair, and found it open. The gate-posts were of iron, and the gates; of iron, too, were all the beams in the house, which was dug down into the earth. There Sigurth found a mighty store of gold, and he filled two chests full thereof; he took the fear-helm and a golden mail-coat and the sword Hrotti, and many other precious things, and loaded Grani with them, but the horse would not go forward until Sigurth mounted on his back.

1. Another periphrasis for gold.
2. A periphrasis for fire.
3. Of Skioldungs.

Sigrdrífumál: The Lay of Sigrdrifa

Sigurd rode up the Hindarfiall, and directed his course southwards towards Frankland. In the fell he saw a great light, as if a fire were burning, which blazed up the sky. On approaching it, there stood a *skialdborg*, and over it a banner. Sigurd went into the skialdborg, and saw a warrior lying within it asleep, completely armed. He first took the helmet off the warrior's head, and saw that it was a woman. Her corslet was a s fast as if it had grown to her body. With his sword Gram he ripped the corslet from the upper opening downwards, and then though both sleeves. He then took the corslet off from her, when she awoke, sat up and, on seeing Sigurd, said:

> 1. What has my corslet cut?
> why from sleep have I started?
> who hast cast from me
> the fallow bands?
>
> Sigurd
> Sigmund's son
> hast just now ript
> the raven's perch,[1]
> with Sigurd's sword.
>
> She
> 2. Long have I slept,
> long been with sleep oppressed,
> long are mortals' sufferings!
> Odin is the cause
> that I have been unable
> to cast off torpor.

Sigurd sat down and asked her name. She then took a horn filled with mead, and gave him the *minnis-cup*.

> She
> 3. Hail to Day!
> Hail to the sons of Day!
> To Night and her daughter hail!
> With placid eyes
> behold us here,
> and here sitting give us victory.

---

1. The original words, *hrafns hrælundir*, the raven's corpse-trees. So Grimm understands the line; because that bird hops about upon the armour as upon a tree.

> 4. Hail to the Æsir!
> Hail to the Asyniur!
> Hail to the bounteous earth!
> Words and wisdom
> give to us noble twain,
> and healing hands[2] while we live.

She was named Sigrdrífa, and was a Valkyria. She said that two kings had made war on each other, one of whom was named Hiálmgunnar; he was old and a great warrior, and Odin had promised him victory. The other was Agnar, a brother of Höda, whom no divinity would patronize. Sigrdrífa overcame Hiálmgunnar in battle; in revenge for which Odin pricked her with a sleep-thorn, and declared that thenceforth she should never have victory in battle, and should be given in marriage. "But I said to him, that I had bound myself by a vow not to espouse any man who could be made to fear." Sigurd answers, and implores her to teach him wisdom, as she had intelligence from all regions:

> Sigrdrifa
> 5. Beer I bear to thee,
> column[3] of battle!
> with might mingled,
> and with bright glory:
> 'tis full of song,
> and salutary saws,
> of potent incantations,
> and joyous discourses.
>
> 6. Sig-runes thou must know,
> if victory (sigr) thou wilt have,
> and on thy sword's hilt grave them;
> some on the chapes,
> some on the guard,
> and twice the name of Tý.
>
> 7. Öl- (beer-) runes thou must know,
> if thou wilt not that another's wife,
> thy trust betray, if thou in her confide.
> On the horn must they be graven,
> and on the hand's back,
> and Naud[4] on the nail be scored.

---

2. The superstition of the *healing hand* is not yet extinct in Iceland. Dr. Maurer relates a story of a man in Reykjavik to whom it would seem to have been communicated by an elfin, in a dream.
3. Literally *apple-tree*.
4. The name of a rune.

8. A cup must be blessed,
and against peril guarded,
and garlick in the liquor cast:
then I know
thou wilt never have
mead with treachery mingled.

9. Biarg- (help-) runes thou must know,
if thou wilt help,
and loose the child from women.
In the palm they must be graven,
and round the joints be clasped,
and the Dísir prayed for aid.

10. Brim- (sea-) runes thou must know,
if thou wilt have secure
afloat thy sailing steeds.
On the prow they must be graven,
and on the helm-blade,
and with fire to the oar applied.
No surge shall be so towering,
nor waves so dark,
but from the ocean thou safe shalt come.

11. Lim- (branch-) runes thou must know,
if thou a leech wouldst be,
and wounds know how to heal.
On the bark they must be graven,
and on the leaves of trees,
of those whose boughs bend eastward.

12. Mál- (speech-) runes thou must know,
if thou wilt that no one
for injury with hate requite thee.
Those thou must wind,
those thou must wrap round,
those thou must altogether place
in the assembly,
where people have
into full court to go.

13. Hug- (thought-) runes thou must know,
if thou a wiser man wilt be
than every other.
Those interpreted,
those graved,
those devised Hropt,
from the fluid,
which had leaked
from Heiddraupnir's head,
and from Hoddropnir's horn.

14. On a rock he stood,
with edged sword,
a helm on his head he bore.
Then spake Mim's head
its first wise word,
and true saying uttered.

15. They are, it said, on the shield graven,
which stands before the shining god,
or Arvakr's ear,
and on Alsvid's hoof,
on the wheel which rolls
under Rögnir's ear,
on Sleipnir's teeth,
and on the sledge's bands.

16. On the bear's paw,
and on Bragi's tongue,
on the wolf's claws,
and the eagle's beak,
on bloody wings,
and on the bridge's end,
on the releasing hand,
and on the healing's track.

17. On glass and on gold,
on amulets of men,
in wine and in wort,
and in the welcome seat,
on Gúngnir's point,
and on Grani's breast,
on the Norn's nail,
and the owl's neb.

18. All were erased
that were inscribed,
and mingled with the sacred mead,
and sent on distant ways:
they are with the Æsir,
they are with the Alfar,
some with the wise Vanir,
some human beings have.

19. Those are bók-runes,
those are biarg-runes,
and all öl- (beer-) runes,
and precious megin- (power-) runes,
for those who can,
without confusion or corruption,
turn them to his welfare.
Use, if thou hast understood them,
until the powers perish.

20. Now thou shalt choose,
since a choice is offered thee,
keen armed warrior!
my speech, or silence:
think over it in thy mind.
All evils[5] have their measure.

---

5. An allusion to Sigurd's unhappy end.

Sigurd
21. I will not flee,
though thou shouldst know me doomed.
I am not born a craven.
Thy friendly counsels all
I will receive,
as long as life is in me.

Sigrdrifa
22. This I thee counsel first:
that towards thy kin
thou bear thee blameless.
Take not hasty vengeance,
although they raise up strife:
that, it is said, benefits the dead.

23. This I thee counsel secondly:
that no oath thou swear,
if it be not true.
Cruel bonds
follow broken faith:
accursed is the faith-breaker.

24. This I thee counsel thirdly:
that in the assembly thou
contend not with a fool;
for an unwise man
oft utters words
worse than he knows of.

25. All is vain,
if thou holdest silence;
then wilt thou seem a craven born,
or else truly accursed.
Doubtful is a servant's testimony,
unless a good one thou gettest.
On the next day
let his life go forth,
and so men's lies reward.

26. This I counsel thee fourthly:
if a wicked sorceress
dwells by the way,
to go on is better
than there to lodge,
though night may overtake thee.

27. Of searching eyes
the sons of men have need,
when fiercely they have to fight:
oft pernicious women
by the way-side sit,
who swords and valour deaden.

28. This I thee counsel fifthly:
although thou see fair women
on the benches sitting,
let not their kindred's silver
over thy sleep have power.
To kiss thee entice no woman.

29. This I thee counsel sixthy:
although among men pass
offensive tipsy talk,
never while drunken quarrel
with men of war:
wine steals the wits of many.

30. Brawls and drink
to many men have been
a heart-felt sorrow;
to some their death,
to some calamity:
many are the griefs of men!

31. This I thee counsel seventhly:
if thou hast disputes
with a daring man,
better it is for men
to fight than to be burnt
within their dwelling.

32. This I thee counsel eighthly:
that thou guard thee against evil,
and eschew deceit.
Entice no maiden,
nor wife of man,
nor to wantoness incite.

33. This is thee counsel ninthly:
that thou corpses bury,
wherever on the earth thou findest them,
whether from sickness they have died,
or from the sea,
or are from weapons dead.

34. Let a mound be raised
for those departed;
let their hands and head be washed,
combed, and wiped dry,
ere in the coffin they are laid:
and pray for their happy sleep.

35. This I thee counsel tenthly:
that thou never trust
a foe's kinsman's promises,
whose brother thou hast slain,
or sire laid low:
there is a wolf
in a young son,
though he with gold be gladdened.

36. Strifes and fierce enmities
think not to be lulled,
no more than deadly injury.
Wisdom and fame in arms
a prince not easily acquires,
who shall of men be foremost.

37. This I counsel thee eleventhly:
that thou at evil look,
what course it may take.
A long life, it seems to me
the prince may (not) enjoy;
fierce disputes will arise.

Sigurd said: "A wiser mortal exists not, and I swear that I will possess thee, for thou art after my heart." She answered: "Thee I will have before all others, though I have to choose among all men." And this they confirmed with oaths to each other.

Fragments of the Lays of Sigurd and Brynhild

Sigurd then rides away from Hindarfiall, and journeys on till he comes to the habitation of Heimir, who was married to Beckhild, Brynhild's sister. Alsvid, Heimir's son, who was at play when Sigurd arrived at the mansion, received him kindly, and requested him to stay with him. Sigurd consented, and remained there a short time. Brynhild was at that time with Heimir, and was weaving within a gold border the great exploits of Sigurd.

One day, when Sigurd was come from the forest, his hawk flew to the window at which Brynhild sat employed on weaving. Sigurd ran after it, saw the lady, and appeared struck with her handiwork and beauty. On the following day Sigurd went to her apartment, and Alsvid stood outside the door shafting arrows. Sigurd said: "Hail to thee, lady!" or "How fares it with thee?" She answered: "We are well, my kindred and friends are living, but it is uncertain what any one's lot may be till their last day." He sat down by her. Brynhild said: "This seat will be allowed to few, unless my father comes." Sigurd answered: "Now is that come to pass which thou didst promise me." She said: "Here shalt thou be welcome." She then arose, and her four maidens with her, and, approaching him with a golden cup, bade him drink. He reached towards her and took hold of her hand together with the cup, and place her by him, clasped her round the neck, kissed her, and said: "A fairer than thou was never born." She said: "it is not wise to place faith in women, for they so often break their promise." He said: "Better days will come upon us, so that we may enjoy happiness." Brynhild said: "It is not ordained that we shall live together, for I am a shield-maiden *(skjaldmær)*." Sigurd said: "Then will our happiness be best promoted, if we live together; for harder to endure is the pain which herein lies than from a keen weapon." Brynhild said: "I shall be called to the aid of warriors, but thou wilt espouse Gudrún, Giuki's daughter." Sigurd said: "No king's daughter shall ensnare me, therefore have not two thoughts on that subject; and I swear by the gods that I will possess thee and no other woman." She answered to the same effect. Sigurd thanked her for what she had said to him, and gave her a gold ring. He remained there a short time in great favour.

Sigurd now rode to Heimir's dwelling with much gold, until he came to the palace of King Giuki, whose wife was named Grimhild. They had three sons, Gunnar, Högni, and Guthorm. Gudrún was the name of their daughter. King Giuki entreated Sigurd to stay there, and there he remained a while. All appeared low by the side of Sigurd. One evening the sorceress Grimhild rose and presented a horn to Sigurd, saying: "Joyful for us is thy presence, and we desire that all good may befall thee. Take this horn and drink." He took it and drank, and with that drink forgot both his love and his vows to Brynhild. After that, Grimhild so fascinated him that he was induced to espouse Gudrún, and all pledged their faith to Sigurd, and confirmed it by oaths. Sigurd gave Gudrún to eat of Fafnir's heart, and she became afterwards far more austere then before. Their son was named Sigmund.

These fragments from the *Volsunga-Saga*, which are inserted in some paper manuscripts of the *Edda*, and containing matter probably derived from the lost poems relative to Sigurd and Brynhild, are printed in the Stockholm edition of the *Edda*. they are also given by Afzelius in his Swedish version, and partially in Danish by Finn Magnusen in his edition. A complete translation into Danish of the entire Saga has since been given by Prof. Rafn at Copenhagen.

Grimhild now counseled her son Gunnar to woo Brynhild, and consulted with Sigurd, in consequence of this design. Brynhild had vowed to wed that man only who should ride over the blazing fire that was laid around her hall. They found the hall and the fire burning around it. Gunnar rode Goti, and Högni Hölknir. Gunnar turns his horse towards the fire but it shrinks back. Sigurd said "Why dost thou shrink back, Gunnar?" Gunnar answers: "My horse will not leap this fire," and prays Sigurd to lend him Grani. "He is at thy service," said Sigurd. Gunnar now rides again towards the fire, but Grani will not go over. They then changed forms. Sigurd rides, having in his hand the sword Gram, and golden spurs on his heels. Grani runs forward to the fire when he feels the spur. There was now a great noise, at it is said:

> 1. The fire began to rage,
> and the earth to tremble,
> high rose the flame
> to heaven itself:
> there ventured few
> chiefs of people
> through that fire to ride,
> or to leap over.

> 2. Sigurd Grani
> with his sword urged,
> the fire was quenched
> before the prince,
> the flame allayed
> before the glory-seeker
> with the bright saddle
> that Rök owned.

Brynhild was sitting in a chair as Sigurd entered. She asks who he is, and he calls himself Gunnar Giuki's son. "And thou art destined to be my wife with my father's consent. I have ridden through the flickering flame *(vafrlogi)* at they requisition." She said: "I know not well how I shall answer this." Sigurd stood erect on the floor resting on the hilt of his sword. She rose embarrassed from her seat, like a swan on the waves, having a sword in her hand, a helmet on her head, and wearing a corslet. "Gunnar," said she, "speak not so to me, unless thou art the foremost of men; and then thou must slay him who has sought me, if thou hast so much trust in thyself." Sigurd said: "Remember now thy promise, that thou wouldst go with that man who should ride through the flickering flame." She acknowledged the truth of his words, stood up, and gave him a glad welcome. He tarried there three nights, and they prepared one bed. He took the sword Gram and laid it between them. She inquired why he did so. He said that it was enjoined him so to act towards his bride on their marriage, or he would receive his death. He then took from her the ring called Andvaranaut, and gave her another that had belonged to Fafnir. After this he rode away through the same fire to his companions, when Gunnar and he again changed forms, and they then rode home.

Brynhild related this in confidence to her foster-father Heimir, and said: "A king named Gunnar has ridden through the flickering flame, and is come to speak with me; but I told him that Sigurd alone might so do, to whom I gave my vow at Hindarfiall, and that he only was the man." Heimir said that what had happened must remain as it was. Brynhild said: "Our daughter Aslaug thou shalt rear up here with thee." Brynhild then went to her father, King Budli, and he with his daughter Brynhild went to King Giuki's palace. A great feasting was afterwards held, when Sigurd remembered all his oaths to Brynhild, and yet kept silence. Brynhild and Gunnar sat at the drinking and drank wine.

One day Brynhild and Gudrún went to the river Rhine, and Brynhild went farther out into the water. Gudrún asked why she did so? Brynhild answered: "Why shall I go on along with thee in this more than in anything else?" "I presume that my father was more potent than thine, and my husband has performed more valorous deeds, and ridden through the blazing fire. They husband was King Hiálprek's thrall." Gudrún answered angrily: "Thou shouldst be wiser than to venture to vilify my husband, as it is the talk of all that no one like to him in every respect has ever come into the world; nor does it become thee to vilify him, as he was thy former husband, and slew Fafnir, and rode through the fire, whom though thoughtest was King Gunnar; and he lay with thee, and took from thee the ring Andvaranaut, and here mayest thou recognize it." Brynhild then looking at the ring, recognized it, and turned pale as though she were dead. Brynhild was very taciturn that evening, and Gudrún asked Sigurd why Brynhild was so taciturn. He dissuaded her much from making this inquiry, and said that at all events it would soon be known.

On the morrow, when sitting in their apartment, Gudrún said: "Be cheerful, Brynhild! What is it that prevents thy mirth?" Brynhild answered: "Malice drives thee to this; for thou hast a cruel heart." "Judge not so," said Gudrún. Brynhild continued: "Ask about that only which is better for thee to know; that is more befitting women of high degree. It is good, too, for thee to be content, as all goes according to thy wishes." Gudrún said: "It is premature to glory in that: this forebodes something; but what instigates thee against us?" Brynhild answered: "Thou shalt be requited for having espoused Sigurd; for I grudge thee the possession of him." Gudrún said: "We knew not of your secret." Brynhild answered: "We have had no secret, though we have sworn oaths of fidelity; and thou knowest that I have been deceived, and I will avenge it." Gudrún said: "Thou art better married than thou deservest to be, and thy violence must be cooled." "Content should I be," said Brynhild, "didst thou not posses a more renowned husband than I." Gudrún answered: "Thou hast as renowned a husband; for it is doubtful which is the greater king." Brynhild said: "Sigurd overcame Fafnir, and that is worth more than all Gunnar's kingdom, as it is said:

> "Sigurd the serpent slew,
> and that henceforth shall be
> by none forgotten,
> while mankind lives:
> but thy brother
> neither dared
> through the fire to ride,
> nor over it to leap."

Gudrún said: "Grani would not run through the fire under King Gunnar: but he (Gunnar) dared to ride." Brynhild said: "Let us not contend: I bear no good will to Grimhild." Gudrún said: "Blame her not; for she is towards thee as to her own daughter." Brynhild said: "She is the cause of all the evil which gnaws me. She presented to Sigurd the pernicious drink, so that he no more remembrest me." Gudrún said: "Many an unjust word thou utterest, and this is a great falsehood." Brynhild said: "So enjoy Sigurd as thou hast not deceived me, and may it go with thee as I imagine." Gudrún said: "Better shall I enjoy him than thou wilt wish; and no one has said he has had too much good with me at any time." Brynhild said: "Thou sayest ill and will repent of it. Let us cease from angry words, and not indulge in useless prattle. Long have I borne in silence the grief that dwells in my breast: I have also felt regard for thy brother. But let us talk of other things." Gudrún said: "Your imagination looks far forward."

Brynhild then lay in bed, and King Gunnar came to talk with her, and begged her to rise and give vent to her sorrow; but she would not listen to him. They then brought Sigurd to visit her and learn whether her grief might not be alleviated. They called to memory their oaths, and how they had been deceived, and at length Sigurd offered to marry her and put away Gudrún; but she would not hear of it. Sigurd left the apartment, but was so greatly affected by her sorrow that the rings of his corslet burst asunder from his sides, as is said in the *Sigurðarkviða*:

> "Out went Sigurd
> from that interview
> into the hall of kings,
> writhing in anguish;
> so that began to start
> the ardent warrior's
> iron-woven sark
> off from his sides."

Brynhild afterwards instigated Gunnar to murder Sigurd, saying that he had deceived them both and broken his oath. Gunnar consulted with Högni, and revealed to him this conversation. Högni earnestly strove to dissuade him from such a deed, on account of their oaths. Gunnar removed the difficulty, saying: "Let us instigate our brother Guthorm; he is young and of little judgement, and is, moreover, free of all oaths; and so avenge the mortal injury of his having seduced Brynhild." They then took a serpent and the flesh of a wolf, and had them cooked, and gave them to him to eat, and offered him gold and a large realm, to do the deed, as is said:

> "The forest-fish they roasted,
> and the wolf's carcase took,
> while some to Guthorm
> dealt out gold;
> gave him Geri's[2] flesh

---

2. The name of one of Odin's wolves; here used poeitically for *wolf* in general.

>with his drink,
>and many other things
>steeped therein."

With this food he became so furious, that he would instantly perpetrate the deed. On this it is related as in the *Sigurðarkviða*, when Gunnar and Brynhild conversed together.

SigurÞarkviða Fafnisbana Þriðja

The Third Lay of Sigurd Fafnicide

1. It was of old that Sigurd,
the young Völsung,
Giuki sought,
after his conflict,
received the pledge of friendship
from the two brothers;
oaths exchanged
the bold of deed.

2. A maid they offered him,
and treasures many,
Gudrún, Giuki's
youthful daughter.
Drank and conversed,
many days together,
Sigurd the young
and Giuki's sons.

3. Until they went
to woo Brynhild,
and with them Sigurd,
the youthful Völsung,
rode in company,
who knew the way.
He would have possessed her,
if her possess he might.

4. Sigurd the southern
laid a naked sword,
a glittering falchion,
between them;
nor the damsel
did he kiss,
nor did the Hunnish king
to his arm lift her.
He the blooming maid
to Giuki's son delivered.

5. She to herself a body
was of no sin conscious,
nor at her death-day,
of any crime,
that could be a stain,
or thought to be:
intervened therein
the grisly fates.

6. Alone she sat without,
at eve of day,
began aloud
with herself to speak:
"Sigurd must be mine;
I must die,
or that blooming youth
clasp in my arms."

7. "Of the words I have uttered
I now repent;
he is Gudrún's consort,
and I am Gunnar's.
The hateful Norns
long suffering have decreed us."

8. Oftentimes she wandered,
filled with evil thoughts,
o'er ice and icebergs,
every eve,
when he and Gudrún
had to their couch withdrawn
and Sigurd her
in the coverings wrapt,
the Hunnish king
his wife caressed.

9. "Devoid I go
of spouse and pleasure;
I will beguile myself
with vengeful thoughts."

10. By those fits of fury
she was impelled to murder.
"Thou, Gunnar! shalt
wholly lose
my land,
and myself also.
Never shall I be happy,
king! with thee.

11. I will return
thither from whence I came,
to my near kindred,
my relations;
there will I remain,
and slumber life away,
cause to be slain,
and a king become
than the other greater.

12. Let the son go
together with the father,
the young wolf may not
longer be fostered.
For whom will vengeance
be the easier
to appease,
if the son lives?"

13. Wroth was Gunnar,
and with grief borne down;
in his mind revolved,
sat the whole day;
he knew not well,
nor could devise,
what were most desirable
for him to do,
or were most fitting
to be done,
when he should find himself
of the Völsung bereft,
and in Sigurd
a great loss sustain.

14. Much he thought,
and also long,
that it did not
often happen,
that from their royal state
women withdrew.
Högni he then
to counsel summoned,
in whom he placed
the fullest trust.

15. "Of all to me Brynhild,
Budli's daughter
is the dearest;
she is the chief of women:
rather will I
my life lay down
than that fair one's
treasures lose.

16. "With thou the prince
for his wealth circumvent?
good 'tis to command
the ore of Rhine,
and at ease
over riches rule,
and in tranquillity
happiness enjoy."

17. This alone Högni
for answer gave:
"It beseems us not
so to do,
by the sword to break
sworn oaths,
oaths sworn,
and plighted faith.

18. "We know not on earth
men more fortunate,
while we four
over the people rule,
and the Hun lives,
that warlike chief;
nor on earth,
a race more excellent,
if we five sons
long shall foster,
and the good progeny
can increase."

19. I know full well
whence the causes spring:
Brynhild's importunity
is over-great.

20. We will Guthorm,
our younger brother,
and not over-wise,
for the deed prepare:
he is free from
sworn oaths,
sworn oaths,
and plighted faith."

21. Easy it was to instigate
the ferocious spirit:
in the heart of Sigurd
stood his sword.

22. On vengeance bent,
the warrior in his chamber
hurled his brand after
the fierce assassin;
to Guthorm flew
dartlike Gram's
gleaming steel
from the king's hand.

23. Fell the murderer
in two parts,
arms and head
flew far away,
but his feet's part
fell backwards on the place.

24. Sunk in sleep was Gudrún,
in her bed,
void of cares,
by Sigurd's side:
but she awoke
of joys bereft,
when in the blood
of Frey's friend she swam.

25. So violently struck she
her hands together,
that the stout of heart
rose in his bed.
"Weep not, Gudrún!
so cruelly,
my blooming bride!
thy brothers live.

26. An heir I have,
alas! too young;
he cannot flee from
the hostile house;
among themselves they
recently have
dark and evil
counsels devised.

27. Never henceforth,
although seven thou bear,
will such a son
to the trysting with them ride.
Full well I know
how this has befallen:
Brynhild the sole cause is
of all the evil.

28. Me the maiden loved
more than any man;
but towards Gunnar
I sinned not;
affinity I held sacred,
and sworn oaths;
thenceforward I was called
his consort's friend."

29. The woman gave forth sighs,
and the king his life.
So violently she struck
her hands together,
that the beakers on the wall
responsive rang,
and in the court
the geese loudly screamed.

30. Laughed then Brynhild,
Budli's daughter,
once only,
from her whole soul,
when in her bed
she listened to
the loud lament
of Giuki's daughter.

31. Then said Gunnar,
the hawk-bearing prince:
"Laugh not thereat,
thou barbarous woman!
glad on thy couch,
as if good awaited thee.
Why hast thou lost
that beauteous colour?
authoress of crime!
Methinks to death thou art doomed.

32. Well doest thou deserve,
above all women,
that before thy eyes,
we should lay Atli low,
that thou shouldst see thy brother's
blood-streaming sore,
his gory wounds
shouldst have to bind."

33. Then said Brynhild, Budli's daughter:
"No one provokes thee, Gunnar!
complete is thy work of death.
Little does Atli
thy hatred fear;
his life will
outlast thine,
and his might
be ever greater.

34. Gunnar! I will tell thee,
though thou well knowest it,
how early ye
resolved on crimes.
I was o'er-young
and unrestrained,
with wealth endowed,
in my brother's house.

35. Nor did I desire
to marry any man,
before ye Giukungs
rode to our dwelling,
three on horseback,
powerful kings:
would that journey
had never been!

36. Then myself I promised
to the great king,
who with gold sat
on Grani's back.
In eyes he did not
you resemble,
nor was at all
in aspect like:
yet ye thought yourselves
mighty kings.

37. And to me apart
Atli said,
that he would not have
our heritage divided,
nor gold nor lands,
unless I let myself be married,
nor grant me any part
of the acquired gold,
which he to me a girl
had given to possess,
and to me a child
in money counted.

38. Then distracted was
my mind thereon,
whether I should engage in conflict,
and death dispense,
valiant in arms,
for my brother's quarrel.
That would then
be world-widely known,
and to many a one
bring heartfelt anguish.

39. Our reconciliation
we let follow:
to me it had been more pleasing
the treasures to accept,
the red-gold rings
of Sigmund's son:
nor did I another's
gold desire;
him alone I loved,
none other.
Menskögul[1] had not
a changing mind.

40. All this will Atli
hereafter find,
when he shall hear of
my funeral rites completed;
for never shall
the heavy-hearted woman
with another's husband
pass her life.
Then will my wrongs
be all avenged."

41. Up rose Gunnar,
prince of warriors,
and round his consort's neck
laid his hands;
all drew nigh,
yet each one singly,
through honest feeling,
to dissuade her.

42. She from her neck
those about her cast;
she let no one stay her
from her long journey.

---

1. That is, Skogul with the necklace; Brynhild applies this name to herself, which is a compound of *men*, necklace, *monile*, and Skogul, the name of a Valkyria.

43. He then called Högni
to consultation.
"I will that all our folk
to the hall be summoned,
thine with mine
now 'tis most needful
to see if we can hinder
my consort's fatal course,
till from our speech
a hindrance may come:
then let us leave
necessity to rule."

44. To him Högni
answer gave:
"Let no one hinder her
from the long journey,
whence may she never
born again return.
Unblest she came
on her mother's lap,
born in the world
for ceaseless misery,
for many a man's
heart-felt sorrow."

45. Downcast he
from the meeting turned
to where the lady
treasures distributed.
She was viewing
all she owned:
hungry female thralls
and chamber-women.
She put on her golden corslet
no good meditated
ere herself she pierced,
with the sword's point.

46. On the pillow she
turned to the other side,
and, wounded with the glave,
on her last counsels thought.

47. "Now let come those
who desire gold,
and aught less precious,
to receive from me.
To every one I give
a gilded necklace,[2]
needle-work and coverlets,
splendid weeds."

48. All were silent,
thought on what to do,
and all together
answer gave:
"Too many are there dead:
we will yet live,
still be hungry hall-servants,
to do what fitting is."

49. At length after reflection,
the lady linen-clad,
young in years,
words in answer uttered:
"I desire that none,
dead to entreaty, should
by force, for our sake,
lose their life.

50. Yet o'er your bones
will burn
fewer ornaments,
Menia's good meal,[3]
when ye go hence
me to seek.

---

2. Necklaces usually consisted in gold and silver chains or laces with ornaments attached to them; if these resembled the sun or moon they were called *Sigli, suns* (such were those here spoken of); and such was the necklace worn by Freyja, the bright goddess of the Vanir.
3. Menia's meal, or flour, is gold.

51. Gunnar! sit down,
I will tell to thee,
that of life now hopeless is
thy bright consort.
Thy vessel will not be
always afloat,
though I shall have
my life resigned.

52. With Gudrún thou wilt be reconciled,
sooner than thou thinkest:
that wise woman has
by the king
sad memorials,
after her consort's death.

53. There is born a maid,
which her mother rears;
brighter far
than the clear day,
than the sun's beam,
will Svanhild be.

54. Gudrún thou wilt give
to an illustrious one,
a warrior, the bane
of many men:
not to her wish
will she be married;
Atli will come
her to espouse,
Budli's son,
my brother.

55. Much have I in memory
how I was treated,
when ye me so cruelly
had deceived:
robbed I was of happiness,
while my life lasted.

56. Thou will desire
Oddrún to possess,
but Atli will
permit it not;
in secret ye will
each other meet.
She will love thee,
as I had done,
if us a better fate
had been allotted.

57. Thee will Atli
barbarously treat;
in the narrow serpent-den
wilt thou be cast.

58. It will too come to pass,
not long after,
that Atli will
his soul resign,
his prosperity,
and cease to live;
for Gudrún in her vengeance
him in his bed will slay,
through bitterness of spirit,
with the sword's sharp edge.

59. More seemly would appear
our sister Gudrún,
had she in death
her first consort followed,
had but good counsel
been to her given,
or she a soul possessed
resembling mine,

60. Faintly now I speak
but for our sake
she will not
lose her life.
She will be borne
on towering billows

to King Jonakr's
paternal soil.
Doubts will be in the resolves
of Jonakr's sons.

61. She will Svanhild
send from the land,
her daughter,
and Sigurd's.
Her will destroy
Bikki's counsel;
for Jörmunrek
for evil lives.
Then will have passed away
all Sigurd's race,
and Gudrún's tears
will be the more.

62. One prayer I have to thee
yet to make,
in this world 't will be
my last request:
Let in the plain be raised
a pile so spacious,
that for us all
like room may be,
for those who shall have died
with Sigurd.

63. Bedeck the pile about
with shields and hangings,
a variegated corpse-cloth,
and multitude of slain.
Let them burn the Hun[4]
on the one side of me;

64. Let them with the Hun
burn on the other side,
my household slaves,
with collars splendid,

---

4. Sigurd.

two at our heads,
and two hawks;
then will all be
equally distributed.

65. Let also lie
between us both
the sword with rings adorned,
the keen-edged iron,
so again be placed,
as when we both
one couch ascended,
and were then called
by the name of consorts.

66. Then will not clang
against his heel
the hall's bright gates,
with splendid ring,
if my train
him hence shall follow.
Then will our procession
appear not mean.

67. For him will follow
five female thralls,
eight male slaves
of gentle birth,
fostered with me,
and with my patrimony,
which to his daughter
Budli gave.

68. Much I have said,
and more would say,
if the sword would grant me
power of speech.
My voice fails,
my wounds swell:
truth only I have uttered;
so I will cease."

Brot af Brynhildarkviða

Fragments of the Lay of Brynhild

Gunnar
1. "Why art thou, Brynhild!
Budli's daughter!
absorbed in evil
and murderous thoughts?
What injury
has Sigurd done thee,
that thou the hero wilt
of life bereave?"

Brynhild
2. "Sigurd to me
oaths has sworn,
all falsehoods.
He at a time deceived me
when he should have been
of all oaths
most observant."

Högni
3. "Thee Brynhild has
in anger instigated
evil to perpetrate,
harm to execute.
She grudges Gudrún
her happy marriage,
and thee,
possession of herself."
****
****

4. Some a wolf roasted,
some a snake cut up,
some to Guthorm
served the wolf,
before they might,
eager for crime,
on the mighty man
lay their hands.

5. Without stood Gudrún,
Giuki's daughter,
and these words
first of all she uttered:
"Where is now Sigurd,
lord of warriors,
seeing that my kinsmen
foremost ride?"

6. Högni alone to her
answer gave:
"Asunder have we Sigurd
hewed with our swords;
his grey steed bends
o'er the dead chief."

7. Then said Brynhild,
Budli's daughter,
"Well shall ye now enjoy
arms and lands.
Sigurd would alone
over all have ruled,
had he a little longer
life retained.

8. Unseemly it had been
that he should so have ruled
over Giuki's heritage
and the Goths' people,
when he five sons,
for the fall of hosts,
eager for warfare,
had begotten."

9. Then laughed Brynhild
the whole burgh resounded
once only
from her whole heart:
"Well shall ye enjoy
lands and subjects,
now the daring king
ye have caused to fall."

10. Then said Gudrún,
Giuki's daughter:
"Much thou speakest,
things most atrocious:
may fiends have Gunnar,
Sigurd's murderer!
Souls malevolent
vengeance awaits."

11. Sigurd had fallen
south of the Rhine:
loud from a tree
a raven screamed:
"With your blood will Atli
his sword's edge redden;
the oaths ye have sworn
your slaughter shall dissolve."

12. Evening was advanced,
much was drunken,
then did pleasant talk
of all kinds pass:
all sank in sleep,
when to rest they went.
Gunnar alone was wakeful
longer than all:

13. He began his foot to move,
and much with himself to speak;
the warlike chief
in his mind pondered,
what during the conflict
the raven and the eagle
were ever saying,
as they rode home.

14. Brynhild awoke,
Budli's daughter,
daughter of the Skiöldungs,
a little ere day:
"Urge me or stay me
the mischief is perpetrated
my sorrow to pour forth,
or so suppress it."

15. All were silent
at these words;
few understood
the lady's conduct,
that weeping she
should begin to speak
of what she laughing
had desired.

16. "In my dream, Gunnar!
all seemed so horrid;
in the chamber all was dead;
my bed was cold;
and thou, king! wast riding
of joy bereft,
with fetters loaded,
to a hostile host.
So will ye all,
race of Niflungs!
be of power deprived,
perjurers as ye are!

17. Ill Gunnar!
didst thou remember,
when blood ye in your footsteps
both let flow;
now hast thou him
ill for all that requited,
because he would
prove himself foremost.

18. Then was it proved,
when the hero had
ridden to see me,
to woo me,
how the warlike chief
whilom held sacred
his oath towards
the youthful prince.

19. Laid his sword,
with gold adorned,
the illustrious king
between us both:
outward its edges were
with fire wrought,
but with venom drops
tempered within."

From this lay, in which the death of Sigurd is related, it appears that he was slain without doors, while some relate that he was slain sleeping in his bed: but the Germans say he was slain out in the forest; and it is told in the *Guðrúnarkviða hin Forna*, that Sigurd and the sons of Giuki had ridden to the public assembly *(Þing)* when he was slain. But it is said by all, without exception, that they broke faith with him, and attacked him while lying down and unprepared.

GuÞrúnarkviða Fyrsta: The First Lay of Gudrún

Gudrún sat over Sigurd dead; she wept not as other women, although ready to burst with sorrow. Both men and women, came to console her, but that was not easy. It is said by some that Gudrún had eaten of Fafnir's heart, and therefore understood the talk of birds. This is also sung of Gudrún:

    1. Of old it was that Gudrún
    prepared to die,
    when she sorrowing
    over Sigurd sat.
    No sigh she uttered,
    nor with her hands beat,
    nor wailed,
    as other women.

    2. Jarls came forward
    of great sagacity,
    from her sad state of mind
    to divert her.
    Gudrún could not
    shed a tear,
    such was her affliction;
    ready she was to burst.

    3. Sat there noble
    wives of jarls,
    adorned with gold,
    before Gudrún;
    each of them
    told her sorrows,
    the bitterest
    she had known.

    4. Then said Giaflaug,
    Giuki's sister:
    "I know myself to be
    on earth most joyless:
    of five consorts I
    the loss have suffered;
    of two daughters,
    sisters three,

and brothers eight;
I alone live."

5. Gudrún could not
shed a tear,
such was her affliction
for her dead consort,
and her soul's anguish
for the king's fall.

6. Then said Herborg,
Hunaland's queen:
"I a more cruel grief
have to recount:
my seven sons,
in the south land,
my spouse the eighth,
in conflict fell.

7. My father and my mother,
my brothers four,
on the sea
the wind deluded;
the waves struck
on the ship's timbers.

8. Their last honours
'twas mine to pay,
'twas mine to see them tombed,
their funeral rites
to prepare was mine.
All this I underwent
in one half-year,
and to me no one
consolation offered.

9. Then I became a captive,
taken in war,
at the close
of the same half-year.
Then had I to adorn,
and tie the shoes,

of the hersir's wife,
each morn.

10. From jealousy
she threatened me,
and with hard blows
drove me:
nowhere master
found I a better,
but mistress
no where a worse."

11. Gudrún could not
shed a tear,
such was her affliction
for her dead consort,
and her soul's anguish
for the king's fall.

12. Then said Gullrönd,
Guiki's daughter:
"Little canst thou, my fosterer,
wise as thou art,
with a young wife
fittingly talk."
The king's body she forbade
to be longer hidden.

13. She snatched the sheet
from Sigurd's corse,
and turned his cheek
towards his wife's knees:
"Behold thy loved one,
lay thy mouth to his lip,
as if thou wouldst embrace
the living prince."

14. Gudrún upon him
cast one look:
she saw the prince's locks
dripping with blood,
the chief's sparking eyes

closed in death,
his kingly breast
cleft by the sword.

15. Then sank down Gudrún
back on her pillow,
her head-gear was loosed,
her cheeks grew red,
and a flood of tears
fell to her knees.

16. Then wept Gudrún,
Giuki's daughter,
so that the tears
spontaneously flowed,
and at the same time screamed
the geese in the court,
the noble birds,
which the lady owned.

17. Then spake Gullrönd
Giuki's daughter:
"Your loves I know
were the most ardent
among living beings
upon earth:
thou hadst delight nowhere,
sister mine!
save with Sigurd."

18. Then said Gudrún,
Giuki's daughter:
"Such was my Sigurd
among Giuki's sons,
as is the garlick
out from the grass which grows,
or a bright stone
on a thread drawn,
a precious gem
on kings.

19. I also seemed
to the prince's warriors
higher than any
of Herian's Dísir;
now I am as little
as the leaf oft is
in the storm-winds,
after the chieftain's death.

20. Sitting I miss,
and in my bed,
my dearest friend.
Giuki's sons have caused,
Giuki's sons have caused
my affliction,
and their sister's
tears of anguish.

21. So ye desolate
the people's land,
as ye have kept
your sworn oaths.
Gunnar! thou wilt not
the gold enjoy;
those rings will
be thy bane,
for the oaths thou
to Sigurd gavest.

22. Oft in the mansion was
the greater mirth,
when my Sigurd
Grani saddled,
and Brynhild
they went to woo,
that witch accursed,
in an evil hour!"

23. Then said Brynhild,
Budli's daughter:
"May the hag lack
spouse and children,

who thee, Gudrún!
has caused to weep,
and this morning
given the runes of speech!"[1]

24. Then said Gullrönd,
Giuki's daughter:
"Cease, thou loathed of all!
from those words.
The evil destiny of princes
thou hast ever been;
thee every billow drives
of an evil nature;
thou sore affliction
of seven kings,
the greatest bane of friendship
among women!"

25. Then said Brynhild,
Budli's daughter:
"Atli my brother,
Budli's offspring,
is the sole cause
of all the evil;

26. When in the hall
of the Hunnish folk,
with the king we beheld
the fire of the serpent's bed.[2]
Of that journey,
I have paid the penalty,
that sight
I have ever rued."

27. She by a column stood,
the wood violently clasped.
From the eyes of Brynhild,
Budli's daughter,
fire gleamed forth;

---

1. Power of speech.
2. A periphrasis of gold.

> venom she snorted,
> when she beheld
> the wounds of Sigurd.

Gudrún then went away to the forest and deserts, and travelled to Denmark, where she stayed seven half-years with Thora, Hakon's daughter. Brynhild would not outlive Sigurd. She caused her eight thralls and five female slaves to be killed, and then slew herself with a sword, as it is related in the *Sigurðarkviða in Skemma (the Short Lay of Sigurd)*.

Helreið Brynhildar: Brynhild's Hel-ride.

After Brynhild's death two piles were made, one for Sigurd, which was the first burnt; but Brynhild was burnt afterwards, and she was in a chariot, which was hung with precious tapestry; so that it was said that Brynhild drove in a chariot on the way to Hel, and passed through a place: in which a giantess dwelt. The giantess said:

1. "Thou shalt not
pass through
my stone-supported
dwelling-place.
Better had it beseemed thee
to work broidery,
than to seek after
another's husband.

2. Why dost thou,
vagrant woman!
from Valland,
my dwelling visit?
Thou hast, golden dame!
if thou desirest to know,
gentle one! from thy hands
washed human blood."

Brynhild
3. "Upbraid me not,
woman of the rock!
although I have
in warfare been.
Of us, I trow,
I shall the better seem,
wherever men
our conditions know."

Giantess
4. "Thou, Brynhild!
Budli's daughter!
wast in evil hour
born in the world;
thou hast been the bane
of Giuki's children,
and their happy
house subverted."

Brynhild
5. "From my chariot I
will truly tell thee,
thou witless crone!
if thou desirest to know,
how Giuki's heirs
made me both
lovelorn
and perjured.

6. The bold-hearted king[1]
caused the garbs
of us eight sisters
under an oak to be borne.
Twelve years old was I,
if thou desirest to know,
when to the youthful king
oaths I gave.

7. By all in Hlymdalir
I was called
Hild with the helm,
by all who knew me.

8. Then caused I next,
in the Gothic realm,
the old Hiálmgunnar
to Hel to journey:
I gave victory to

---

1. By depriving them of swan-plumage, for they were Valkyriur like the wives of Völund and his brothers, Agnar reduced them under his subjection.

the youthful
brother of Öda,
whereat Odin became
hostile to me.

9. He with shields encompassed me,
red and white,
in Skatalund;
their surfaces enclosed me;
him he ordained
my sleep to break,
who in no place
could be made to fear.

10. He made around my hall,
towards the south,
towering burn
the destroyer of all wood:
then bade that man only
over it to ride,
who me the gold should bring,
that under Fafnir lay.

11. On Grani rode the chief,
the gold-disperser,
to where my foster-father
ruled o'er the dwellings.
He alone seemed there
to all superior,
the Danish warrior,
of the court.

12. We slept and were content
in the same bed,
as if he had
my born brother been;
neither of us might
on the other,
for eight nights,
lay a hand.

13. Reproached me Gudrún,
Giuki's daughter,
that I had slept
in Sigurd's arms;
then was I made aware
of what I fain would not,
that they had deceived me,
when a mate I took.

14. To calamities
all too lasting
men and women ever will
be while living born.
We two shall now,
Sigurd and I,
pass our life together.
Sink thou of giant-kind!"

Drap Niflunga: The Slaughter of the Niflungs.

Gunnar and Högni then took all the gold, Fafnir's heritage. Dissension prevailed afterwards between the Giúkungs and Atli. He charged them with being the cause of Brynhild's death. By way of reconciliation, it was agreed that they should give him Gudrún in marriage, to whom they administered an oblivious potion, before she would consent to espouse Atli. Atli had two sons, Erp and Eitil, but Svanhild was the daughter of Sigurd and Gudrún. King Atli invited gunnar and Högni to his residence, and sent to them Vingi, or Knefröd. Gudrún was aware of the treachery, and sent them word in runes not to come; and to Högni, as a token, she sent the ring Andvaranaut, in which she had tied some wolf's hair. Gunnar had sought the hand of Oddrún, Atli's sister, but did not obtain it. He then married Glaumvör, and Högni took Kostbera to wife. Their sons were Sólar, Snævar, and Giúki. When the Giúkungs came to Atli, Gudrún besought his sons to intercede for their lives, but they would not. The heart of Högni was cut out, and Gunnar was cast into a pen of serpents. He struck his harp and lulled the serpents, but an adder stung him in the liver.

Guðrúnarkviða Önnur: The Second Lay of Gudrún

King Theodric was with Atli, and had there lost the greater number of his men. Theodric and Gudrún mutually bewailed their afflictions. She related to him and said:

1. A maid above all maids I was;
my mother reared me
bright in her bower;
my brothers I much loved,
until me Giúki,
with gold adorned,
with gold adorned,
to Sigurd gave.

2. Such as Sigurd
above Giúki's sons,
as the green leek is,
springing from the grass,
or the high-limbed hart
above the savage beasts,
or the gleed-red gold
above grey silver.

3. Until my brothers
the possession grudged me
of a consort
to all superior.
They could not sleep,
nor on affairs deliberate,
before they Sigurd
had caused to die.

4. Grani to the assembly ran,
his tramp was to be heard;
but Sigurd then
himself came not.
All the saddle-beasts
were splashed with blood,
and with sweating faint,
from the murderers.

5. Weeping I went
to talk to Grani,
with humid cheeks,
I prayed the steed to tell:
then Grani shuddered,
in the grass bowed down his head.
The steed knew
that his master was no more.

6. Long I wandered,
long was my mind distracted,
ere of the people's guardian
I inquired for my king.

7. Gunnar hung his head,
but Högni told me
of Sigurd's cruel death.
"Beyond the river
slaughtered lies
Guthorm's murderer,
and to the wolves given.

8. Yonder beyond Sigurd,
towards the south,
there thou wilt hear
the ravens croak,
the eagles scream,
in their feast exulting;
the wolves howling
round thy consort."

9. "Why wilt thou, Högni!
to a joyless being
such miseries recount?
May thy heart by ravens
be torn and scattered
over the wide world,
rather than thou shouldst
walk with men."

10. Högni answered,
for once cast down,
from his cheerful mood
by intense trouble:
"Gudrún! thou wouldst have
greater cause to weep,
if the ravens
should tear my heart."

11. Alone I turned
from that interview
to the wolves'
scattered leavings.
No sigh I uttered,
nor with my hands beat,
nor wailed,
as other women,
when I heart-broken sat
by Sigurd.

12. Night seemed to me
of blackest darkness,
when I sorrowing sat
by Sigurd.
Better by far
it seemed to me
had the wolves
taken my life,
or I had been burnt
as a birchen tree.

13. From the fell I journeyed
five long days and nights,
until the lofty hall
of Hálf I recognized.
Seven half-years
I with Thora stayed,
Hákon's daughter,
in Denmark.

14. She for my solace
wrought in gold
southern halls,
and Danish swans.

15. We had in pictures
the game of warriors,
and in handiworks
a prince's nobles;
red shields,
Hunnish heroes,
a sworded host, a helmed host,
a prince's following.

16. Sigmund's ships
from the land sailing,
with gilded heads,
and carved prows.
We on our canvas wrought
how Sigar and Siggeir
both contended
southward in Fyen.

17. When Grimhild,
the Gothic woman,
heard how greatly
I was affected,
she cast aside her needlework,
and her sons called
oft and earnestly,
that she might know,
who for her son would
their sister compensate,
or for her consort slain
the blood-fine pay?

18. Gunnar was ready
gold to offer,
for the injuries to atone,
and Högni also.
****
****

She then inquired
who would go
the steeds to saddle,
the chariot to drive,
on horseback ride,
the hawk let fly,
arrows shoot
from the yew bow?

19. Valdar and the Danes
with Jarizleif,
Eymód the third
with Jarizkar,
then entered,
to princes like.
Red mantles had
the Langbard's men,
corslets ornamented,
towering helms;
girded they were with falchions,
brown were their locks.

20. For me each one would choose
precious gifts,
precious gifts,
and to my heart would speak,
if for my many woes
they might
gain my confidence,
and I would in them trust.

21. Grimhild to me brought
a potion to drink
cold and bitter,
that I my injuries might forget;
it was mingled
with Urd's power,
with cold sea-water,
and with Són's blood.

22. In that horn were
characters of every kind
graven and red-hued;
nor could I comprehend them:
the long lyng-fish[1]
of the Haddings' land,
an uncut ear of corn:
the wild-beasts' entrance.

23. In that potion were
many ills together,
a herb from every wood,
and the acorn,
the fire-stead's dew,[2]
entrails of offerings,
swine's liver seethed;
for that deadens strife.

24. And then I forgot,
when I had taken it,
all the king's words
in the hall spoken.
There to my feet
three kings came,
before she herself
sought to speak with me.

25. "Gudrún! I will give thee
gold to possess,
of all the riches much
of thy dead father;
rings of red gold,
Hlödver's halls,
all the hangings
left by the fallen king.

---

1. That is the long fish of the heath, or ling, a snake or serpent.
2. Soot.

26. Hunnish maids,
those who weave tapestry,
and in bright gold work,
so that I may delight thee.
Over Budli's wealth
thou alone shalt rule,
adorned with gold,
and given to Atli."

27. "I will not
have any man,
nor Brynhild's
brother marry:
it beseems me not
with Budli's son
to increase a race,
or life enjoy."

28. "Take care not to pay
the chiefs with hate;
for 'tis we who have
been the aggressors:
so shouldst thou act
as if yet lived
Sigurd and Sigmund,
if sons thou bearest."

29. "Grimhild! I cannot
in mirth indulge,
nor, for my hero's sake,
cherish a hope,
since the bloodthirsty (wolf and) raven
have together
cruelly drunk
my Sigurd's heart's blood."

30. "Him[3] of all
I have found to be
a king of noblest race,
and in much most excellent:
him shalt thou have
until age lays thee low,
or mateless be,
if him thou wilt not take."

31. "Cease to offer
that cup of ills
so pertinaciously,
that race to me:
he will Gunnar's
destruction perpetrate,
and will cut out
Högni's heart.
I will not cease
until the exulting
strife-exciter's life
I shall have taken."

32. Weeping Grimhild
caught the words,
by which to her sons
Gudrún forboded evil,
and to her kindred
dire misfortunes.
"Lands I will also give thee,
people and followers,
Vinbiörg and Valbiörg,
if thou wilt accept them;
for life possess them,
and be happy, daughter!"

33. "Him then I will choose,
among the kings,
and from my relatives
reluctantly receive him.
Never will he be to me

---

3. Atli: Grimhild speaks.

a welcome consort,
nor my brothers' bale
a protection to our sons."

34. Forthwith on horseback was
each warrior to be seen;
but the Walish women
were in chariots placed.
For seven days
o'er a cold land we rode;
but the second seven,
we beat the waves;
and the third seven,
we reached dry land.

35. There the gate-wards
of the lofty burgh
the latticed entrance opened,
ere the court we entered.
****
****

36. Atli waked me,
but I seemed to be
full of evil thoughts,
for my kinsmen's death.

37. "So me just now[4]
have the Norns waked,
a grateful interpretation
I fain would have.
Methought that thou, Gudrún!
Giuki's daughter!
with a treacherous sword
didst pierce me through."

38. "Fire it forebodes,[5]
when one of iron dreams,
arrogance and pleasure,

---

4. Atli speaks.
5. Gudrun answers.

a woman's anger.
Against evil
I will go burn thee,
cure and medicate thee,
although to me thou art hateful."

39. "Seemed to me here in the garden[6]
that young shoots had fallen,
which I wished
to let grow:
torn up with their roots
reddened with blood,
to table were they brought,
and offered me to eat.

40. Seemed to me that hawks
flew from my hand,
lacking their quarry,
to the house of woes;
seemed to me I ate
their hearts with honey
swollen with blood,
with sorrowing mind.

41. Seemed to me from my hand
whelps I let slip;
lacking cause of joy,
both of them howled:
seemed to me their bodies
became dead carcases:
of the carrion
I was compelled to eat."

42. "There will warriors[7]
round thy couch converse,
and of the white-locked ones
take off the head;
death-doomed they are
within a few nights,
a little ere day:
thy court will eat of them."

---

6. Atli speaks.
7. Gudrun answers.

43. "Lie down I would not,[8]
nor sleep after,
obstinate in my fate
That I will execute!"

---

8. Atli speaks.

Guðrunarkviða Þriðja: The Third Lay of Gudrún

Atli had a serving-woman named Herkia[1], who had been his concubine. She informed Atli that she had seen Thiodrek and Gudrún together; whereat Atli was much afflicted. Then Gudrún said:

1. What ails thee ever, Atli!
Budli's son!
Hast thou sorrow in thy heart?
Why never laughest thou?
To thy jarls it would
seem more desirable,
that thou with men wouldst talk,
and on me wouldst look.

Atli
2. It grieves me, Gudrún!
Giuki's daughter!
that in my palace here,
Herkia has said,
that thou and Thiodrek have
under one covering slept,
and wantonly
been in the linen wrapt.

Gudrún
3. For all this charge
I will give my oaths
by the white
sacred stone,
that with me and Thiodrek
nothing has passed,
which to man and wife
only belongs;

---

1. Herkia, the Erka or Helche of the German tradition, who here appears as a slave or servant, is, according to that tradition, the queen of Etzel or Atli, who did not marry Kreimhilt (Gudrun) until after her death. The falsification of the story, the pitiful subordinate part acted by Thiodrek, the perfect silence of all the other poems on this event, and the ordeal of the cauldron, sufficiently show that the poem is a later composition. P. E. Muller (II., p. 319) ascribes it to Sæmund himself.

4. Save that I embraced
the prince of armies,
the honoured king,
a single time.
Other were
our cogitations,
when sorrowful we two
sat to converse.

5. Hither came Thiodrek,
with thirty warriors;
now there lives not one
of those thirty men.
Surround me with thy brothers,
and with mailed warriors;
surround me with all
thy noblest kinsmen.

6. Send to Saxi
the Southmen's prince,
he can hallow
the boiling cauldron."

7. Seven hundred men
entered the hall,
ere in the cauldron
the queen dipt her hand.

8. "Now Gunnar comes not,
nor call I Högni:
I shall not see again
my loved brothers:
with his sword would Högni
such wrong avenge:
now I must myself
purify from crime."

9. She to the bottom plunged
her snow-white hand,
and up she drew
the precious stones.[2]
"See now, ye men!
I am proved guiltless
in holy wise,
boil the vessel as it may."

10. Laughed then Atli's
heart within his breast,
when he unscathed beheld
the hands of Gudrún.
"Now must Herkia
to the cauldron go,
she who Gudrún
had hoped to injure."
No one has misery seen
who saw not that,
how the hand there
of Herkia was burnt.
They then the woman led
to a foul slough.[3]
So were Gudrún's
wrongs avenged.

---

2. The iarknastein of the original was a milk-white opal.
3. This punishment was known to the old Germans.

Oddrúnargrátr: Oddrún's Lament

There was a King named Heidrek, who had a daughter named Borgný. Her lover was named Vilmund. She could not give birth to a child until Oddrún, Atli's sister, came. She had been the beloved of Gunnar, Giuki's son. Of this story it is here sung:

    1. I have heard tell,
    in ancient storied
    how a damsel came
    to the eastern land:
    no one was able,
    on the face of earth,
    help to afford
    to Heidrek's daughter.

    2. When Oddrún,
    Atli's sister, heard
    that the damsel
    had great pains,
    from the stall she led
    her well-bridled steed,
    and on the swart one
    the saddle laid.

    3. She the horse made run
    on the smooth, dusty way,
    until she came
    to where a high hall stood.
    She the saddle snatched
    from the hungry steed,
    and in she went
    along the court,
    and these words
    first of all she uttered:

    4. "What is most noteworthy
    in this country?
    or what most desirable
    in the Hunnish land?"

Borgný
5. Here lies Borgný
with pains o'erwhlemed,
thy friend, Oddrún!
See if thou canst help her.

Oddrún
6. What chieftain has on thee
brought this dishonour?
Why so acute
are Borgný's pains?

Borgný
7. Vilmund is named
the falcon-bearers' friend:
he the damsel wrapt
in a warm coverlet
five whole winters,
so that from her father she was hidden.

8. They, I ween, spoke not
more than this:
kindly she went to sit
at the damsel's knee.
Vehemently sang Oddrún,
fervently sang Oddrún
songs of power
over Borgný.

9. A girl and boy might then
tread the mould-way,
gentle babes,
born of Högni's bane.
Then began to speak
the death-sick damsel,
who before had
no word uttered.

10. "So may thee help
the benignant genii,
Frigg and Freyja,
and other gods besides,
as thou hast from me
peril removed!"

11. "I was not inclined
to give thee help,
because thou never wast
of succour worthy:
I vowed, and have performed
what I then said
when the princes
the heritage divided,
that I would ever
help afford."

Borgný
12. Mad art thou, Oddrún!
and hast lost thy wits,
when in hostile spirit
most of thy words thou utterest;
for I have been thy companion
upon the earth,
as if from brothers
we both were born.

Oddrún
13. I remember yet
what thou one evening saidst,
when I for Gunnar,
a compotation made.
Such a case, saidst thou,
would not thenceforth happen
to any maiden,
save to me alone."

14. Then sat down
the sorrowing lady
to tell her woes,
for her great grief:

15. "I was nurtured
in the kingly hall,
I was the joy of many
in the council of men.
Life I enjoyed,
and my father's wealth,
five winters only,
while my father lived.

16. These last words
the noble-hearted king
strove to utter,
ere he departed hence.

17. He bade me be endowed
with ruddy gold,
and in the south be given
to Grimhild's son.
He said no maiden
could more excellent
in the world be born,
if fate willed it not otherwise.

18. Brynhild in her bower
was occupied to broidery:
she had people
and lands around her.
Earth slumbered,
and the heavens above,
when Fafnir's bane
her burgh first saw.

19. Then was conflict waged
with the Walish sword,
and the burgh taken
which Brynhild owned.
It was not long
which was not surprising
ere she discovered
all those frauds.

20. These she caused
cruelly to be avenged,
so that we all have
great afflictions.
Know it will be
through every land of men,
that she caused herself to die
with Sigurd.

21. But I for Gunnar,
rings' dispenser,
love conceived,
such as Brynhild should.
But he Brynhild bade
a helmet take,
said she a Valkyria
should become.

22. They forthwith offered[1]
ruddy rings
to my brother,
and indemnity not small.
He[2] besides offered for me
fifteen vills,
and the load of Grani's sides,
if he would accept them.

23. But Atli said
he never would
a marriage-gift receive
from Giuki's son.
Still we could not
our loves withstand,
but I my head must lay
upon the ring-breaker.

---

1. For Brynhild's death.
2. Gunnar.

24. Many things said
my relations;
declared they had surprised us
both together;
but Atli said,
that I would not
crime commit,
nor scandal perpetrate.
But such should no one
ever deny,
when love has part.

25. Atli sent
his emissaries
about the Murk-wood,
that he might prove me;
and they came to where
they ought not to have come,
to where we had
one couch prepared.

26. To the men we offered
red-gold rings,
that they it might not
to Atli tell;
but they forthwith
hastened home,
and it quickly
to Atli told.

27. But they from Gudrún
carefully concealed it,
yet rather by half
she should have known it.[3]
****
****

28. A sound was heard
of gold-shod hoofs,
when into the court
rode Giuki's heirs.

3. From here the narrative appears to be very fragmentary.

****
****
Of Högni they
the heart cut out,
and into a serpent-pen
the other cast.
****
****

29. I had gone
yet once again
to Geirmund,
to prepare a banquet.
****
****
****

The brave king began[4]
the harp to sound;
for the prince of noble race
hoped that I
to his aid might come.

30. I it heard
from Hlesey,
how of trouble there
the harp-strings sang.

31. I my thralls bade
all be ready;
I the prince's
life would save.
The vessel we let float
past the forest,[5]
until I saw
all Atli's courts.

---

    4. Gunnar while in the serpent-pen.
    5. For *lund (forest, wood)*, which is the reading of the MSS., the Copenhagen editor favours the correction to sund (a *sound* or *straight, the Sound*)?

32. Then came Atli's
miserable mother
crawling forth:
may she perish!
she Gunnar
pierced to the heart;
so that the hero
I could not save.

33. Oftentimes I wonder,
woman gold-adorned![6]
how I after can
life retain;
for I seemed
the formidable
sword-dispenser
as myself to love:

34. Thou sitst and listenest,
while I recount to thee
many and evil fate,
my own and theirs."
Each one lives
as he best may.
Now is ended
Oddrún's lament.

---

6. Borgny.

Atlakviða: The Lay of Atli

Gudrún, Giuki's daughter, avenged her brothers, as is well known. She first killed Atli's sons, and afterwards Atli himself, and burnt the palace with all the household. On these events was this lay composed.

1. Atli sent riding
a messenger to Gunnar,
a crafty man,
Knefrud was his name.
To Giuki's courts he came,
and to Gunnar's hall,
to the seats of state,[1]
and the glad potation:

2. There drank the courtiers
wine in their Valhall
but the guileful ones[2] silence kept
the Huns' wrath they[3] feared.
Then said Knefrud,
with chilling voice:
the southern warrior
on a high bench sat

3. "Atli has sent me hither
on his errand riding
on a bit-griping steed,
through the unknown Myrkwood,
to pray you, Gunnar!
that to his bench ye come,
with helms of state,
Atli's home to visit.

---

1. The ephithet *aringreypr* is applied both to benches and helmets (see Strophes 3 and 16). Its meaning is doubtful: it has been rendered *iron-bound, brass-bound, hearth-encircling, curved like an eagle's beak*, etc. Benches and helmets of ceremony are evidently intended, probably ornamented with brass-work or figures of eagles. But to whichever substantive applied, I take its meaning to be the same.
2. The messengers of Atli.
3. The Giukings.

4. Shields ye there can choose,
and smooth-shaven spears,
gold-red helms,
and of Huns a multitude,
silver-gilt saddle-cloths,
sarks gory-red,
the dart's obstruction,
and bit-griping steeds.

5. The plain he will also give you,
the broad Gnítaheid,
whistling javelins,
and gilded prows,
vast treasures,
and Danp's towns,
with that famed forest,
which men the Murkwood call."

6. Gunnar his head then turned,
and to Högni said:
"What counselest thou, bold warrior?"
now suchlike we hear?
Of no gold I knew
on Gníta's heath,
to which we possess not
other equal.

7. Seven halls have we
filled with swords,
of each of which
the hilt is gold.
My horse I know the best,
and my sword the keenest;
my bow adorns my seat,
my corslets are of gold,
my helm and shield the brightest,
brought from the hall of Kiar:
mine alone are better
than all the Hunnish ones.

8. What thinkest thou the woman[4] means,
by sending us a ring
in a wolf's clothing wrapt?
I think that she caution enjoins.
Wolf's hair I found
twined in the red-gold ring:
wolfish is the way
we on our errand ride."

9. No sons persuaded Gunnar,
nor other kinsman,
interpreters nor counsellors,
nor those who potent were.
Then spake Gunnar,
as beseemed a king,
great in his mead-hall,
from his large soul:

10. "Rise now up, Fiörnir!
let along the benches pass
the golden cups of heroes,
from the attendants' hands.

11. The wolf shall rule
the Niflungs' heritage,
O bearded sages!
if Gunnar perish;
black-coated bears
earth's fruit tear with their teeth,
to the dogs' delight,
if Gunnar come not back."

12. Honoured men,
weeping led
the land's ruler
from the Huns' court.
Then said Högni's
youthful heir:
"Go now, prudent and prosperous,
whither your wishes lead."

---

4. Gudrun: she had sent, by Atli's messengers, a ring to her brothers, as a warning, in which a wolf's hair was entwined, together with a note in runes, which were falsified by Vingi.

13. The warriors made
their bit-griping steeds
over the mountains fly,
through the unknown Murkwood.
The whole Hunnish forest trembled
where'er the warriors rode;
over the shrubless, all-green plains
they sped.

14. Atli's land they saw,
and the high watch-towers;
Bikki's people stood
on that lofty fortress;
the south people's hall
was round with benches set,
with well-bound bucklers,
and white shields,
the javelin's obstruction.
There Atli drank
wine in his Valhall:
his guards sat without,
Gunnar and his men to watch,
lest they there should come
with yelling dart,
to excite their prince to conflict.

15. Their sister forthwith saw,
when the hall they had entered,
her brothers both
beer had she little drunken
"Betrayed art thou now Gunnar!
though strong, how wilt thou contend
with the Huns' deadly wiles?
Go quickly from this hall!

16. Better hadst thou, Gunnar!
in corslet come,
than with helm of state,
to see the home of Atli;
thou in the saddle wouldst have sat
whole sun-bright days,
and o'er the pallid dead

let the Norns weep,
the Hunnish shield-maids
misery suffer;
but Atli himself thou shouldst
into the serpent-pen have cast;
but now the serpent-pen
is for you two reserved."

17. "Sister! 'tis now too late
the Niflungs to assemble,
long 'tis to seek
the aid of men,
of valiant heroes,
over the rugged fells of Rhine."

18. Then the Burgundians' friends[5]
Gunnar seized,
in fetters laid,
and him fast bound.

19. Högni hewed down seven,
with the keen sword,
but the eighth he thrust
into the raging fire.
So should a valiant man
defend himself from foes.

20 Högni had Gunnar's
hands[6] protected.
The bold chief they asked,
if the Goths' lord
would with gold
his life redeem?
****
****

21. "Högnis heart
in my hand shall lie,
cut bloody from the breast
of the valiant chief,

---

5. Atli's men.
6. That is Gunnar himself.

the king's son,
with a dull-edged knife."
****
****

They the heart cut out
from Hialli's breast;
on a dish bleeding laid it,
and to Gunnar bare.

23. Then said Gunnar,
lord of men:
"Here have I the heart
of the timid Hialli,
unlike the heart
of the bold Högni;
for much it trembles
as in the dish it lies:
it trembled more by half,
while in his breast it lay."

24. Högni laughed,
when to his heart they cut
the living crest-crasher;
no lament uttered he.
All bleeding on a dish they laid it,
and it to Gunnar bare.

25. Calmly said Gunnar,
the warrior Niflung:
"Here have I the heart
of the bold Högni,
unlike the heart
of the timid Hialli;
for it little trembles,
as in the dish it lies:
it trembled less,
while in his breast it lay.

26. So far shalt thou, Atli!
be from the eyes of men
as thou wilt
from the treasures be.
In my power alone
is all the hidden
Niflungs' gold,
now that Högni lives not.

27. Ever was I wavering,
while we both lived;
now am I so no longer,
as I alone survive.
Rhine shall possess
men's baleful metal,
the mighty stream, the Ás-known
Niflungs' heritage.
In the rolling water
the choice rings shall glitter,
rather than on the hands
of the Huns' children shine.

28. Drive your wheel-chariots,
the captive is now in bonds."

29. Atli the mighty,
their sister's husband,
rode with resounding steeds,
with strife-thorns[7] surrounded.
Gudrún perceived
the heroes' peril
she from tears refrained,
on entering the hall of tumult.

30. "So be it with thee, Atli!
as toward Gunnar thou hast held
the oft-sworn oaths,
formerly taken
by the southward verging sun,
and by Sigtý's hill,

---

7. Spears.

the secluded bed of rest,
and by Ullr's ring."
Yet thence the more
did the bit-shaker[8]
the treasure's guardian,
the warrior chief,
drag to death.

31. The living prince
then did a host of men
into a pen cast down,
which was within
with serpents over-crawled.
But Gunnar there alone
a harp in wrathful mood
with his hand struck:
the strings resounded.
So should a daring chief,
a ring-dispenser,
gold from men withhold.

32. Atli turned
his brass-shod[9] steed,
his home to re-visit,
back from the murder.
Din was in the court
with horses thronged,
men's weapon-song,
from the heath they were come.

33. Out then went Gudrún,
Atli to meet,
with a golden cup to do
her duty to the king.
"Thou canst, o king!
joyful in thy hall
receive from Gudrún
the arms of the departed."

---

8. The horse.
9. The original word is *eyrskan*, a word of doubtful signification.

34. The drinking-cups of Atli
groaned with wine heavy,
when in the hall together
the Huns were counted.
Long-bearded, bold,
the warriors entered.

35. Hastened the bright-faced dame
to bear their potions to them,
the wondrous lady to the chiefs;
and reluctantly to the pallid Atli
the festal dainties offered,
and uttered words of hate.

36. "Thou, swords' dispenser! hast
thy two sons' hearts,
slaughter-gory,
with honey eaten.
I resolved that thou, bold chief!
shouldst of a human dish
eat at thy feasting,
and to the place of honour send it.

37. Henceforth thou wilt not
to thy knees call
Erp and Eitil,
joyous with beer the two:
thou wilt not henceforth see them
from thy middle seat,
gold-dispersing,
javelins shafting,
manes clipping,
or horses urging."

38. Uproar was on the benches,
portentous the cry of men,
noise beneath the costly hangings.
The children of the Huns wept,
all wept save Gudrún,
who never wept,
or for her bear-fierce brothers,
or her dear sons,

young, simple,
whom she had borne to Atli.

39. Gold scattered
the swan-fair dame;
with ruddy rings
the household gifted.
Fate she let ripen,
but the bright gold flow.
The woman spared not
the treasure-houses.

40. Atli incautious had
himself drunk weary;
weapon he had none,
nor was 'gainst Gudrún guarded.
Oft had their sport been better,
when they lovingly
embraced each other
before the nobles.

41. With the sword's point she gave
the bed of blood to drink
with death-bent hand,
and the dogs loosed,
out at the hall-door drove them,
and the lady wakened
the household with burning brand.
That vengeance she for her brothers took.

42. To fire she then gave all
that were therein,
and from her brothers' murder
were from the dark den[10] returned.
The old structures fell,
the treasure-houses smoked,
the Budlungs' dwelling.
Burnt too were the shield-maids
within, their lives cut short;
in the raging fire they sank.

---

10. The serpent-pen.

43. Of this enough is said.
No such woman will henceforth
arms again bear,
to avenge her brothers.
That bright woman had
to three kings of men
the death-doom borne,
before she died.

Yet more clearly is this told in *Atlamálum inum Groenlenzkum (the Groenland lay of Atli).*

Atlamál in Groenlenzku

The Groenland Lay of Atli

1. Of those misdeeds men have heard tell,
when warriors of old
a compact made,
which by pledges they confirmed,
a secret consultation held:
terrible it was to them after,
and to Giuki's sons likewise,
who were betrayed.

2. The warriors' fate ripened,
they were death-doomed:
ill advised was Atli,
though he possessed sagacity:
he felled a mighty column,
strove hardly against himself;
with speed he messengers despatched,
that his wife's brothers should come quickly.

3. Wise was the house-dame,
prudently she thought;
the words in order she had heard,
that in secret they had said:
the sage lady was at a loss:
fain would she help them:
they[1] o'er the sea must sail,
but she herself could not go.

4. Runes she graved,
Vingi them falsified,
before he gave them from him;
of ill he was the bearer.
Then departed
Atli's messengers,
through the branched firth,
for where the bold warriors dwelt.

---

1. The messengers.

5. They with beer were cheered,
and fires they kindled,
naught thought they of guile,
when they were come;
they the gifts accepted,
which the prince sent them,
and of no evil thought.

6. Then came Kostbera,
she was Högni's wife,
a woman greatly cautious,
and them both greeted.
Glad was also Glaumvör,
Gunnar's consort,
the prudent dame her duty forgot not,
she to the guests' need attended.

7. Högni they home invited,
if he would be pleased to go.
Treachery was manifest,
had they but reflected!
Gunnar then promised,
if only Högni would,
but Högni refused
what the other proposed.

8. The noble dames bore mead,
of many things there was abundance,
many horns passed round,
until it seemed they had full drunken.

9. The household prepared their couches,
as to them seemed best.
Cunning was Kostbera,
she could runes interpret;
she the letters read
by the bright fire;
her tongue she had to guard
between both her gums
so perverted were they,
it was difficult to understand them.

10. To their bed they went,
she and Högni.
The gentle lady dreamed,
and concealed it not,
to the prince wisely said it
as soon as she awoke.

11. "From home thou art going, Högni!
give ear to counsel;
few are fully prudent:
go another time.

12. I have the runes interpreted,
which thy sister graved:
that fair dame has not
this time invited thee.
At one thing I wonder most,
I cannot even conceive,
why so wise a woman
so confusedly should grave;
for it is so set down
as if it intimated
death to you both,
if you should straightway come.
Either she has left out a letter,
or others are the cause. [2]

13. "They are," said Högni, "all suspicious;
I have no knowledge of them,
nor will I into it inquire,
unless we have to make requital.
The king will gift us
with gleed-red gold.
I never fear,
though we may hear of terror."

---

[2] It would seem that the original runes, as graved by Gudrun, had not been so completely erased as to leave no traces of them; but that they were still sufficiently legible to enable Kostbera to ascertain the real purport of the communication.

14. "Tottering ye will go,
if thitherward ye tend.
No kind entertainment there
will ye at this time find.
Högni! I have dreamed,
I will not conceal it:
in an evil hour ye will go,
or so at least I fear.

15. Methought thy coverlet was
with fire consumed;
that the towering flame
rushed through my dwelling."

Högni
16. "Here lie linen cloths,
which thou hadst little noticed:
these will quickly burn
where thou the coverlet sawest."

Kostbera
17. "Methought a bear came in,
and broke down the columns;
and so his talons shook,
that we were terror-stricken;
by his mouth held many of us,
so that we were helpless:
there, too, was a din
far from little."

Högni
18. "A tempest there will be
furious and sudden:
the white bear thou sawest
will be a storm from the east."

Kostbera
19. "Methought an eagle flew herein,
all through the house:
that will largely concern us.
He sprinkled all with blood:
from his threats I thought it

to be the 'ham'[3] of Atli."

Högni
20. "We often slaughter largely,
and then red we see:
often are oxen meant,
when we of eagles dream.
Sound is the heart of Atli,
dream thou as thou mayest."
With this they ended:
all speeches have an end.
****

21. The high-born awoke,
there the like befell:
Glaumvör had perceived
that her dreams were ill-boding,
adverse to Gunnar's
going to and fro.

22. "Methought a gallows was for thee erected,[4]
thou wentest to be hanged,
that serpents ate thee,
that I inter'd thee living,
that the Powers' dissolution came
Divine thou what that portends.

23. Methought a bloody glave
from thy sark was drawn
ill 'tis such a dream
to a consort to recount
methought a lance was
thrust through thy middle:
wolves howled
on every side."

---

3. *Ham* (*hamr*. fem. *hamingja*) a gaurdian angel, an attendant spirit.
4. Here a gallows in our sense of the word, but usually a stake on a scaffold, to which the condemned to a death of torture was bound hand and foot.

Gunnar
24. "Where dogs run
they are wont to bark:
oft bodes the bay of dogs
the flight of javelins."

Glaumvör
25. "Methought a river ran herein,
through the whole house,
that it roared violently,
rushed o'er the benches,
brake the feet of you
brothers twain;
nothing the water spared:
something will that portend!

26. Methought dead women
in the night came hither;
not ill-clad were they:
they would choose thee,
forthwith invited thee
to their seats.
I ween thy Dísir
have forsaken thee."

Gunnar
27. "Too late it is to speak,
it is now so resolved;
from the journey we shall not shrink,
as it is decreed to go:
very probable it seems
that our lives will be short."
****

28. When colours were discernible,
those on journey bent
all rose up:
the others fain would stay them.
The five journeyed together,
of 'hús-carls' there were present
twice that number.
It was ill devised

Snævar and Sólar,
they were Högni's sons;
Orkning he was named,
who them accompanied,
a gentle shield-bearer was he,
the brother of Högni's wife.

29. They went fair-appointed,
until the firth them parted:
ever would their wives have stayed them,
they would not be stayed.

30. Glaumvör then spake,
Gunnar's consort,
Vingi she addressed,
as to her seemed fitting:
"I know not whether ye will requite us
as we would:
with treachery came the guest,
if aught of ill betide."

31. Then Vingi swore,
little spared he himself:
"May him the Jötuns have,
if towards you he lies!
the gallows hold him,
if aught against peace he meditates!"

32. Bera took up the word,
she of gentle soul:
"Sail ye prosperous,
and may success attend you:
may it be as I pray,
and it nothing hinder!"

33. Högni answered
he to his kin meant well
"Be of good cheer, ye prudent!
whatever may befall.
Many say the same,
though with great difference;
for many little care
how they depart from home."

34. On each other then they looked
before they parted:
then, I ween, their fates were severed,
and their ways divided.

35. Vigorously they rowed,
their bark was well nigh riven;
backward bending the waves they beat,
ardently plied:
their oar-bands were broken,
the rowlocks shattered.[5]

36. A little after
I will the end relate
they saw the mansion stand
that Budli had possessed.
Loud creaked the latticed gates,
when Högni knocked.

37. Then said Vingi,
what he had better not,
"Go far from the house,
'tis perilous to enter;
I quickly enticed you to perdition;
ye shall forthwith be slain.
With fair words I prayed your coming,
though guile was under them.
But just bide here,
while a gallows I prepare."

38. Högni answered
little thought he of yielding,
or of aught fearful
that was to be proved:
"Think not to frighten us;
try that seldom.
If one word thou addest,
thou wilt thy harm prolong."

---

5. So great was their haste to land.

39. They rushed on Vingi,
and struck him dead,
laid on their axes,
while life within him throbbed.

40. Atli his men assembled,
in their byrnies they issued forth,
went prepared so
that a fence was between them.
Words they bandied,
all with rags boiling:
"Already had we resolved
to take your lives away."

Högni
41. "It looks but ill,
if ye before have counseled:
e'en now ye are unprepared,
and we one have felled,
smitten to death:
one of your host was he."

42. Furious they became,
when those words they heard;
their fingers they stretched forth,
and their bow-strings seized;
sharply shot,
and with shields themselves protected.

43. In then came the tale
of what without was passing;
loud before the hall
they a thrall heard speak.

44. Then incensed was Gudrún,
when the sad news she heard:
adorned with necklaces,
she tore them all asunder;
so hurled the silver,
that the rings in shivers flew.

45. Then she went out,
not gently moved the doors;
went forth void of fear,
and the comers hailed,
turned to the Niflungs:
that was her last greeting,
truth attended it;
more words she said:

46. "I sought by symbols
to prevent your leaving home,
fate may no one resist
and yet must you come hither."
Wisely she asked:
might they not be appeased?
No one consented,
all answered no.

47. Saw then the high-born lady
that a hard game they played;
a deadly deed she meditated,
and her robe dashed aside,
a naked falchion seized,
and her kinsmen's lives defended:
skilful she was in warfare,
where her hand she applied.

48. Giuki's daughter caused
two warriors to fall;
Atli's brother she struck down,
he must thenceforth be borne
so she the conflict managed,
that she his foot struck off.
Another too she smote,
so that he never rose,
to Hel she sent him:
her hand trembled not.

49. A conflict then ensued,
which was widely famed,
but that excelled all else
which Giuki's sons performed.
So 'tis said the Niflungs,
while yet they lived,
with swords maintained the fight,
corslets rent,
helmets hewed,
as their hearts prompted.

50. At morning most they fought,
until mid-day had passed;
all early morn,
and the forenoon,
ere the fight was ended,
the field flowed with blood,
until eighteen had fallen:
Bera's two sons,
and her brother,
had them overcome.

51. Then the fierce Atli spoke,
wroth though he was:
"'Tis ill to look around;
this is long of you.
We were thirty
warlike thanes,
eleven survive:
the chasm is too great.
We were five brothers,
when Budli died;
now has Hel the half,
two lie slain.

52. "A great affinity I obtained,
that I cannot deny,
pernicious woman!
of which I have no benefit:
peace we have seldom had,
since thou among us camest.
Of kinsmen ye have bereft me,
of riches often wronged.
To Hel my sister ye have sent;
that is to me most bitter."

Gudrún
53. "This thou callest to mind, Atli!
but thou so first didst act:
my mother thou didst take,
and for her treasures murder;
my gifted niece with hunger
thou didst cause to perish.
Laughable to me it seems,
when thou sorrows doest recount.
The gods are to be thanked,
that it goes ill with thee."

Atli
54. "Jarls! I exhort you
the sorrow to augment
of that presumptuous woman:
I would fain see it.
Strive so to do,
that Gudrún may lament.
Might I but see
that in her lot she joys not!

55. Take ye Högni,
and with a knife hack him:
cut out his heart:
this ye shall do.
Gunnar the fierce of soul
to a gallows fasten;
do the work thoroughly,
lure up the serpents."

Högni
56. Do as thou listest,
glad I will await it;
stout I shall prove myself:
I have ere now things much harder proved.
Ye had a hindrance
while unscathed we were:
now are we so wounded
that our fate thou mayest command.

57. Beiti spake,
he was Atli's steward
Take we Hialli,
but Högni let us save.
Let us do half the work;
he is death-worthy.
As long as he lives
a slug he will ever be.

58. Terrified was the kettle-watcher
the place no longer held him:
he could be a whiner,
he clomb into every nook:
their conflict was his bane,
as he the penalty must pay;
and the day sad,
when he must from the swine die,
from all good things,
which he had enjoyed.

59. Budli's cook they took,
and the knife brought towards him.
Howled the wretched thrall,
ere the point he felt;
declared that he had time
the gardens to manure,
the vilest offices to do,
if from death he might escape.
Joyful indeed was Hialli,
could he but save his life.

60. Högni all this observed
few so act,
as for a slave to intercede,
that he may escape
"Less 'tis, I say, for me
to play this game myself.
Why shall we here desire
to listen to that screaming?"

61. Hands on the good prince they laid.
Then was no option
for the bold warriors,
the sentence longer to delay.
Then laughed Högni;
heard the sons of day
how he could hold out:
torment he well endured!

62. A harp Gunnar took,
with his foot-branches touched it.
He could so strike it,
that women wept,
and the men sobbed,
who best could hear it.
He the noble queen counseled:
the rafters burst asunder.

63. There died the noble,
at the dawn of day;
at the last they caused
their deeds to live.

64. Atli thought himself great:
over them both he strode,
to the sagacious woman told the evil,
and bitterly reproached her.
"It is now morning, Gudrún!
thy loved ones thou hast lost;
partly thou art the cause
that it has so befallen."

Gudrún
65. Joyful art thou, Atli!
slaughter to announce:
repentance shall await thee,
when thou hast all proved.
That heritage shall be left thee
that I can tell thee
that ill shall never from thee go,
unless I also die.

Atli
66. That I can prevent;
another course I see,
easier by half:
the good we oft reject.
With slaves I will console thee,
with things most precious,
with snow-white silver,
as thou thyself mayest desire.

Gudrún
67. Of that there is no hope;
I will all reject;
atonement I have spurned
for smaller injuries.
Hard I was ever thought,
now will that be aggravated.
I every grudge concealed,
while Högni lived.

68. We were both nurtured
in one house;
many a play we played,
and in the wood grew up;
Grimhild us adorned
with gold and necklaces;
for my brothers' death
never wilt thou indemnify me,
nor ever do
what shall to me seem good.

69. Mens' too great power
women's lot oppresses;
on the knee the hand sinks,
if the arms wither;
the tree inclines,
if its root-fibres are severed.
Now, Atli! thou mayest alone
over all here command.

70. Most unwise it was,
when to this the prince gave credit:
the guild was manifest,
had he been on his guard.
Dissembling then was Gudrún,
against her heart she could speak,
made herself gay appear,
with two shields she played.[6]

71. A banquet she would prepare,
her brothers' funeral feast;
the same would Atli also
for his own do.

72. With this they ended;
the banquet was prepared;
the feasting was
too luxurious.
The woman great of heart was stern,
she warred on Budli's race;
on her spouse she would
cruel vengeance wreak.

73. The young ones she enticed,
and on a block laid them,
the fierce babes were terrified,
and wept not,
to their mother's bosom crept,
asked what was she was going to do.

---

6. She played a double game.

74. "Ask no questions,
both I intend to kill;
long have I desired
to cut short your days."

75. "Slay as thou wilt thy children,
no one hinders it;
thy rage will have short peace,
if thou destroyest us
in our blooming years,
thou desperate woman!"
It fell out accordingly:
she cut the throats of both.

76. Atli oft inquired
whither his boys
were gone to play,
as he nowhere saw them?

Gudrún
77. Over I am resolved to go,
and to Atli tell it.
Grimhild's daughter
will not conceal from thee.
Little glad, Atli! wilt thou be,
when all thou learnest;
great woe didst thou raise up,
when thou my brothers slewest.

78. Very seldom have I slept
since they fell.
Bitterly I threatened thee:
now I have reminded thee.
'It is now morning', saidst thou:
I yet it well remember;
and it now is eve,
when thou the like shalt learn.

79. Thou thy sons hast lost,
as thou least shouldest;
know that their skulls thou
hast had for beer-cups;

thy drink I prepared,
I their red blood have shed.

80. I their hearts took,
and on a spit staked them,
then to thee gave them.
I said they were of calves,
it was long of thee alone
thou didst leave none,
voraciously didst devour,
well didst ply thy teeth.

81. Thy children's fate thou knowest,
few a worse awaits.
I have my part performed,
though in it glory not.

Atli
82. Cruel was thou, Gudrún!
who couldst so act,
with thy children's blood
my drink to mingle.
Thou hast destroyed thy offspring,
as thou least shouldest;
and to myself thou leavest
a short interval from ill.

Gudrún
83. I could still desire
thyself to slay;
rarely too ill
it fares with such a prince.
Thou hast already perpetrated
crimes unexampled among men
of frantic cruelty,
in this world:
now thou hast added
what we have just witnessed.
A great misdeed hast thou committed,
thy death-feast thou hast prepared.

Atli
84. On the pile thou shalt be burnt,
but first be stoned;
then wilt thou have earned
what thou hast ever sought.

Gudrún
85. Tell to thyself such griefs
early to-morrow:
by a fairer death I will
pass to another light.

86. In the same hall they sat,
exchanged hostile thoughts,
bandied words of hate:
each was ill at ease.

87. Hate waxed in a Hniflung,
a great deed he meditated;
to Gudrún he declared
that he was Atli's deadly foe.

88. Into her mind came
Högni's treatment;
happy she him accounted,
if he vengeance wreaked.
Then was Atli slain,
within a little space;
Högni's son him slew,
and Gudrún herself.

89. The bold king spake,
roused up from sleep;
quickly he felt the wounds,
said he no binding needed.
"Tell me most truly
who has slain Budli's son.
I am hardly treated:
of life I have no hope."

Gudrún

90. I, Grimhild's daughter,
will not from thee hide,
that I am the cause
that thy life passes away;
but partly Högni's son,
that thy wounds make thee faint.

Atli

91. To the slaughter thou hast rushed,
although it ill beseemed thee;
'tis bad to circumvent a friend,
who well confided in thee.
Besought I went from home,
to woo thee, Gudrún!

92. A widow thou wast left,
fierce thou was accounted,
which was no falsehood,
as we have proved.
Hither home thou camest,
us a host of men attended;
all was splendid
on our journey.

93. Pomp of all kinds was there,
of illustrious men,
beeves in abundance:
largely we enjoyed them.
Of all things there was plenty
partaken of by many.

94. A marriage gift to my bride I gave,
treasures for her acceptance,
thralls thrice ten,
seven fair female slaves:
in such things was honour;
silver there was yet more.

95. All seemed to thee
as it were naught,
while the lands untouched lay,
which Budli had left me.
So didst thou undermine,
didst allow me nothing to receive.
Thou didst my mother let
often sit weeping:
with heart content I found not
one of my household after.

Gudrún
96. Now, Atli! thou liest,
though of that I little reck.
Gentle I seldom was,
yet didst thou greatly aggravate it.
Young brothers ye fought together,
among yourselves contended;
to Hel went the half
from thy house:
all went to ruin
that should be for benefit.

97. Brothers and sisters we were three,
we thought ourselves invincible:
from the land we departed,
we followed Sigurd.
We roved about,
each steered a ship;
seeking luck we went,
till to the east we came.

98. The chief king we slew,
there a land obtained,
the 'hersar' yielded to us;
that manifested fear.
We from the forest freed
him whom we wished harmless,
raised him to prosperity
who nothing had possessed.

99. The Hun king[7] died,
then suddenly my fortune changed:
great was the young wife's grief,
the widow's lot was hers.
A torment to me it seemed
to come living to the house of Atli.
A hero had possessed me:
sad was that loss!

100. Thou didst never from a contest come,
as we have heard,
where thou didst gain thy cause,
or others overcome;
ever wouldst thou give way,
and never stand,
lettest all pass off quietly,
as ill beseemed a king.

Atli
101. Gudrún! now thou liest.
Little will be bettered
the lot of either:
we have all suffered.
Now act thou, Gudrún!
Of thy goodness,
and for our honour,
when I forth am borne.

Gudrún
102. I a ship will buy,
and a painted cist;[8]
will the winding-sheet well wax,
to enwrap thy corse;
will think of every requisite,
as if we had each other loved.

---

7. Sigurd.
8. The ancient usage of laying the body in a ship and sending it adrift, seems inconsistent with the later custom of depositing it in a cist or coffin.

103. Atli was now a corpse,
lament from his kin arose:
the illustrious woman did
all she had promised.
The wise woman would
go to destroy herself;
her days were lengthened:
she died another time.

104. Happy is every one hereafter
who shall give birth to such
a daughter famed for deeds,
as Giuki begat:
ever will live,
in every land,
their oft-told tale,
wherever people shall give ear.

Gudrúnarhvöt: Gudrún's Incitement

Having slain Atli, Gudrún went to the sea-shore. She went out into the sea, and would destroy herself, but could not sink. She was borne across the firth to the land of King Jonakr, who married her. Their sons were Sörli, Erp, and Hamdir. There was reared up Svanhild, the daughter of Sigurd. She was given in marriage to Jörmunrek the Powerful. With him lived Bikki, who counseled Randver, the king's son, to take her. Bikki told that to the king, who caused Randver to be hanged, and Svanhild trodden under horses' feet. When Gudrún heard of this she said to her sons:

> 1. Then heard I tell
> of quarrels dire,
> hard sayings uttered
> from great affliction,
> when her sons
> the fierce-hearted Gudrún,
> in deadly words,
> to slaughter instigated.
> ****************************
>
> 2. "Why sit ye here?
> why sleep life away?
> why does it pain you not
> joyous words to speak,
> now Jörmunrek
> your sister
> young in years
> has with horses trodden,
> white and black,
> in the public way,
> with grey and way-wont
> Gothic steeds?
>
> 3. Ye are not like
> to Gunnar and the others,
> nor of soul so valiant,
> as Högni was.
> Her ye should
> seek to avenge,
> if ye had the courage
> of my brothers,
> or the fierce spirit
> of the Hunnish kings."

4. Then said Hamdir,
the great of heart:
"Little didst thou care
Högni's deed to praise,
when Sigurd he
from sleep awaked.
They blue-white
bed-clothes were
red with thy husband's gore,
with death-blood covered.

5. For thy brothers thou didst
o'er-hasty vengeance take,
dire and bitter,
when thou thy sons didst murder.
We young ones[1] could
on Jörmunrek,
acting all together,
have avenged our sister.

6. Bring forth the arms
of the Hunnish kings:
thou hast us stimulated
to a sword-mote."

7. Laughing Gudrún
to the storehouse turned,
the kings' crested helms
from the coffers drew,
their ample corslets,
and to her sons them bore.
The young heroes loaded
their horses' shoulders.

8. Then said Hamdir,
the great of heart:
"So will no more come
his mother to see,
the warrior felled
in the Gothic land,

---

1. Themselves and the two sons of Atli.

so that thou the funeral-beer
after us all my drink,
after Svanhild
and thy sons."

9. Weeping Gudrún,
Giuki's daughter,
sorrowing went,
to sit in the fore-court,
and to recount,
with tear-worn cheeks,
sad of soul, her calamities,
in many ways.

10. "Three fires I have known,
three hearths I have known,
of three consorts I have been
borne to the house.
Sigurd alone to me was
better than all,
of whom my brothers
were the murderers.

11. Of my painful wounds
I might not complain;
yet they even more
seemed to afflict me,
when those chieftains
to Atli gave me.

12. My bright boys
I called to speak with me;
for my injuries I could not
get revenge,
ere I had severed
the Hniflungs heads.

13. To the sea-shore I went,
against the Norns I was embittered;
I would cast off
their persecution;
bore, and submerged me not

the towering billows;
up on land I rose,
because I was to live.

14. To the nuptial couch I went
as I thought better for me,
for the third time,
with a mighty king.
I brought forth offspring,
guardians of the heritage,
guardians of the heritage,
Jonarkr's sons.

15. But around Svanhild
bond-maidens sat;
of all my children her
I loved the best.
Svanhild was,
in my hall,
as was the sun-beam,
fair to behold.

16. I with gold adorned her,
and with fine raiment,
before I gave her
to the Gothic people.
That is to me the hardest
of all my woes,
that Svanhild's
beauteous locks
should in the mire be trodden
under horses' feet.

17. But that was yet more painful,
when my Sigurd they
ingloriously
slew in his bed;
though of all most cruel,
when of Gunnar
the glistening serpents
to the vitals crawled;
but the most agonizing,

which to my heart flew,
when the brave king's heart
they while quick cut out.

18. Many griefs I call to memory,
many ills I call to memory.
Guide, Sigurd!
thy black steed,
thy swift courser,
hither let it run.
Here sits
no son's wife, no daughter,
who to Gudrún
precious things may give.

19. Remember, Sigurd!
what we together said,
when on our bed
we both were sitting,
that thou, brave one,
wouldst come to me
from Hel's abode,
but I from the world to thee.

20. Raise, ye Jarls!
an oaken pile;
let it under heaven
the highest be.
May it burn
a breast full of woes!
the fire round my heart
its sorrows melt!"

21. May all men's lot
be bettered,
all women's
sorrow lessened,
to whom this tale of woes
shall be recounted.

Hamðismal: The Lay of Hamdir.

1. In that court[1] arose
woeful deeds,
at the Alfar's
doleful lament;[2]
at early morn,
men's afflictions,
troubles of various kinds;
sorrows were quickened.

2. It was not now,
nor yesterday,
a long time since
has passed away,
few things are more ancient,
it was by much earlier
when Gudrún,
Giuki's daughter,
her young sons instigated
Svanhild to avenge.

3. "She was your sister,
her name Svanhild,
she whom Jörmunrek
with horses trod to death,
on the public way,
with grey and way-wont
Gothic steeds.

4. Thenceforth all is sad to you,
kings of people!
Ye alone survive,

5. "Branches of my race.
Lonely I am become,
as the asp-tree in the forest,

---

[1]. See Str. 10, and Ghv. 9, and, Luning, Glossar.
[2]. *The Alfar's Lament* is the early dawn, and is in apposition to "early morn," in the following line. The swart Alfar are meant, who were turned to stone if they did not flee from the light of day. This is the best interpretation I can offer of this obscure strophe.

of kindred bereft,
as the fir of branches;
of joy deprived,
as is the tree of foliage,
when the branch-spoiler
comes in the warm day."

6. Then spake Hamdir,
the great of soul,
"Little, Gudrún! didst thou care
Högni's deed to praise,
when Sigurd they
from sleep awaked.
On the bed thou satst,
and the murderers laughed.

7. Thy bed-clothes,
blue and white,
woven by cunning hands,
swam in thy husband's gore.
When Sigurd perished,
o'er the dead thou satst,
caredst not for mirth
So Gunnar willed it.

8. Atli thou wouldst afflict
by Erp's murder,
and by Eitil's
life's destruction:
that proved for thyself the worse:
therefore should every one
so against others use,
a sharp-biting sword,
that he harm not himself."

9. Then said Sörli
he had a prudent mind
"I with my mother will not
speeches exchange:
though words to each of you
to me seem wanting.
What, Gudrún! dost thou desire,
which for tears thou canst not utter?

10. For thy brothers weep,
and thy dear sons,
thy nearest kin,
drawn to the strife:
for us both shalt thou, Gudrún!
also have to weep,
who here sit fated on our steeds,
far away to die."

11. From the court they went,
for conflict ready.
The young men journeyed
over humid fells,
on Hunnish steeds,
murder to avenge.

12. Then said Erp,
all at once
 the noble youth was joking
on his horse's back
"Ill 'tis to a timid man
to point out the ways."
They said the bastard[3]
was over bold.

13. On their way they had found
the wily jester.
"How will the swarthy dwarf
afford us aid?"

14. He of another mother answered:
so he said aid he would
to his kin afford,
as one foot to the other[4]
(or, grown to the body,
one hand the other.)

---

3. In this and the four following strophes the person alluded to is their half-brother Erp, of whose story nothing more is known. He, it appears, had preceded or outridden the others.
4. Malmesbury relates a similar story of king Æthelstan and his cupbearer.

15. "What can a foot
to a foot give;
or, grown to the body,
one hand the other?"

16. From the sheath they drew
the iron blade,
the falchion's edges,
for Hel's delight.
They their strength diminished
by a third part,
they their young kinsman caused
to earth to sink.

17. Their mantles then they shook,
their weapons grasped;
the high-born were clad
in sumptuous raiment.

18. Forward lay the ways,
a woeful path they found,
and their sister's son
wounded on a gibbet,
wind-cold outlaw-trees,[5]
on the town's west.
Ever vibrated the ravens' whet:
there to tarry was not good.

19. Uproar was in the hall,
men were with drink excited,
so that the horses' tramp
no one heard,
until a mindful man
winded his horn.

20. To announce they went
to Jörmunrek
that were seen
helm-decked warriors.

---

5. Lit. *wolf-trees*; a fugitive criminal being called *vargr* wolf.

"Take ye counsel,
potent ones are come;
before mighty men ye have
on a damsel trampled."

21. Then laughed Jörmunrek,
with his hand stroked his beard,
asked not for his corslet;
with wine he struggled
shook his dark locks,
on his white shield looked,
and in his hand
swung the golden cup.

22. "Happy should I seem,
if I could see
Hamdir and Sörli
within my hall.
I would them then
With bowstrings bind,
The good sons of Giuki
on the gallows hang."

23. Then said Hródrglöd,
on the high steps standing;
"Prince," said she
to her son
for that was threatened
which ought not to happen
"shall two men alone
bind or slay
ten hundred Goths
in this lofty burgh?"

24. Tumult was in the mansion,
the beer-cups flew in shivers,
men lay in blood
from the Goths' breasts flowing.

25. Then said Hamdir,
the great of heart:
"Jörmunrek! thou didst

desire our coming,
brothers of one mother,
into thy burgh;[1]
now seest thou thy feet,
seest thy hands
Jörmunrek! cast
into the glowing fire.

26. Then roared forth
a godlike[2]
mail-clad warrior,
as a bear roars:
"On the men hurl stones,
since spears bite not,
nor edge of sword, nor point,
the sons of Jonakr."

27. Then said Hamdir,
the great of heart:
"Harm didst thou, brother!
when thou that mouth didst ope.
Oft from that mouth
bad counsel comes."

28. "Courage hast thou, Hamdir!
if only thou hadst sense:
that man lacks much
who wisdom lacks.

29. Off would the head now be,
had but Erp lived,
our brother bold in fight,
whom on the way we slew,
that warrior brave
me the Dísir instigated
that man sacred to us,
whom we resolved to slay.

---

6. According to the *Skalda* it would appear that they cut off his hands and feet while he was asleep. Erp, had they not murdered him, was to have cut off his head.
7. Odin, as in the Battle of Bravalla.

30. I ween not that ours should be
the wolves' example,
that with ourselves we should contend,
like the Norns' dogs,
that voracious are
in the desert nurtured."

31. "Well have we fought,
on slaughtered Goths we stand,
on those fallen by the sword,
like eagles on a branch.
Great glory we have gained,
Though now or to morrow we shall die.
No one lives till eve
against the Norns' decree."

32. There fell Sörli,
at the mansion's front;
but Hamdir sank
at the house's back.

This is called the Old Lay of Hamdir.

Gunnars Slagr: Gunnar's Melody.

1. It of old befell that Gunnar,
Giuki's son,
was doomed to die
In Grábak's halls.
The feet were free
of the king's son,
but his hands were bound
with hard bonds.

2. A harp he seized,
the warrior king
his skill displayed,
his foot-branches moved,
the harp-strings
sweetly touched:
that art had not been practised
save by the king's son.

3. Then sang Gunnar,
in these strains:
the harp got voice,
as it had been a man;
yet not a sweeter sound,
had it been a swan;
the hall of serpents echoed
to the golden strings:

4. "I my sister know
wedded to the worst of men,
and to the Niflungs'
base foe espoused.
To his home bade Atli
Högni and Gunnar,
his relations,
but murdered both.

5. Slaughter he made them
take for festivity,
and conflict for
convivial potations.
Ever will that survive
while men shall live:
so did relations never
any one delude.

6. Why, Atli! dost thou
so wreak thy anger?
Herself did Brynhild
cause to die,
and Sigurd's
cruel death.
Why wouldst thou Gudrún
cause to weep?

7. Long since the raven told,
from the high tree,
our calamities,
at our relation's death;
Brynhild told me,
Budli's daughter,
how Atli would
deceive us both.

8. This also Glaumvör said,
when we both reposed,
for the last time,
in the same bed,
my consort had
portentous dreams
'Go not Gunnar!
Atli is now false to thee.

9. A lance I saw
red with thy blood,
a gallows ready
for Giuki's son:
I thought for thee the Dísir
prepared a feast;
I ween that for you brothers
treachery is at work.'

10. Said also Kostbera
she was Högni's wife
the runes were falsely graved,
and the dreams interpreted.
But the heart beat high
In the princes' breast,
neither knew fear
of a cruel death.

11. The Norns have for us,
Giuki's heirs,
a life-time appointed,
at Odin's will;
no one may
against fate provide,
nor, of luck bereft,
in his valour trust.

12. Atli! I laugh
that thou hast not
the red-gold rings
that Hreidmar owned;
I alone know where that treasure
hidden lies,
since that Högni
to the heart ye cut.

13. Atli! I laugh,
that ye Huns
the laughing Högni
to the heart cut.
The Hniflung shrank not
from the scooping wound,
nor flinched he from
a painful death.

14. Atli! I laugh,
that thou hast lost
many of thy men
that choicest were,
beneath our swords,
before thy own death.
Our noble sister has
thy brother maimed.

15. Yet shall not Gunnar,
Giuki's son,
fear express
in Grafvitnir's dwelling;
nor dejected go
to the sire of hosts:
Already is the prince
inured to suffering.

16. Sooner shall Góin
pierce me to the heart,
and Nidhögg
such my reins,
Linn and Lángbak
my liver tear,
than I will abandon
my steadfastness of heart.

17. Gudrún it will
grimly avenge,
that Atli us
has both deceived;
she to thee, king! will
give the hearts
of thy cubs,
hot at the evening meal;

18. And their blood
thou from cups shalt drink
formed of their skulls.
That mental anguish shall
bite thee most cruelly,
when Gudrún sets
such crimes before thee.

19. Short will be thy life
after the princes' death;
an ill end thou wilt have,
for breach of our affinity:
such is befitting thee,
through the deed
of our sister sorely impelled
thy treachery to requite.

20. Gudrún will thee
with a lance lay low,
and the Niflung
stand hard by;
in thy palace
will the red flame play;
then in Náströnd thou shalt
be to Nidhögg given.

21. Now is Grábak lulled,
and Grafvitnir,
Góin and Móin,
and Grafvöllud,
Ofnir and Svafnir,
with venom glistening,
Nad and Nidhögg,
and the serpents all,
Hring, Höggvard,
by the harp's sound.

22. Alone wakeful remains
Atli's mother,
she has pierced me
to the heart's roots,
my liver sucks,
and my lungs tears.

23. Cease now, my harp!
hence I will depart,
and in the vast
Valhall abide,
with the Æsir drink
of costly cups,
be with Sæhrimnir sated
at Odin's feast.

24. Now is Gunnar's melody
all sung out;
I have men delighted
for the last time.
Henceforth few princes will
with their foot-branches
the sweetly sounding
harp-strings strike."

Gróttasöngr: The Lay of Grótti, or The Mill-Song

King Fródi succeeded to the kingdom of Denmark at the time when the emperor Augustus had proclaimed peace over all the world; and as Fródi was the most powerful king in the North, the peace was attributed to him and called Fródi's peace, where-ever the Danish tongue was spoken. When on a visit to king Fiölnir in Sweden, he bought two female slaves, whose names were Fenia and Menia, both of great strength and stature. At this time two mill-stones were found in Denmark so large that no one could drag them. These stones possessed the property of grinding whatever the grinder wished. Fródi set the two slaves to work at the quern, or mill, which was named Grótti and commanded them to grind gold, peace, and prosperity to Fródi; but he allowed them not a moment's rest nor even sleep longer than while the cuckoo was silent, or a song might be sung. They then sang the song called *Gróttasöngr*, and ceased not before they had ground an army against Fródi, so that in the night a sea-king, named Mýsing, came, slew Fródi, and carried off great booty. Such was the end of Fródi's peace. Mýsing took Grótti, together with Fenia and Menia, and caused white salt to be ground in his ships, until they sank in Pentland Firth. There is ever since a vortex where the sea falls into Grótti's eye; there the sea roars as it (Grótti) roars, and then it was that the sea first became salt. *Skalda*, edit. Rask, p. 146.

1. Now are come
to the king's house
two prescient damsels,
Fenia and Menia;
they are with Fródi,
Fridleif's son,
the powerful maidens,
in thraldom held.

2. To the mill
they both were led,
and the grey stone
to set a going ordered;
he to both forbade
rest and solace,
before he heard
the maidens' voice.

3. They made resound
the clattering quern,
with their arms
swung the light stones.
The maidens he commanded
yet more to grind.

4. They sung and swung
the whirling stone,
until Fródi's thralls
nearly all slept.
Then said Menia
to the meal 'twas come

5. "Riches we grind for Fródi,
all happiness we grind,
wealth in abundance,
in gladness' mill.
On riches may he sit,
on down may he sleep,
to joy may he wake:
then 'tis well ground!

6. Here shall not one
another harm,
evil machinate,
nor occasion death,
nor yet strike
with the biting sword,
although a brother's slayer
he find bound."

7. He had not yet said
one word before:
"Sleep ye not longer
than the gowks round the house,
or than while
one song I sing."

8. "Thou was not, Fródi!
for thyself over-wise,
or a friend of men,
when thralls thou boughtest;
for strength thou chosest them,
and for their looks,
but of their race
didst not inquire.

9. Stout was Hrúngnir,
and his father,
yet was Thiassi
stronger than they;
Idi and Örnir
our relations are,
brothers of the mountain-giants
from whom we are born.

10. Grótti had not come
from the grey fell,
nor yet the hard
stone from the earth;
nor so had ground
the giant maid,
if her race had
aught of her known.

11. Nine winters we
playmates were,
strong and nurtured
beneath the earth.
We maidens stood
at mighty works;
ourselves we moved
the fast rock from its place.

12. We rolled the stone
o'er the giants' house,
so that earth thereby
shrank trembling;
so hurled we
the whirling rock,
that men could take it.

13. But afterwards, in Sweden,
we prescient two
among people went,
chased the bear,
and shattered shields;
went against
a grey-sarked host,
aided one prince,
another overthrew,
afforded the good
Guthrom help.
Quiet I sat not
ere we warriors felled.

14. Thus we went on
all those winters,
so that in conflicts
we were known;
there we carved,
with our sharp spears,
blood from wounds,
and reddened brands.

15. Now are we come
to a king's house,
unpitied both,
and in thraldom held;
gravel gnaws our feet,
and above 'tis cold;
a foe's host we drew.
Sad 'tis at Fródi's!

16. Hands must rest,
the stone shall stand still;
for me I have
my portion ground.
To hands will not
rest be given,
until Fródi thinks
enough is ground.

17. Hands shall hold
falchions hard,
the weapon slaughter-gory.
Wake thou, Fródi!
wake thou, Fródi!
if thou wilt listen
to our songs
and sagas old.

18. Fire I see burning
east of the burgh;
tidings of war are rife:
that should be a token;
a host will forthwith
hither come,
and the town burn
over the king.

19. Thou wilt not hold
the throne of Lethra,
rings of red gold,
or mighty mill-stone.
Let us ply the winch,
girl! yet more rapidly;
are we not grown up
in deadly slaughter?

20. My father's daughter
has stoutly ground,
because the fate
of many men she saw.
Huge fragments
spring from the mill-stone
into the Örnefiörd.
Let us grind on!

21. Let us grind on!
Yrsa's son,
Hálfdan's kinsman,
will avenge Fródi:
he will of her
be called
son and brother:
we both know that."

22. The maidens ground,
their might applied;
the damsels were
in Jotun-mood,
the axes trembled;
the stone fell from above,
the ponderous rock
was in shivers split.

23. But the mountain-giants'
maiden said;
"Frodi! we have ground;
together we cease,
the maidens have
stood at the grinding long."

www.ingramcontent.com/pod-product-compliance
Lightning Source LLC
Chambersburg PA
CBHW080910170426
43201CB00017B/2278